I0896531

Praise for *The Root of Trauma*

"Whether you're a therapist helping others or simply seeking to understand and heal your own wounds, this book is a valuable contribution to the fields of psychology and trauma. Easy-to-read anecdotes illustrate psychological principles and bring them home. Lists of disorders and how to address them make this book comprehensive. The lower chakras, often overlooked and misaligned, are given the attention needed to heal from the ground up. Like having a compassionate and skilled therapist in your own hands, this book is essential reading for everyone who wants to live a life of wholeness. Should be required reading for all therapists!"
—**ANODEA JUDITH, PHD,** author of *Wheels of Life* and *Eastern Body, Western Mind*

"A fiercely honest and luminously grounded guide to healing where it matters most—at the base of the self, where safety is first negotiated and pain quietly roots itself in the body. Melissa Grabau, PhD, weaves personal reckoning, clinical insight, and chakra-based wisdom into a rare synthesis: trauma is not just remembered—it is lived, patterned into our legs, our hunger, our resistance to presence. Through this lens, addiction becomes a form of self-rescue, and healing begins with the courage to be here—in the breath, in the bones, in the stories we thought we could outrun. This book returns us to the raw, unfinished ground of life and teaches us how to stand."
—**SHAI TUBALI, PHD,** author of *Your Chakra Personality*

"*The Root of Trauma* offers a compelling and insightful synthesis of chakra theory and the psychology of trauma. It postulates a unique theory of healing, drawing fascinating parallels between specific energy centers and the psychological impact of traumatic experiences—a framework I believe holds immense potential for future generations. Her reference to Big T and Little t is very clear and informative to understanding trauma. Grabau's wisdom shines through as she articulates practical spiritual work that empowers individuals to actively support their well-being and embark on a path of healing, moving beyond the cycle of suffering often perpetuated by life's traumas. Her perspective feels deeply relevant to the universal human struggle for wholeness."
—**JEAN GRANT SUTTON,** founder and director of BodyWorks Integrative Yoga and Stress Management Center

the ROOT *of* TRAUMA

About the Author

Melissa Grabau, PhD (Davis, CA), received her doctorate degree in clinical psychology from Duquesne University in 1998. She has been working in private practice in Northern California since 2002. She is a certified yoga teacher and integrates mind-body techniques into her work with clients. More recently she has broadened her understanding of consciousness and completed trainings in psychedelic therapy and ketamine therapy. Visit her at melissagrabau.com.

the ROOT *of* TRAUMA

Resolving Pain & Addiction Through *the Lower Chakras*

MELISSA GRABAU, PhD

LLEWELLYN
WOODBURY, MINNESOTA

FIRST EDITION
First Printing, 2025

Cover design by Shannon McKuhen

Llewellyn Publications is a registered trademark of Llewellyn Worldwide Ltd.

Library of Congress Cataloging-in-Publication Data
Names: Grabau, Melissa author
Title: The root of trauma : resolving pain & addiction through the lower chakras / by Melissa Grabau, PhD.
Description: First edition. | Woodbury, Minnesota : Llewellyn Worldwide, [2025] | Includes index. | Summary: "Childhood trauma creates imbalances in the three lower chakras, blocking the higher chakras and stunting an individual's development. Melissa Grabau explains how each chakra is matched with Western psychology diagnoses and then offers client stories that help you understand how to heal it. As the lower chakras heal, energy naturally moves upward into the higher chakras, allowing you to blossom and find new possibilities in your life"— Provided by publisher.
Identifiers: LCCN 2025024386 (print) | LCCN 2025024387 (ebook) | ISBN 9780738781389 paperback | ISBN 9780738781549 ebook
Subjects: LCSH: Chakras | Psychic trauma in children | Mental healing
Classification: LCC BF1442.C53 G733 2025 (print) | LCC BF1442.C53 (ebook) | DDC 294.5/43--dc23/eng/20250924
LC record available at https://lccn.loc.gov/2025024386
LC ebook record available at https://lccn.loc.gov/2025024387

Llewellyn Publications
A Division of Llewellyn Worldwide Ltd.
2143 Wooddale Drive
Woodbury, MN 55125-2989
www.llewellyn.com

Printed in the United States of America

GPSR Representation:
UPI-2M PLUS d.o.o., Medulićeva 20, 10000 Zagreb, Croatia
matt.parsons@upi2mbooks.hr

For my parents, their darkness and their light.

For Peter. This book could not have been borne without you.

Disclaimer

All characters in this book, except for the author, are fictional. This book is intended to be informational only and not to diagnose or treat an emotional or physical condition. The material in this book is based upon the writer's professional and personal experience and is not intended as medical advice or to be prescriptive with regard to the reader's psychological, medical, or personal self-care. It is recommended that readers consult appropriate professionals before embarking on any of the techniques discussed.

Yoga, sauna, cold plunge, and even breathwork can have unexpected, sometimes deleterious effects when applied without proper screening and oversight. Undiagnosed medical conditions and pregnancy preclude the engagement with several of these activities described in this book. The author and publisher encourage you to consult a professional if you have any questions about the use or efficacy of the techniques or theories presented in this book.

Contents

Introduction

I wrote this book as I was emerging from a very dark period in my life. In fact, writing the book, and developing the ideas conveyed in it, was an integral part of my emergence. I found that these ideas also resonated with my clients and seemed applicable to many who were facing crisis, breakdown, and a necessary reconstitution of a self. It is my hope that others beyond my limited scope will find the ideas here useful in understanding personal struggles, as well as the struggles of loved ones grappling with addiction and mental health disorders.

The book has a dual purpose. First, it is an educational guide through the lower three chakras and expands upon Eastern views of the chakras to incorporate psychological issues resulting from the impact of trauma on development. The intent is to demystify mental health issues, and also to demonstrate how both addiction and mental health dysfunctions are understandable responses to trauma and make sense when understood contextually. The second, and perhaps more important, intention is to provide guidance for the reader to address blockages in their own healing and suggest both tools and hope for finding a way forward.

This book is not a spiritual text in any traditional sense; however, there is an underpinning of faith implicit in the writing that suggests that when you let go, face uncomfortable truths, and reach out for help, the universe will support you. In my own process, I have experienced miracles large and small that have provided sustenance and hope and kept my feet moving forward toward a better future. I believe there is an evolutionary process occurring on the microlevel of the individual that mirrors the evolutionary process occurring on the macro level of the planet. Although globally it may appear that we are presently in a very dark time and headed toward imminent peril, my experience as a person and a clinician tells me that often things need to get very bad in order to tip the scales and allow a change process to take hold.

Whether sustained change and a global shift in consciousness will occur remains an unanswered question at this time, and therein lies both the mystery and the dynamism of the human experience. It is an unfolding drama in which we are all playing an infinitesimally small but potentially potent part. The potency of our part rests upon whether we are able and willing to surrender to the burdens of being vested with both free will and choice. There is an inherent vulnerability in being on the side of hope and daring to embrace free will and make new choices. However, this vulnerability also has power that is distinctly felt and lends a palpable vitality to one's life. A healing momentum is kindled that galvanizes further growth. As free will and choice are accepted, and eventually are embraced, the once unimaginable manifests. Let's hold that out as a planetary prayer that starts with each one of us here and now.

What to Expect in This Book

The concepts in this book are illustrated through the stories of three fictional clients. The characters I have developed are designed to help you learn about the energy of each chakra, the key developmental challenges each chakra encompasses, how trauma affects a person's ability to meet the developmental challenges of that chakra, and the addictions and mental health problems that compensate for imbalances in the foundational chakras. The people in this book are all products of my imagination, informed by my own struggles and the numerous individuals I have known during my thirty-year career as a therapist. My characters do not include any people of color or individuals from other cultures, which is a limitation of my own imagination as well as my personal and professional experience. Likewise, none of my characters have any kind of physical or intellectual disability, which again is a limitation of my imagination and personal/professional experience. I hope that I will be forgiven for my admittedly biased view and joined in the aspiration that someone with wider experiences could apply the chakra system to more diverse populations.

Ultimately, this book is my autobiography, and I hope yours as well. My intent is to capture something that is universal to the experience of being human and experiencing trauma. I believe everyone experiences trauma of one variety or another. After all, this planet is composed of forces of great darkness and great light. The two are clashing, interfacing, and reconfiguring all the time. Our challenge as humans is to navigate these polarities without becoming vapidly positive or burdened with the morose darkness that is all too easy to succumb to. The deeply visceral challenge of being human is learning to deal with the darkness by keeping our emotional processing systems alive and strong. We have emotional digestive systems and need emotional livers with honed emotional peristalsis to move the darkness through our minds and bodies by bringing language, story, and consciousness to the darkness. As we share these experiences with others, we enter into a universal bond that all humans, past and present, participate in. This is where being human becomes an exciting, unscripted adventure that rises out of biological programming toward something less predictable and instead expressive of the possible.

Structure and Layout of the Book

The Initiation gives the reader a basic understanding of the concepts this book is based on, including chakra theory, addiction, Big T and Little t, and legacy trauma. You will be introduced to Belle, who is one of the main characters in the book. Her first session of therapy is used to illustrate how breakdown begets eventual breakthrough. I also include my story, both as a tool to help concretize the esoteric ideas presented and to lend credibility and authenticity to the genesis of these ideas.

Part I, "The Root Chakra: Where Your Mind-Body Forms," contains six chapters that explain the way this foundational chakra is damaged by the impact of trauma. In chapter 1, "Big T and the Root Chakra," you meet No Roots Riley. Through her story, you learn about the impact of trauma and how it affected her nervous system, personality development, and trajectory of social and intellectual learning. Chapter 2, "Root Chakra Damage via Big T," illustrates how Riley's addictions are related to the damage her first chakra sustained during her childhood due to abuse and neglect. These damages became embedded in the structure of her nervous system, which influenced her ability to self-regulate and left her vulnerable to addiction. Chapter 3, "Little t and the Root Chakra," takes a detour from Riley's story to introduce our third character, Joe, and also to delve more into Belle's story. Their stories illustrate how root chakra addictions can take hold in people who did not suffer severe trauma in childhood yet find themselves using substances to manage stress and boredom. This chapter illustrates how childhood emotional invalidation (Little t) impacts the relationship a person has with themselves and can make them vulnerable to addiction later in life.

Chapter 4, "Mental Health Disorders and Root Chakra Trauma," discusses the mental health disorders associated with root chakra trauma—borderline personality disorder, dissociative identity disorder, and complex post-traumatic stress disorder—with Riley as the example. Chapter 5, "The Legacy Download," discusses the impact of modeling by early caregivers, as well as generational trauma. Riley demonstrates how individuals can move beyond anger and blame and live in a different way than was modeled. Finally, in chapter 6, "Healing Your Root Chakra," I share exercises that will help you address the traumas you experienced as a child and provide you with tools to begin addressing the addictions you adopted as a way to cope.

Part II, "The Sacral Chakra: Your Power Source," focuses on the sacral chakra and has four chapters. Chapter 7, "The Sacral Chakra and Emotional Processing," describes the fundamental importance of your sacral chakra and further explains the concept of emotional processing and its centrality to the human experience. You learn how childhood emotional invalidation creates weakness in the sacral chakra and the consequences this has on the rest of a person's life. Riley illustrates the perils of emotional turbulence, and Belle demonstrates the consequences of having an overly rigid and contracted emotional system. Joe illustrates how rigidity and a lack of emotional language can translate into a lack of confidence and, most tragically, a lack of being comfortable with oneself. Joe also demonstrates how moderate addiction can foreclose growth, while Belle illustrates how gratifying the change process can be when old mandates are released and a new communication with the self is established. Chapter 8, "Mental Health Disorders and Sacral Chakra Dysfunction," examines depressive disorders and anxiety through the lens of a weak sacral chakra. Chapter 9, "Emotional Legacies," discusses the invisible energetic legacy left by sacral chakra impairment, which later affects an individual's ability to feel and regulate their impulses and desires. Part II concludes with chapter 10, "Healing Your Sacral Chakra," which provides you with specific tools to develop more energetic strength and resilience. This protocol focuses on balance in the nervous system and emphasizes the importance of integrating restorative practices into your daily life. The importance of cultivating a relationship with your internal body is also emphasized.

Part III, "The Solar Plexus Chakra: Stoking the Fire of Your Purpose," includes four chapters. Chapter 11, "The Solar Plexus Chakra and the Realm of Identity," explores the solar plexus chakra and the challenges of selfhood. The perils of having a performance-based identity and the importance of being able to take initiative in the face of uncertainty are primary themes of this chapter. Joe and Belle exemplify how gender roles influence the expression an outside-in identity takes, with Joe manifesting a more forceful, achievement-driven personality and Belle taking a more codependent, relationship-oriented approach. The difficulties of change are addressed through a discussion of self-reinforcing paradigms and the inevitable dialectic between disorganization and reorganization when a change process is initiated. Chapter 12, "Mental Health Disorders and Solar Plexus Chakra Impairment," addresses the compulsive and codependent disorders associated with solar plexus chakra rigidity, while chapter 13, "The Legacy of the Conditioned Mind," explores how, if the solar plexus is weak, messages from the cultural zeitgeist can gain too much traction in the individual psyche and subvert a more creative expression of selfhood. Part III concludes with chapter 14, "Healing Your Solar Plexus Chakra: Identity Re-Formation," which provides tools to address healing your solar plexus chakra. You can use these tools to address motivation, develop purpose and community, and strengthen the relationship of your past, present, and future selves.

The conclusion, "Base Camp at Mount Everest," is short and reinforces how the gifts of the upper chakras, requiring their own kind of work, are the next phase of your journey.

The Initiation

Belle popped up on my screen right on time for our initial consult. These days, post-pandemic, I am used to making introductory connections over the internet. The challenge of a first session is greater for me virtually because I have to feel my way into who the person is and where their pain is without the benefit of warm tea and a soothing room to cue my client that they are safe to reveal their troubles. But it turned out that Belle didn't need any nonverbal cues. The more pressing need to express herself to an assumed sympathetic ear trumped any reticence on her part. Even if she had wanted to keep up a shield, she likely couldn't have, given her high level of distress.

"I don't understand what's happening to me," she began. "I mean, I've always had anxiety, but this is different. I'm just not myself." She described intense anxiety to the point that she almost vibrated. The pressure in her upper chest, she said, was so bad at times that she felt like she might explode. She was treating her symptoms with various medications, including antianxiety medication, antidepressants, and sleep aids. She was understandably worried about becoming dependent on these medications and felt that they weren't particularly helpful anyway. "I'm desperate," she finally concluded, glancing up at me woefully as she dabbed mascara off her face, adding, with a mixture of regret and perhaps a twinkle of insight, "I knew I shouldn't have worn makeup," and then she cracked a half smile.

Wearing makeup to our first session was a telling indicator of how Belle had been functioning lately. Determined to make a good impression, she put on her customary affable face and continued to show up to her stressful job, online now, which made the performance easier but also blurred the division between her work self and her home self, which she found confusing. She did less well maintaining this face with her two boys and her husband, but she still attempted to carry on with business as usual. She churned out dinner, checked the boys' homework nightly, and coordinated their slimmed-down activity schedule. They were playing way too many video games now, which bothered her a lot, but she didn't have the energy to take it on. "That's not like me," she said. "I always felt like a good parent. But now," she shook her head, "it's just not me." Her husband, she said, wasn't much help with the kids. He left most of the parenting to her, an arrangement that had worked well in the past. "His job is just so busy. And this is the way it's always been, so I can't really complain. I always wished he would be more involved with the boys and their activities, but I understood. I really need him now, though, and I don't think he gets this." She finally said, "I don't know," shaking her head slightly. "I mean, we have a great marriage, but, well, I guess it's just too much togetherness." She sighed, looking down as she shook her head again, stumped by her unhappiness, her unfamiliarity with her own life.

Prior to the pandemic, Belle had been doing well enough. She worked as a manager in a branch of state government. Balancing her career and parenting had never been easy, she reported, and her self-care had always taken low priority, but never before had she experienced so much unrelenting distress. She knew she should exercise more and make an effort to see her friends, but she just couldn't seem to find the time. She and her husband got along well, but, "You know," she said, "it's hard with his job and we have different interests." Her husband liked to watch TV in the little downtime he had, and she was usually reading a book. "I mean, we rarely fight and he tries to be supportive." She seemed a little confused and I thought it best not to push further. Instead, I gathered more information about her symptoms and the mental health treatment she'd had in the past. She had been diagnosed with depression a few years prior and had begun taking antidepressants even before the coronavirus hit. Although the medication seemed to help her get through her days and nights, the gnawing in her heart and gut was increasingly hard to ignore. What was new was her escalating anxiety, and she was bewildered about what was causing it, because nothing had really changed.

I assured Belle that her experience of increased distress since the pandemic was not unique. Inquiries into my services increased threefold after it hit, and the level of people's expressed distress was markedly higher. This was true even among individuals who had not experienced job loss or housing problems. The coronavirus, it seemed, had churned up all the things people had been living with, both individually and collectively, perhaps knowing that things weren't great, maybe even knowing that things were pretty bad, but it hadn't had the same level of urgency it suddenly took on in the pandemic pressure cooker. Thinking that the situation could be fixed later was no longer good enough. It appeared that later had come for Belle.

I wrote this book because later also came for me. Later, it seems to me, eventually comes for all of us, even if we manage to tiptoe through the minefields of our own concessions and compromises for a very long time. Later came for me in the form of divorce. Followed by the pandemic. Preceded by the recent deaths of both parents. Culminating when my daughter left for college. Before her departure, following the divorce, I enjoyed what I now refer to as the post-divorce bump. This is the period when you feel that you have a new lease on life now that you have been relieved of the anchor of your tiresome spouse. I reveled in being able to do whatever I wanted, whenever I wanted, without fear of judgment or censure. Me, myself, and I were getting along just fine, and I was intoxicated with the limitless possibilities that now lay within my purview. I considered absconding to Mexico and working remotely from the exotic city of San Miguel de Allende. Or perhaps I would use the inheritance from my father to buy a Sprinter van and take to the mountains, conducting therapy via laptop as I gazed upon snow-capped peaks. What could go wrong?

Everything, it turned out, even when nothing all that bad actually happened to me. You see, far from being relieved of the responsibilities and accountability of marriage, I now found myself subjected to my own unchecked neurosis, lack of competence, and indecision. My confidence, you see, had rested on the structure and security provided by marriage. Going it alone wasn't so easy, and my bravado soon faltered and then dissolved into a silent, seemingly eternal scream of terror that was deafening only to my own ears. I was confronted with the reality that there are no shortcuts in life and you are responsible for every single thing you do. Without anyone else to blame for my own unhappiness, I found myself caught in a house of mirrors that confronted me with an anguished, disoriented, and impoverished reflection of myself whichever way I turned to escape. It appeared there was no exiting from myself.

Reflecting upon my unhappiness in my marriage, I was forced to the sorry conclusion that, indeed, it had been me all along. I was the progenitor of my own misery. This self-evident conclusion was an agonizing reckoning to endure. It became stunningly clear to me that we are all fully and eternally responsible for our own energy. What we create in the world of form is only a reflection of our own internal energetic world. This is why there was nowhere to run to and nowhere to hide and why Sprinter vans and exotic cities in Mexico could do nothing to relieve, and would likely only exacerbate, my internal distress.

Lest you fall into despair and throw up your hands regarding my plight, know that alongside the relentlessness of karma, which I define as the inevitability of eventual reckoning, there is also forgiveness. Healing is possible, progressive, and forever accessible. All you need do is take the first step. Figuring out how and where to begin is why this book was born. It was inspired by my need to understand my own breakdown and quest to find a way through it.

The healing paradigm I offer to you here is based upon my own trauma, how it manifested, and how I managed to climb out of it. In my better moments, I began to wrap the disintegration I was experiencing in the loose structure of a theory I was developing regarding what was happening to me and why. Having always been drawn to Eastern psychology, I began to conceptualize myself within the framework of the chakras, which

I will explain in more detail in the next section. Briefly, the seven chakras represent nodal centers in the flow of life energy circulating through all human beings. Each chakra builds upon the one preceding it, so the capacity of the higher chakras rests upon the foundation provided below. I realized that my fantasies of Mexico and the Sprinter van existed in the realm of my imagination. This realm is a wonderful place and rests in the third eye, which is the sixth chakra, residing between the eyebrows.

Many people are blessed with a strong imaginative capacity and enjoy story, art, writing, painting, interior design, and other creative commitments. The challenge of manifestation is that the lower chakras must be strong enough to afford you the time, energy, and resources to bring this visionary capacity into the world of form. So I, like a lot of people, had plenty of imagination about what I could do, but I lacked the experiential skills and competence to undertake the project of successfully executing my visions. This became humiliatingly obvious after I rented a Sprinter van to try it out before buying one, promptly damaged it in a parking lot getting gas, and spent a miserable night at a campground with no idea how to heat the damn thing or use the stove. I was just grateful to get the wounded van back to the heartbroken owners without further threat to life or limb. Suffice it to say, my lower chakras were not strong enough to carry out the vision of my upper chakras.

I will segue from my story now into an explanation of the fundamentals of an embodied spiritual paradigm. We will explore what the chakras are, how they function, and how they are impacted by trauma during childhood.

First Steps: Understanding Chakra Theory, Trauma, and Addiction

This section will give you a primer on key principles used in the book. First you will be introduced to the concept of the chakras and given a brief description of how they are understood in Eastern philosophy. Then the concepts of addiction and trauma will be explained with regard to the unique way they are used in this book.

Chakra Theory

Chakra theory arises out of Eastern psychology and yogic theory as a system for understanding the human experience that is grounded in the body, integrates the concept of energy, and posits spiritual opening as the crowning jewel of a well-lived life. The chakras are seven energetic centers that traverse the body from the bottom of the spine to the top of the head. Each energetic center, or chakra, is thought to contain the energy of key developmental challenges inherent to human life. These challenges highlight core conflicts that human beings face as they move from birth to death. How you resolve each of these conflicts sets the stage for the next challenge you encounter as you progress through your life. The upper chakras open you to higher levels of consciousness, culminating in the opening of your crown chakra, located at the top of the head, which portends unification with the divine.

The first three chakras create the foundation for your human incarnation. The first chakra, often referred to as the root chakra, is located at the bottom of the spine and includes the buttocks, hips, legs, and feet. It establishes your sense of safety in your body and the world, and its balance rides on your earliest experiences in childhood, starting with infancy. The second chakra, referred to as the sacral chakra, is located right below the navel and includes the lower abdomen and pelvis. It holds your capacity to feel and process all the energies and emotions inherent to human life and is the hub of your energetic capacity. The third chakra, or solar plexus chakra, is located at the solar plexus and includes the stomach and digestive organs. It houses the fire of your motivation and capacity to take initiative in the world.

When any one of these foundational chakras is impaired, it affects the course of your entire development. This is because each chakra builds upon the next, so that when one chakra is weak or imbalanced, you encounter the next developmental challenge at a deficit. Having a shaky foundation makes it difficult for you to function effectively in your life and also impairs your ability to develop your higher chakras, which open you to the expressive and imaginative potentialities of human consciousness.

Instability in the lower chakras also renders you vulnerable to the conditioning of the larger culture, which is decidedly not a good thing. We live in a world with an economy that is based on consumption and runs on sound bites peddling people as products in order to keep the machine running. People who are not strong in their own bodies and confident in their instinctive feelings—capacities of the first and second chakras—are like lambs being led on a soul-slaughtering quest to secure safety and status in a cutthroat world. This leaves the formation of identity, the challenge of the solar plexus chakra, in the hands of mass culture. An identity formed from the values of mass culture is an identity predicated on superficial values whose existence remains forever contingent on the approval of others. This is an inherently vulnerable self, because it rests upon an outside-in identity rather than an identity based on interior values fueled by the capacity for self-initiated action.

The first three chakras can become impaired through trauma, insensitive parenting, and the impersonal, conformity-based influence of the larger culture. Impairment in these chakras creates a weak foundation for the self, which relegates you to living in survival-based consciousness. Survival-based consciousness is typified by feeling continually in danger, unsafe in your own skin, without the right to your own feelings, and in need of constant external validation that you are good enough. This survival-based way of living can occur regardless of the material circumstances of your life. This is because consciousness informs perception, so when your psyche is wired for survival, you feel continually in danger, regardless of how much money you have, where you live, and any other accoutrements of success you may have gathered. When you are so afflicted, your nervous system becomes wired around anxious, survival-based energy and your habits and lifestyle follow suit.

Types of Trauma: Big T/Little t and Legacy Trauma

All humans carry trauma, and the challenge of being human is to not shut down in the face of it. People who experience a difficult childhood are at a deficit because their foundational chakras are impaired, and as you learned above, this impacts the development of the rest of the chakra system. Big T/ Little t is a useful way to understand and delineate different forms of trauma, and we can extrapolate from this how they affect the different chakras. *Big T* refers to physical and sexual abuse, as well as poverty, racism or discrimination, and neglect. Big T affects the root chakra because it interferes with basic safety and trust. Of course, the timing, chronicity, and severity of the trauma determine how much it disrupts the root chakra, as well as whether the trauma is occurring at home with primary caregivers or in the larger community. *Little t* refers to emotional invalidation, including ridicule, bullying, colluding with or denying abuse, and ignoring or diminishing feelings. Little t affects the sacral chakra, which involves trust in your own instincts and feelings. Usually, but not always, Big T includes Little t. For example, when someone is being sexually abused, which is Big T, if others in the surrounding environment are denying or colluding with the abuse, this creates Little t. For the survivors of childhood sexual abuse whom I have worked with, the scalding pain and psychological scarring are not so much due to what actually happened; rather, it is the ignoring, minimizing, covering up, denying, and obfuscating of it by others that creates long-term damage.

Little t also exists on its own without Big T. It can be challenging to name and identify Little t because it is so ordinary and typically falls under a misguided understanding of "good parenting." As a younger therapist, I got into too many fruitless discussions with defensive clients who refused to talk about or acknowledge that there was anything amiss in their early life. When "good parenting" includes techniques that are coercive, critical, or done without sensitivity, empathy, and good humor, it is very damaging to the emotional processing system of the child. The adult whom this child becomes does not recognize the Little t because it is all they have ever known and constitutes "normal" for them. "They didn't really mean it" or "Everyone disciplined their kids that way where I grew up" are common ways people minimize and dismiss the impact that coercion and humiliation have on the developing psyche.

Trauma is intergenerational. *Legacy trauma* is a term that conveys how, as a child, you were an innocent receptacle for your parent's unhealed wounds. Your parents did not download their trauma into you because they were mean-spirited or had ill intentions. In fact, they were likely doing the best they could given what they knew and the resources they had at the time. Parents download their trauma into their offspring because they have no awareness that they are doing so if they have not been afforded the opportunity to bring consciousness to their wounds and process them. If your parents did not recognize their own trauma, then they raised you from their own unconscious, and therefore unquestioned, script. To add to this, during child-rearing years, parents are also dealing with the daily stressors of social expectations, financial demands, poverty, and unforeseen mental health and addiction issues in themselves and their partners. When people are overwhelmed with external stressors, they default to their programming and often resort to crude techniques of control and coercion to cope.

The first step in healing is recognizing your legacy trauma and working through the anger and grief that you likely feel about it. You may go through a period of intense anger toward your parents and family, which is often necessary and useful. The next step is finding a way to move forward in your life from a new perspective that recognizes the trauma you inherited, the damages incurred, and the mistakes you, as well as your loved ones, have made. Taking responsibility for your own life entails recognizing that people do the best they can from the level of consciousness they have at the time. This includes you and your parents. A spiritual perspective proposes that the process of moving forward with greater awareness and responsibility for your own life heals your parents and ancestors as well. Most parents gave better than they got. By reaping the benefits of the gifts they were able to bequeath to you, and by forgiving them for how they erred, you simultaneously heal them as you heal yourself by moving their gifts forward and improving upon them. From a spiritual perspective, not only does this move the evolution of consciousness forward for your parents, even if they have passed away, but it also contributes to the evolution and well-being of human consciousness as a whole.

The Result of Unprocessed Trauma: Addiction

In this paradigm, *addiction* refers to any repetitive behavior that compensates for weakness in one of the first three chakras. Addiction is defined as a repetitive energetic-behavioral pattern that lodges in the mind-body and provides temporary relief from the inevitable pains and discomforts of life. It can be understood as an attempt to avoid, circumvent, or outwit the natural pains and losses of life. When addiction takes root in your mind-body, it interferes with the natural function of emotional processing and congests your emotional digestive system, located in your sacral chakra. Over time, this weakens your overall pranic/energetic system, which results in a depletion of life energy in your mind-body system. I will contextualize these ideas by showing how they played out in my life.

My Story: How Unprocessed Trauma Leads to Addiction

I was raised by a very anxious mother and a preoccupied father. I was an anxious child and looked to my mother for a lot of soothing. Bless her heart, she was very attentive in my early years and my home offered many pleasures, not least of which was good home cooking and baking. My mother was very food-oriented, as was my father. Eating is a natural and wonderful part of life, and it served as the axis around which our family rotated. It was only after my parents divorced and my root chakra blew up as an adolescent that it became a problem.

The root chakra encompasses the structure and possessions of your home and your physical surroundings. At age thirteen I moved from a rural country home in Vermont to an apartment in a suburb of Chicago. Food became a lifeline for me, providing me with a way to self-soothe, re-create the past, and manage the emotional pain I was feeling. Hence, I developed an over-fixation on food, which focused energy in my root and sacral chakras in a repetitive, nonproductive way that interfered with other age-appropriate activities. Instead of dealing with my feelings of loss and learning how to cope with the new challenges of adolescence (sacral and solar plexus chakra issues), I became obsessed with my weight, food, and the eating of it and not eating of it (all root chakra issues). Energy that should have been going outward into the world instead went inward in a repetitive and nonproductive way. This is how all addictions are born. The same concept can apply to alcohol, cigarettes, or any other substance that directly impacts the biology and can be passively applied, meaning you don't have to do anything other than consume, inject, swallow, or apply the agent to get the desired effect.

In this paradigm, any substance that affects the body in an immediate, chemical way is categorized as a root chakra addiction. Root chakra addictions involve all addictions that require a substance and meet a primitive need for soothing in a way that is instant, requires little effort, and is very gratifying, much like a baby suckling at the breast. At its inception, the addiction promises a solution to, or a release from, an unsolvable problem or inescapable life condition. Just as food provided me with an anchor after my parents' divorce, other substances such as cannabis, alcohol, and cigarettes also provide coping tools that relieve pain and seemingly allow you to endure your current situation.

Obviously, this pseudo-coping tool is also deeply problematic because you are not facing the real problem and are instead creating a dependency on a substance. The wiring and neurochemistry of your mind and body are then influenced by your dependency, which over time influences how your mind-body develops. This is especially damaging when the addiction begins early in life, because it can have long-term effects on your appetite, energy, and neurochemistry. As your mind and body habituate to the substance, your dependency influences your willingness to take risks and engage with life in an open, free way. It is not uncommon for individuals with root chakra addictions to habituate to avoidance of other activities due to fears of not having access to their chosen form of soothing. For example, a person may turn down a dinner invitation if it interferes with their food patterns or if alcohol won't be provided. A person may also find themselves gravitating toward others who also have an addiction and build their own lifestyles around heavy use, thus reinforcing the dependency. College students, entertainers, and people who work in late-night clubs often thrive on this normalization of heavy substance usage, which adds fuel to the fire for any budding addict.

Because each chakra builds upon the prior one, sacral chakra addictions can develop out of root chakra addiction, which I can illustrate again using my own experience. In later adolescence I started running in order to manage my weight. Healthy, right? Most certainly it was a step up from obsessing about, restricting, and over- and under-consuming food. But—and this is important—over time it became the primary way for me to manage my emotional and energetic system (sacral chakra). Exercise, work, gambling, and sex all require more skill and effort than do root chakra addictions. You have to go to the gym, put on your running shoes, or have the skill and competence to win money, hold a job, or woo sexual partners. However, all these activities, when relied upon excessively, can become habitual, nonproductive ways of managing feelings and energy. This creates rigidity in your sacral chakra and leads you to avoid facing the necessarily uncomfortable challenges required for solar plexus chakra development. Turning down social or leisure engagements because they interfere with your exercise or work schedule is an example of how sacral chakra addictions can slowly winnow down your life and interfere with your overall development. Over time, cumulative damage to relationships and finances inevitably occurs.

The solar plexus chakra builds upon the balance and stability of the first two chakras and involves solidification of your sense of identity. This includes cultivating your ability to self-motivate, set intentions based on your values, and self-validate in the face of opposition. When your root and sacral chakras are impaired due to energy congestion caused by trauma or addiction, this by default impairs your solar plexus chakra. If you are feeling self-conscious about your body, are obsessing about food, or are too busy working or exercising to engage with others, your confidence and your perception of what is possible for you will be deleteriously impacted. Over time, this also affects the reality of what is actually possible for you. The more you avoid development of skills, capacities, and relationships, the more devoid your life becomes of life-giving interests, skills capacities, and relationships. You also become addicted to comfort and increasingly resistant to anything that might interfere with this. Engagement with possibility requires stepping outside your comfort zone, while addiction, by definition, is default into the comfort zone.

In order to cope with my root chakra addiction, I became rigidly dependent on exercise to regulate my energetic system, which helped me manage my obsession with food. My solar plexus chakra, which encompassed my identity and sense of self, became rigidly identified with exercise and weight management through control. As I intimated earlier, all compromises, when executed unconsciously, eventually exact a karmic toll. Aging challenges the system, and when it is rigidly structured and lacks the flexibility to adjust to new demands, things do not go well. The karmic reckoning I was forced to endure had certainly been coming for a long time. Bereft of my marriage and home, which had provided for so many of my root and sacral chakra needs, my solar plexus chakra, the realm of identity and purpose, exploded. Me, myself, and I turned on one another and twisted in the wind as I literally and figuratively gasped for air and sought a way out. And out, I learned, can only be through. This entailed finding ways to engage with life beyond my addictions, making new friends, and taking on new activities. You must return to the scene of the crime and do the remedial work required to shore up the cracks in the foundation.

On a practical level, addiction of any kind creates numerous problems in living, including health, financial, and relational dysfunction. This is because your addictions interfere with your capacity to do the work necessary to shore up your lower chakras. By numbing the pain required to fuel growth and waylaying the energy that is necessary for growth, your addictions keep you stuck in the status quo. Pain motivates change. If you are numbing pain with addiction, your life energy will continually be drawn into the addiction, which temporarily negates your pain and absorbs your energy. This interferes with your natural ability to process your feelings, as well as with your motivation to address your pain, because you are constantly avoiding it. Hence, you do not engage in the new behaviors required to generate growth and change. Instead, you stay stuck in patterns that reinforce your dependency on your addictions and you likely create a story that legitimizes the behaviors that are keeping you stuck. After all, everyone needs something to unwind at the end of the day, right?

Next Steps: Integrating Legacy Trauma

Living though the intense disorientation and gradual reconstruction that I experienced following my divorce shifted my level of consciousness. Consciousness can be partially understood as the lens through which you see yourself and the world. It is your frame of reference and informs what you perceive and how you interpret what you perceive. We all see the world from our own peculiar frame of reference and this constitutes our reality. When your everyday life and sense of normalcy is disrupted, as happens when there is any extreme change in your circumstances, your frame of reference changes. This in turn changes your level of consciousness. It messes with the structures that you have imposed upon the world and also shifts your understanding of who you are. This is a very big deal, because when your sense of self changes and your reference point changes, everything else changes.

I never fully appreciated this until I experienced the upside-down world I found myself in, and the upside-down self I now resided in, following my divorce. The woman I had become bore little resemblance to the well-controlled, firmly oriented woman I had curated over a lifetime. "Well, Mom," I would at times reflect to my now dead mother, "perhaps I have at last been changed for Mabel." This had been a standing joke between us when I was a child, a reference to Alice in Wonderland falling down the rabbit hole and wondering, as she attempted to orient herself in the new world where she had landed, if she had become the rather dreary Mabel whom she had known from afar in her old life. My dead mother didn't respond in any direct way, but a felt ripple of understanding kept my feet moving forward. Early attachments inform our frame of reference and sense of self throughout our lives, which can be both good and bad. In this case it was a good thing, because it referenced a shared idea that signified the beautiful aspects of our bond. Early attachments, however, also portend what is to come, no matter how vigorously we try to avoid this. From my new frame of reference, it was now clear to me that the seeds of my being changed for Mabel had been planted long ago.

When I was a young woman-girl in my early twenties, my father and I would spend time driving the scenic roads of rural Vermont. He would regale me with stories of his recent past, lectures that I would tolerate but barely, as he often repeated his stories and I tired of his endless self-analysis. Following my parents' divorce, my father had experienced a breakdown, which led to a thankfully uncompleted suicide attempt, after which he was able to reconstitute a self. One of his oft-repeated stories was that after he and my mother divorced, he had felt like an astronaut cut loose from the mother ship, suspended in the atmosphere, untethered by gravity, location, or destination. I envisioned a puffy, suited figure gently undulating in an endless, deceptively tranquil silence. It was a story to me then, and though it was my father who went through this, I held the story and him at arm's length. It was him, after all, not me, and I was nothing like him. Little did I know then what I had in store.

Since legacy trauma is a relatively new concept that is just entering mainstream psychology, it has not been integrated into treatment protocols or the mainstream diagnostic lexicon. It can be helpful, however, to understand one's own struggles in the autobiographical context in which they developed. I can see now that the seeds of my father's breakdown had been planted long ago in me as well. My mother had lost her mother to cancer when she was eleven years old. In response, she desired nothing more than to be a housewife and mother. She managed to have two children; I came following my brother and a miscarriage. I was conceived in my mother's eye, a vision foisted upon a young man who had no clue what he wanted nor any idea of how to manage the burdens of fatherhood and a demanding career pursuing tenure at a university.

A few years following my birth, my father survived a brush with a near-deadly melanoma. This was successfully treated, but the die was cast. He awoke from the life-saving surgery and was furious. For although he had been sedated, the excision of the tumor and scraping of his lymph nodes unleashed the body memory of the brutal abuse he had endured at the hands of his mentally ill mother. Stories of his childhood were communicated to me by osmosis, or perhaps it is a constellation of my own memory, that he had been put in an oven and chased around the kitchen table with a knife as his mother foamed at the mouth. My father recalled his father's admonition, "If your mother says black is white, then black is white!" His father was intent on keeping up appearances, and my father was a necessary casualty. Excommunication was inevitable and eventually happened when my father married my mother, a Protestant, which was anathema to his Italian Catholic family. Hence, the unprocessed traumas of both my parents suffused the home where my brother and I innocently toddled around, oblivious to everything but what was being offered.

And so, my long-term anxiety disorder has its rightful origins and still informs the atmosphere of my inner world. Given all this, is it any wonder that I found myself struggling to breathe, cut loose from the mother ship, in my late fifties after my own marriage went up in flames? I lived through a distilled version of what my father had experienced after his divorce, untethered and floating in the atmosphere, the air sucked out of me. This was bound to come for the anxious little girl I had been, clinging to my mother for life.

This deeper understanding of myself developed slowly as I sought to understand what was happening to me. The material had been there all along, but it was now illuminated by an awareness that had been altogether missing before when I sought to distance myself as much as possible from the past. Consciousness evolves as you accept and process that which has formerly been unconscious. The term *unconscious* refers to that which lives inside but is disowned and hidden from oneself. The unconscious informs your consciousness, but unannounced and surreptitiously, rendering it all the more powerful. Because it is disowned, it suffuses the atmosphere of your mind-body and dictates your habits of daily living without your awareness. For me, the structures provided by rigidly scheduled food, exercise, and work served as bulwarks against the formlessness of space and time that threatened to unleash all the unprocessed traumas, all the unprocessed legacies of my parents, that I had inherited. My marriage and our home had offered the edifice that kept it all contained and looking quite respectable.

Following my divorce, a great conflagration enveloped the edifice I had so carefully constructed and my center could no longer hold. It was only because of this collapse that I was forced to come to terms with the unacknowledged fragility and fear at my core. This breakdown also allowed me to bring consciousness to the traumas that had lived unprocessed in my parents' own psyches. Giving word, story, and deep acknowledgment to what lived inside the darkness allowed a shift in my consciousness, and perhaps even theirs, though they no longer inhabit bodies. My parents gave better than they got, allowing me the gift of repeating their traumas, albeit in a different way, with a different outcome.

Trauma processing is hard work. "This is rigorous work," I repeatedly tell my clients who are in the throes of recovery from substance addiction or going through their own calamitous breakdowns. In order to process trauma, you must not shut down. Shutting down is when you slow your emotional processing system through numbing agents or behaviors. You numb with your addictions. The worst of them are the root chakra addictions, which slow you at a physical level, bathing you in a soothing balm of oblivion and leaving the traumas stagnant in your unconscious, only to rear their heads the next day, demanding more of the same. If you continue this pattern of numbing and avoidance, the unconscious pain will writhe and howl in the darkness, calling for more numbing, which, if you apply, quells the pain and allows it to grow more malignant outside your awareness.

Consciousness does not evolve by means of thinking. It evolves first by acknowledging your own pain to yourself and then by engaging with others. You cannot genuinely engage with others if you are not being honest with yourself. Your self-honesty encourages the same in others, and slowly relationships evolve to hold you in a network wherein you no longer feel so alone. This process fosters a new energy that begins to carry you along and diminishes your reliance on substances and behaviors that suppress and negate your life energy. Like a quarter turn of a kaleidoscope, the pieces of your life remain largely the same, but your reference point and the overall configuration of your life are altogether different.

Part I
The Root Chakra: Where the Mind-Body Forms

Chapter 1
Big T and the Root Chakra

In this chapter you will meet Riley, a Big T survivor and therapy client. Through her story you will learn how Big T affects nervous system development and can inflict long-term damage on a person's ability to self-regulate. She will demonstrate how the inability to self-soothe structures a chaotic and frantic relationship to oneself and others, resulting in acute psychological pain, difficulty functioning, and problems regulating basic biological needs.

The Root Chakra in Focus

Location in the Body: Base of the spine and the perineum

Developmental Challenges: Establishing safety in the body; capacity to manage bodily functions related to feeding, waste elimination, and motility; capacity to navigate obstacles in the physical world and protect physical integrity; sense of worthiness to have needs met without conditions

Threats to Development: Physical or sexual abuse, physical neglect, or abandonment; disease or deformity during childhood; cultural factors such as war, racism, sexism, homophobia, oppression, and poverty; inherited legacy trauma

Primary Developmental Conflict: Managing the inherent vulnerability of the body versus the imperative to develop mastery over the body and environment

Signs of Overdevelopment: Overeating, hoarding, miserly, priority on safety and security over the risk of new experiences, materialism, hypervigilance

Signs of Underdevelopment: Ignoring the physical body and basic material needs; inability to manage basic tasks such as cooking, cleaning, and organizing; inability to function in the world, e.g., shop for and prepare food, pay rent, have a job, or drive a car; inability to transform ideas into concrete actions leading to a desired goal

Conditioned Beliefs: You are your body and your material possessions. Your worth is earned and defined through your physical looks and prowess, the amount of money you have, and your possessions. Might makes right.

Associated Addictions: Root chakra addictions, which are defined as the passive application of a substance to the body that provides immediate relief from core anxiety; includes alcohol, nicotine, snorted or injected drugs, and food

Associated Mental Health Disturbances: Post-traumatic stress disorder, borderline personality disorder, dissociative identity disorder

Gifts of the Root Chakra: Trust in the face of uncertainty; ability to let go; ability to value what is without clinging; satisfaction with enough; ability to depend on others

No Roots Riley

Riley is a large, muscular woman in her mid-thirties. Her body is a mosaic of tattoos. A picture of a lean tiger ripples on her arm, in addition to a howling wolf on her ankle and birds in flight across her upper back. She has a formidable presence and penetrating green eyes and moves as though she is prepared for attack. She emanates an evocative intensity that is both attractive and mildly off-putting, like a hot fire you are drawn to but must maintain a safe distance from. She is like one of the animals adorning her body: wild, wary, and possibly dangerous when startled or threatened.

I hesitated before agreeing to work with Riley. She had been referred to me by a colleague who was leaving the area and had been seeing Riley in intensive therapy for several years. My colleague warned me that Riley had a serious history of trauma, with multiple hospitalizations, and carried diagnoses covering the spectrum from bipolar disorder to dissociative personality disorder and borderline personality disorder. Riley was also highly motivated, had been in long-term recovery from alcohol abuse, and, my colleague told me, had made tremendous strides in her emotional awareness and stability. I agreed to meet with her to assess whether I felt comfortable taking her on.

I liked Riley immediately. She was wary with me, I could tell, but I still felt intrigued and wanted to know her better. Many clients open up immediately, like Belle. Their story gushes out and they have an implicit trust in me that I have earned only by virtue of my title or perhaps a referral, but largely it's a leap of faith they are willing to take. Riley, by contrast, was far slower to warm. I knew she was assessing me. For what, I was not sure, but people like Riley, with a history of brutal treatment, do not trust others on faith. You must earn their trust slowly and be aware that such individuals can be hypervigilant about any perceived slight, inconsistency, or insensitivity. People like Riley are also very good at assessing others because of their exquisite attention to detail, as well as an intuitive capacity that has been well honed from early years of living amid the enemy. Such clients require me, as a therapist, to be transparent, accountable, and very present.

As Riley's story unfolded, it became clear that she had survived against all odds. She had cut off from her family long ago after years of their refusal to acknowledge the severe sexual and emotional abuse she had endured at the hands of her elder brother. The abuse began early; Riley was not sure how early. Her first memory was of being held down on her bed by him when he was entrusted with her care. He was ten years older, angry, and addicted to drugs. In addition, physical abuse was common from the nuns and teachers managing the classrooms in the private church school Riley attended throughout her childhood.

Riley's parents were severe, righteous members of a fundamentalist Christian organization. She had been raised attending church services multiple times a week and was educated in privately run church schools that were not overseen by any external body, affording them the latitude to enforce draconian disciplinarian procedures that ranged from inappropriate to downright abusive. Examples of inappropriate discipline were the multiple ruler slaps on some poor child's hands administered in front of a stricken classroom of peers. A full-on, bare-assed beating in the principal's office behind a closed door was the more dreaded, not uncommon occurrence and the sorry outcome of any perceived assertion of autonomy or resistance to the authoritarian rule. And sometimes a beating was just the result of a teacher or school administrator having a bad day, with a commensurate need to vent their interior rage on a helpless child.

Riley endured her childhood by not really being there. She had fragmented memories of her past and described herself as being a "ghost girl." She was vague and even dismissive when I probed for specific memories or descriptions of the rhythms of her early life or details of how she survived. Her history after childhood tells the story of what she was unable to describe. She was in abusive relationships from the beginning. At age fifteen she became secretly involved with an older male who was in his early twenties. She left home as soon as she graduated from high school (barely, it should be noted), having transferred from the church school to a public high school, where her lack of academic competency was roundly ignored. Having no direction or launching pad, she moved in with her boyfriend, which felt inevitable and determined. "I knew that I needed to get out of that house," she later confided in me, "and it didn't matter how or where."

The relationship was brutal from the beginning and lasted, off and on, into her twenties. His treatment of her ran the gamut from closed-fist punches on areas of her body that would not be visible to others to sexual coercion, including sodomy, sex with multiple partners, and a daily barrage of insults. She was vague about the times he sodomized her, again self-protective and not ready to deal with her feelings about the incidents or to let me get that close. Like many women without a strong sense of agency, Riley felt responsible for the occurrences because she didn't resist strongly enough. When asked why she stayed with him, she reported that when it was good, it was really good. She felt understood and safe with him. She felt like she could handle his "moods" and rationalized that if she could just manage her jealousy so as to not set him off, then things would be okay. He was there for her during the first abortion. Not so much with the second one, but she was older then and could handle it on her own.

Throughout the ten-year relationship, she tried to leave him several times. It wasn't until after a brutal beating, when she thought he would kill her, that she finally was able to leave for good. Her parents were of no help in this. She didn't even ask for their assistance at that point, but a local women's shelter provided enough respite and resources that she was able to break the tie of her dependency on him. She told me that she was sure he would have ended up killing her if she had stayed. Her next relationships weren't as clearly dangerous, but she still allowed others to dominate and dismiss her. She considered herself bisexual and had a pattern of becoming enmeshed with hyper-controlling partners, whether they were men or women.

Trauma and Development: Formation of Your Mind-Body

Riley's story illustrates the profound impact that early childhood experiences have on the formation of the mind-body system and how this influences your relationship to your physical body and needs, your expectations of other people, and your overall orientation to life. The term *mind-body system* is used to indicate just how entwined biology is with psychological health and functioning. How you were treated as a child quite literally shapes the resilience, heartiness, and balance of your nervous system, including your hormonal tendencies, neurotransmitter release and uptake, and ability to regulate stress. These biological determinants then affect your psychology, shaping your perception of the world and other people, particularly your tendency to perceive new things as threats versus opportunities. This lens through which you perceive the world has far-reaching consequences that ultimately shape your experience of life.

We will use Riley's story to illustrate the profound and often overlooked role that nervous system functioning has on mental and physical health. Even if you find Riley hard to relate to because her experiences are so extreme, remember that how her body shaped itself around trauma is applicable to you as well, even if you suffered less severe trauma. If you do share experiences similar to Riley's, perhaps you can take comfort in the fact that you are not as alone as you might think and that it is possible to heal.

Getting Through the Day

Riley's struggles illustrate the ramifications of early developmental stress on the daily well-being of an individual. Riley could not go into stores like Costco, Target, or Walmart without first taking a benzodiazepine (a strong antianxiety medication) to calm her reaction to the bright lights and noise. Any sudden movement or unexpected sound created a spike of adrenaline and correlative panic that led to over-reactive and inappropriate behavior, such as yelling at a store clerk, leaving her amped-up and miserable for hours afterward.

In the past, when she was less regulated, Riley would cut herself or binge eat to channel her distress, which she experienced as a racing heart, sweaty palms, and a sense of being trapped in her body. In addition to her reactivity, Riley also experienced chronic sleep issues that began when she was a young child. Although she had no clear memories, it is likely that her brother came to her room in the night to molest her. She also suffered from irritable bowel syndrome (IBS) and was not infrequently in severe pain due to abdominal gas, diarrhea, and constipation. The upshot of the above symptoms was that Riley was not at home in her own body and she shaped much of her daily life around managing, offsetting, and preventing the consequences of her physical reactivity. In essence, her own body was a source of chronic stress.

After Riley began the recovery process, starting with quitting alcohol, she coped with her problems with self-regulation by adopting a very rigid and circumscribed structure for daily living. This was an improvement from the past, when she had engaged in more erratic and risky behaviors. She had suffered from severe eating disorders (anorexic and bulimia), engaged in self-injury through cutting and burning herself, and had a history of reckless sexual behavior, which included meeting people she did not know for sexual trysts. She had not engaged in any of these behaviors for several years but still had to be vigilant with regard to her habits of self-regulation and activity schedule. On good days she rose at 7:00 a.m., stuck to a low-fat, vegan diet, and attended a CrossFit gym, where she performed a rigorous hour-and-a-half workout. Her ideal was to maintain this regimen six days a week and then attend her shift at Walmart, where her duties included restocking and recordkeeping for supplies and maintenance. It was a victory to have kept this job for eight months. Customer service, she had long ago discovered, was definitely not her forte due to her limited ability to interface with the public, which had resulted in being let go from several jobs in the past.

Riley began therapy with me soon after being diagnosed with a back injury that was not responding to intervention and was interfering with her job and overall quality of life. She admitted that it had gotten so bad because of her refusal (or inability) to back off her intense workouts after initial injury. In addition to the back injury, she was then walloped with a deep, enervating fatigue and malaise that was eventually diagnosed as fibromyalgia. This is a mysterious autoimmune disorder that is little understood by the medical community and is often chalked up to being all in the patient's head. Patients with fibromyalgia complain of severe, diffuse pain throughout the body and are sometimes left incapacitated for long periods of time.

This diagnosis was initially frustrating for Riley, as it offered no clear treatment plan. However, after reading about the relationship between childhood trauma and long-term health issues such as fibromyalgia, she began to connect the dots between her history and her symptoms.

Through therapy she came to understand that her rigid habits and lifestyle were actually repeating and reinforcing the abuse she received as a child. She saw that she was not listening to her own body or responding intelligently to signs of pain and distress from her flesh. This recapitulated the trauma of the abuse she had endured and her family's refusal to acknowledge it. This insight enhanced her compassion for herself and gave her a renewed sense of agency in her own life.

Self-Reinforcing Abuse Cycles

Current research links childhood trauma to long-term health problems, most notably autoimmune diseases such as fibromyalgia.[1] Exposure to this literature reinforced Riley's dawning realization that her severe treatment of herself was not her fault but was in fact a repetition of her early childhood that she was now perpetuating: "abuse by my own hand," she later sardonically quipped. Her intent had not been self-abuse; rather, keeping a rigid schedule and forcing compliance was the only way she knew how to avoid the chaos of unstructured time. Because she didn't know how to respond organically and intelligently to her own needs (after all, she had not experienced this during her infancy or childhood and therefore had no reference point), her only known choice was to rely on rigidly prescribed behaviors. But now she had a problem because this coping style was becoming abusive and was making her sick. This outcome underlines a key point of this paradigm for understanding trauma: *We treat ourselves as we were treated.*

Even if you do not have clear memories of your childhood, investigating your self-talk, habits, and lifestyle will give you a window into your past. Riley was never treated with warmth or care and had never experienced responsible limit setting. This left her unable to care for herself, and instead she repeated patterns of force and abuse. This kept the past alive in the present, and Riley was now the unwitting perpetrator of her own abuse. This is how abuse cycles are self-perpetuating and why survivors of abuse often become perpetrators or victims as adults. Another key

1. Dube et al., "Cumulative Childhood Stress and Autoimmune Diseases in Adults."

aspect of this healing paradigm is that *breakdown begets opportunity*, which is also illustrated in Riley's story. I think Riley would agree that, had her body never resisted, she likely would have continued her patterns of force and coercion and never would have let go enough to allow the growth that occurred following the breakdown of her rigid system of coping.

Biological Ramifications of Big T

The intention of the following information is to help you apply science to your own physiological and psychic structure. This will give you greater insight into how you have come to be who you are. This helps alleviate the guilt and shame that often accompany over-reactive nervous system responses and the behavioral peculiarities arising from them. You are then empowered to make mindful lifestyle choices that are not driven by a sense of "should," which is shame-based and corrective, but rather from an intention to care for yourself at a deeper level. As you redesign entrenched patterns based on coercion and correction, you learn to override the default wiring of your nervous system.

The following categories highlight key physiological functions that are deleteriously affected by childhood trauma.

A. Nervous System Development: The autonomic nervous system is comprised of two branches: (1) the sympathetic nervous system, which regulates the "fight, flight, or freeze" response, and (2) the parasympathetic nervous system, which oversees your capacity to "rest and digest" and restores your mind-body from the wear and tear of daily life. These two systems are meant to work in tandem. Ideally, the parasympathetic nervous system provides a resilient and responsive balancing function to offset the activating tendencies of the sympathetic nervous system. The functions and response patterns of your autonomic nervous system are typically not under your conscious control. Some advanced yoga practitioners are able to control their heartbeat and breathing to an astounding degree, but this is highly unusual and takes years of cultivating interior body awareness and self-regulatory skills. For the majority of us, the two systems operate independently of our will and our response patterns are controlled by instinctive survival reflexes that are hardwired during our early life.

Your early childhood environment influences the baseline wiring of your nervous system and establishes the hard drive of your mind-body system. During your early years, your body adapts to the demands of your environment. If you were reared in an environment with chronic stress, you were unable to count on consistent, nurturing care. Sustained periods of enduring hunger or other physical discomfort caused by being too hot or cold or left in an unclean diaper create a psychobiological anxiety that lives in the body. Because you were under chronic stress, your sympathetic nervous system was continually activated and the parasympathetic branch of your nervous system failed to develop a hardy balancing response.

The "use it or lose it" principle applies to the nervous system as well as to more visible functions of the body. A lack of parasympathetic tonality not only degrades the quality of your life and sense of well-being but also damages your body and interferes with the reparative functions that are initiated during resting states. Because you are continually poised for threat, essentially out of habit, relatively small stressors such as bright lights and loud noises can precipitate chemical and hormonal responses that are rooted in the past and not relevant to your current environment. The absence of memories of the pleasures of human interaction in your visceral unconscious also contributes to the deep hopelessness that drives some individuals to severe addiction or suicide.

This nightmare is well illustrated by Riley's story. After she left her family of origin, she chose a man who was similarly abusive and emotionally vacant. And even after she left that relationship, she continued to abuse herself with drugs and alcohol, food, and self-mutilation. As horrific as these behaviors sound, they were actually ways of coping with her overactive stress response and inability to self-regulate. The sympathetic branch of her nervous system was never dormant, so she felt continually under attack. Self-harm actually had the effect of calming her because she could externalize her pain and achieve some relief. Having never known the deep pleasure and relaxation of satisfactory feeding, being clean and safe, snuggled against a familiar-smelling body, or giggling joyfully and being held and tickled in a responsive, sensitive way, she had no reference point of hope stored in her deep memory. Consequently, it became all too easy to re-create what she knew and settle into familiar, albeit dangerous, abuse patterns.

The tragedy of trauma is that it renders you eternally stuck in the past by virtue of your body's ingrained responses, which reinforce terror and helplessness even when you are no longer under threat. Lack of parasympathetic tonality creates an enormous deficit because happiness and well-being are experienced in discrete moments that are rooted in the body. Your body's capacity to regulate also frees your energetic and cognitive capacities to engage with the world in an open, spontaneous way. Put simply, safety is the prerequisite for learning, engagement, and the ability to live in the present. When you are wired for stress, you are at an extreme disadvantage through no fault of your own. You are unable to live in the moment or fully enjoy the small pleasures of your life because you are chronically tense, sleep-deprived, and in a state of internal distress. You may not be fully aware of this because it is all you have ever known; however, this does not mitigate the reality of your condition and its effect on your quality of life.

B. Interoception: The term *interoception* refers to your capacity to track internal sensate experiences, such as feeling cold, warmth, tension, hunger, thirst, and satiety. *Proprioception*, in contrast, refers to your awareness of your body in space and enables you to kick a ball and not bump into things in your path. Both capacities are crucial aspects of nervous system development, although, not surprisingly, caregivers generally pay more attention to a child's proprioception than to teaching them how to track and meaningfully respond to internal states of awareness.

Riley again illustrates how a lack of interoception can have a pernicious effect on a person's overall health and well-being. I remember one session where she was having a harder time than usual staying present and focusing on her feelings. I noticed that she was dressed lightly, and she informed me that she had walked from work to my office, which was several miles. After further questioning, it turned out that she hadn't eaten all day and was also very cold. This opened up a whole new area of insight and work for her, as she recognized that she was often so dissociated from her body that she neglected to care for herself in basic ways. Being too cold and gutting it out, either forgetting to eat or stuffing herself with rich food, were patterns that she had never fully recognized as vestiges of her childhood. After I fixed her some tea and gave her a blanket and some nuts, we had a productive session where she viscerally felt the power of human care and recognized her own capacity to do this for herself. I reminded her of the fact that due to how her nervous system was wired as a child, she had learned to dissociate from her own needs, which led her to inadvertently neglect herself. We discussed ways she could learn to check in with herself to rewire this pattern in her nervous system.

C. The Vagus Nerve: The vagus is a cranial nerve extending down from the brain stem into the rest of the body, where it connects to the internal organs above and below the diaphragm. It relays information from your organs to your brain, giving it a primary role in interoception. It also plays a role in digestion, respiration, and heart rate. When you exist in a state of chronic stress, your vagus nerve loses tonality. Riley experienced this viscerally in sessions when she discovered that, after a very brief meditation and some gentle stretching, she felt much more relaxed and "in her body," as she put it. This enhanced the quality of our sessions and allowed her access to more body awareness outside of sessions. "I never realized how tight my shoulders are," she later shared, "like all the time. I remember having headaches as a kid, and now I know it's because I was clenching practically every muscle in my body." Riley discovered that small increments of attention toward herself enhanced her sense of security and made it easier to cope with the stressors of the day. She even felt that her fibromyalgia symptoms were improving, and I shared with her the recent research linking adverse childhood experiences to chronic health problems in adulthood, including high blood pressure, obesity, and autoimmune disorders.[2]

D. Heart Rate Variability (HRV): When you inhale, your sympathetic nervous system is activated and your heart rate speeds up. As you exhale, your parasympathetic nervous system initiates the vagal brake, which slows your heart rate. The slowing of your heart rate by the vagal brake provides an ongoing check on sympathetic nervous system activation and helps to keep your body in a balanced state. Heart rate variability measures the discrepancy between your heart rate as you inhale and your heart rate as you exhale. Ideally there should be high variability between these two measures, showing that your vagal brake is functioning well and your parasympathetic nervous system is responsive to ongoing fluctuations in sympathetic activation.

Heart rate variability is a good measure of the general tonality of your parasympathetic nervous system and vagus nerve. When your HRV is high, it indicates that your vagal brake is working well and there is a healthy balance between the activating (sympathetic) and corresponding balancing (parasympathetic) capacities of your nervous system. The ability to slow activation, not only of your heart rate but of all the systems in your body that create muscular contraction and release stress hormones, is a crucial determinant of your physical and emotional health. When you are in a state of chronic hyperarousal, particularly when you are not in physically challenging circumstances, it creates a chronic sense of agitation and anxiety. It is understandable that when a young child is under chronic stress, their nervous system acclimates to this state and wires itself accordingly, leading to a loss of vagal tone and low HRV. This vividly illustrates the detrimental biological ramifications of Big T, as Riley's experience also reinforces.

E. Rest and Digest: The parasympathetic nervous system governs these two primary capacities and needs of the body. Sleeping well and digesting

2. Dube et al., "Cumulative Childhood Stress and Autoimmune Diseases in Adults."

well are not only physical necessities but also pleasurable experiences that bring feelings of happiness and well-being to daily living. The feeling of being pleasantly full after a good meal or drifting into peaceful sleep are blessed moments in a human life. When the body is contracted into chronic stress patterns, these capacities degrade and can be all but lost. The inability to digest well and sleep well add two more stressors to your life, because not only do you have to contend with the stress that led you to be poised for threat, but now you are also stressed because your body is not working as it should. Again, the tragedy of a child who has not experienced these pleasures on a consistent basis is illustrated by Riley. Since her biology never knew these gifts, she was not wired to expect or seek them out. This led to a loss of safety and basic enjoyment, and the emotional and psychological ramifications of that will be discussed next.

Psychological Ramifications: Stress Related to Living in the Body

An unidentified aspect of stress is the chronic stress some people experience managing their own bodies. The stress of bathing, grooming, exercising, feeding, dressing, and moving can take a huge unconscious toll on a person's sense of ease and well-being. "Will I be able to sleep tonight?" "Will I fit into my jeans tomorrow?" "What if I don't have the energy to go to the party tonight? "Will I be able to stick to my diet with all that tempting food?" "Will I be able to keep up with everyone on the hike?" These worries can chip away at your self-esteem and confidence and cause you to avoid events that you anticipate will be uncomfortable or embarrassing. The fear of having your anomalies and weaknesses seen by others, and the fear of losing control, exact an internal toll that is often unconscious. Shame about the body's needs and dysfunctions can be so ingrained that it causes some people who are having serious medical events to refuse to call an ambulance or seek immediate medical attention.

Identifying how chronic, internal stress shadows your daily life is the first step of change. The following categories underline how a lack of confidence in your body's functioning may express in your daily life. Note that you may experience some or all of the following conditions even if you did not experience overt trauma or chronic emotional invalidation as a child. This is because difficulty living in and regulating the body is a pervasive problem in this culture due to an overemphasis on the material body, its looks and performance, coupled with the level of daily stress plaguing most individuals. This alienation is further exacerbated by our alienation from the natural world and rhythms of nature.

A. Health Anxiety: Do you often worry that you have a serious disease or physical problem? Do you focus on small discomforts in your body and find yourself ruminating about what the problem might be and how you can fix it? Do you frequently consult Doctor Google, who is an infamous hysteric known for chronicling worst-case scenarios with little to no filter? Do you foresee catastrophic consequences of your supposed ailment? Do you feel shame about it and blame yourself? Do you need to see a doctor or have tests done before you can calm down? Or, conversely, do you avoid seeing the doctor and ignore troubling health issues that you need to address?

An over-preoccupation with health is distinct from realistic concern about a potential health problem because of the frequency with which you identify a problem and the way it sabotages your daily sense of safety and peace. Your preoccupation can result in rigid rituals, including unusual vitamin protocols, eating and exercise routines that interfere with normal activities, or overscheduling invasive medical procedures in response to unfamiliar sensations in your body. Underlying your fixation is a denial of the inherent vulnerability of your body that is manifested in the attempt to circumvent illness through hypervigilant control. The opposite affliction is ignoring your body and neglecting your health. Minimizing the importance of your health and not attending to issues that might be of concern manifests a similar disregard for the ephemeral nature of your own existence and a refusal to acknowledge its fragility and need for attention. This, of course, can result in actual health issues remaining unaddressed until they develop into something serious.

B. Eating Anxiety: Distrust of your appetite and your ability to regulate your need for nourishment often results in anxiety around eating and exercise. This can result in rigid and circumscribed eating and exercise patterns or dissociation from the anxiety altogether, leading you to eat whatever food is offered whenever it is offered. In the former coping style, you track weight, calories, and exercise obsessively as a means to establish a sense of control. Although this creates a temporary illusion of control, your rituals also absorb a large amount of energy and attention and are laden with anxiety. Riley experienced this rigid preoccupation with food and exercise, which she later realized interfered with forming friendships and participating in activities that threatened to disrupt her diet and exercise protocol.

The opposite pattern is living in a state of nonrestraint and dissociation from your appetite and paying no attention at all to health and nutrition. Riley had lived this way during her alcoholism, and her fear of returning to this unregulated state fueled her obsessive regimen. Similar to the pattern of rigid control, this pattern can lead to circumventing social engagements, traveling, clothes shopping, and skipping medical checkups in order to avoid confrontation with your health and/or size. Anxiety eventually crashes in when you have to visit a doctor, glimpse an unwelcome picture of yourself, or need to take an airplane and fit into a small space. Underlying both expressions of eating anxiety is an inability to feel and respond appropriately to hunger, which is a result of dissociation from your body. This problem often bespeaks an overall shame about your needs and a fear that you are unable to regulate them.

C. Sleep Anxiety: When you are unable to sleep, you suffer from an inability to let go and allow your parasympathetic nervous system to assume its rightful dominion. The capacity to soften consciousness and trust your body to release is an essential aspect of mental and physical health. The sleepless individual is trapped in a tense body and a ruminating mind that allows no peace. The desperation to sleep, coupled with the inability to do so, creates even more anxiety and a sense of inner helplessness, which only increases your difficulty falling asleep. You may struggle not to become drug-dependent but feel driven to take sedatives in order to get some rest, which inserts a pernicious gnaw of guilt into your system. The inability of your logical mind to fix this malady is deeply frustrating and perpetuates a negative relationship to your organic self.

Riley had years of reliance on sleep medications, which she continued to use occasionally due to still suffering from intermittent insomnia. "It's not as bad as it used to be," she acknowledged ruefully, "but it still rears up when I am under stress." We further discussed how the hardwiring of the nervous system is pretty cemented, and although it can be altered, it still tends to default to old patterns.

D. Intestinal Anxiety: When you suffer from digestive problems, you bear a secret shame that creates anxiety and rigid lifestyle patterns designed to avoid embarrassment and physical discomfort. If you have IBS-diarrhea, you fear that an attack will strike when a bathroom is unavailable. You may not eat and choose to go hungry rather than risk a sudden attack of diarrhea during a work event or social engagement. The inability to control gas or digestive pain that strikes randomly can create avoidance patterns coupled with shame about the primitive nature of your ailment. Alternatively, when you have IBS-constipation, you suffer the indignity of being unable to move your bowels. This can result in physical and emotional discomfort that verges on torment. Individuals afflicted with either of these dysfunctions often become preoccupied with them and develop strange eating habits and rigid routines to avoid discomfort and embarrassment. These symptoms reinforce distrust in the body and alienation from the natural rhythms of the organic self, as well as alienation from other people and the bonding that occurs through communal rituals around food.

Fortunately, Riley's digestive issues resolved after she began eating and resting in a more regulated and mindful way. She reported being greatly relieved by no longer needing to worry about the availability of toilets or having an onset of debilitating intestinal pain. "It's funny, sometimes now I take it for granted that, you know," she smiled, "things just move along. It's easy to forget just what a shit show it used to be. Sorry," she added, smirking, "I just couldn't resist."

Psychobiological Ramifications of Big T in Early Childhood

Big T: Physical abuse, sexual abuse, or a lack of attention to a child's basic physical need for safety, well-timed, nutritious food, warm clothing, and a safe, comfortable physical environment

Nervous System Wiring: Dominance of the sympathetic nervous system resulting in low parasympathetic tonality and a mental and physical orientation toward threat in the environment

Physical Consequences: Hormonal regulation oriented toward chronic activation; low heart rate variability and low vagal tonality; muscular tension; impaired digestion due to clenching in the belly; constricted breathing

Psychological Consequences: Hyperbolic response to perceived impingements such as loud noises or sudden movements; attention oriented toward threat versus engagement, learning, and pleasure; body not experienced as a friend or a source of pleasure; tendency to dissociate and not attend to the present moment

Relational Consequences: Others perceived as sources of potential threat rather than pleasure and nurture; tending toward isolation due to fear of others or, conversely, being overly clingy with others and unable to read social cues

Functional Difficulties: Problems establishing regulated eating, sleeping, and elimination patterns leading to either rigid patterns of self-care or lack of awareness of the body's needs

Emotional Consequences: Physiological tension and discomfort leading to emotional constriction and lack of humor, imagination, and gratitude; tendency toward anger and negativity; tendency to blame self for feeling bad due to the natural proclivity of children to be self-referential; feeling bad is experienced as being bad. These issues will be explored more thoroughly in chapter 4, when we look at specific mental health conditions connected to the root chakra.

Riley's story illustrates the tragic consequences of a child being subjected to Big T during their crucial developmental years. The nervous system wires itself around the need to be vigilant and hence trends toward hyper-arousal. This leads to imbalances in the central nervous system and a lack of tonality in the parasympathetic branch, which governs the restorative function of the body. This not only has severe health implications but also leads to psychological stress surrounding the inability to manage the body's basic functions. Riley's experience demonstrates how Big T can then predispose a person to develop addiction, which you will learn about next.

Chapter 2
Root Chakra Damage via Big T

In this chapter you will learn about how addiction progresses in individuals with Big T. Riley's story demonstrates how poor attachment to primary caregivers translates into distrust of other people in general. Substances are unconsciously chosen as a substitute for people and become one-stop shopping to get all one's needs met. Modeling of addictive substance use by early caregivers, abuse, and an unregulated nervous system load the gun, while the inability to cope with normative developmental challenges pulls the trigger. You will learn how the sexual abuse Riley endured, coupled with her parents' modeling of substance use, made it all but inevitable that Riley would come to depend on substances. This need not be the end of the story, however, and through Riley you will learn how recovery can and does occur. This involves learning to cope with the inevitable wounding inflicted by other people without falling into self-abuse and despair.

Progression and Recovery in Root Chakra Addiction

This section explores the factors that create a vulnerability to developing an addiction and also illustrates how recovery can later take hold and allow for a healing process.

The Loaded Gun

Due to the faulty foundation that results from Big T, and its physical and relational ramifications, it is not uncommon for survivors of Big T to develop root chakra addictions. This is due to the discomfort of living in a chronically tense body and is also a way to compensate for social difficulties and a lack of pleasure in normative activities, such as playing, learning, and imagining. Root chakra addictions are defined as the application of a substance through the mouth, the nose, or intravenous injection in order to create feelings of pleasure and relaxation. The substance quickly bathes the nervous system and, by virtue of its chemical impact, allows the nervous system to release. Stimulating chemicals are also frequently used to manipulate the sedated nervous system into activation and to enhance social interaction. Keep in mind that all drugs, including stimulants, alcohol, and cigarettes, are also frequently used and abused by individuals who do not have a history of Big T. This is because drugs enhance pleasure, reduce anxiety, and play a big role in social connection.

Riley began drinking and smoking cigarettes in early adolescence even though she didn't particularly enjoy either substance at first. But they allowed her to join with cohorts and gave her a way to bypass feeling like an alien. Her problem was that she didn't know how to regulate her drinking because of her pattern of dissociation and poor interoception. Consequently, she came to depend on both habits rather quickly as a means to feel comfortable around others. Her alcohol and cigarette use slowly edged into her private life as well. "It cushioned things," she later told me. "It gave me something to look forward to and something that I could control, kind of like a punctuation mark at the end of a sentence. Especially after my brother would molest me, it was there like a friend that I could count on to make it go away." She paused for a moment. "You know, I just thought of this: It also let me do something bad to myself, and in that way it gave me a sense of control, almost like an 'F**k you, you're not the only one who can abuse me.'"

Riley was far into her recovery at that time and had developed a language to express and understand her inner chaos, which prior to therapy was inchoate, even to herself. "I just felt so bad inside," she went on. "Just bad. Bad, bad, bad. My therapist called it 'badding' on myself, and that was exactly what it was. She actually told me to say it out loud, and I would. I'd just say it: 'You are so bad. You are bad, bad, bad.' I'd say it over and over again and somehow that diffused it. It's weird," she mused, "but somehow saying it out loud made it less powerful and helped me see that it wasn't true because I was able to hear how absurd it was."

This was actually a very effective intervention by Riley's therapist that did not reinforce her bad feelings but instead brought them to the surface so that she could identify them and work more consciously with them. During her therapy with me, Riley had many years in recovery unfurling the layers of her past trauma. "Yeah, it was pretty ugly," she shook her head and went on. "I'd call myself names like Cunt, Loser, and Waste of Life. I wouldn't mean it. It was like a purge of my brother and of how much I hated myself, but it helped me to see that I didn't really hate myself. I hated what he'd done to me and how he'd made it my fault. And I really hated my parents for sitting on their sorry asses and ignoring the whole shit show. It was so painful to have to feel all that, and sometimes I literally didn't think I could survive it."

"You know, Riley," I responded after a pause, "healing is rigorous work. People think it's some airy-fairy feel-good thing involving massage oils and aromatherapy. How wrong they are. It hurts from the inside out when you come to terms with what was done to you when you had no say in the matter. I guess it's why many people choose not to do the work."

"Yeah," she said, "sometimes I wished I could just go back and get shit-faced, but my therapist would tell me, 'You've come too far. You know too much. You would be going back to an even worse hell because now you know better.' I knew she was right. But man, it's like you've got to relive all the feelings again. When I had to break it off with Rick, who was kicking my ass, it was like coming to terms with what a shitty family I had and my fear that no one would ever be there for me." Rick was the man she left her family to live with in her late teens who ended up repeating the abuse she had grown up with. She continued, "It brought it all back and it just seemed so unfair and really terrifying."

"What got you through?" I queried.

"Oh, it's like Sheila (her therapist) said. I'd come too far and I knew it wouldn't be better to go back on the bottle. I mean, I did go there at first, you know, but I guess between Sheila and my sponsor, I had enough of a foothold to stop the train."

Pulling the Trigger

In her twenties, Riley began drinking regularly to soothe chronic internal tension, though at that time she had no idea why she was drinking. What she did feel was trapped in her body, her life, and even trapped in time, she told me during one session. During her worst periods, she felt that the only relief she had was after drinking several shots of hard alcohol. That was a dark time, she told me, literally moving from one hit to the next to numb the pain. "It stopped even working at the end," she said. "I learned that that happens in late-stage addiction."

Late-stage addiction refers to the period when the substance doesn't even work anymore to make you feel good. At this point you are using it to try to feel normal and avoid withdrawal. "I'd just drink myself into a stupor, feeling as bad as I can imagine anyone has ever felt." She shook her head sadly. "Some people think hell is a place you go to after death, but I think that was hell, pure hell. Because you know you are doing it to yourself, but you don't know what else to do." She looked sober as she said this, dead sober. I reflected that this was what motivated her now in her work with addicts in her church. She had previously expressed to me how much it meant to her to provide others with a safe place as they struggled with the demons she was so familiar with. "Yeah, I'm in a much different place now, and if I can help one person who is in that hell and give them some comfort, well, that's what gives me purpose."

After her final and most serious suicide attempt, Riley ended up in rehab and then became involved in recovery through Alcoholics Anonymous. She was in the program for several years and found it beneficial; however, she also became disillusioned with it after having a falling-out with her sponsor, whom she began to experience as hypercritical and controlling. She lost her community with AA and relapsed briefly, though thankfully she had enough recovery to recognize the misery of that existence and ultimately decided that she didn't want to drink herself to death.

She had maintained her sobriety ever since that pivotal decision, which harkened her eventual entry into therapy with my colleague and then to seeing me.

Through therapy Riley was able to affirm her choice to live on her own terms and establish a foundation from which to build a more meaningful life. She was also able to see that her pattern of addictions, with alcohol, food, and cigarettes (which were all in her playbook at one time and still reared up now and then, especially food), made sense in light of the lack of safety and nurture in her background. She began to have more understanding and empathy for her strong need for soothing and her lack of capacity to self-soothe in any other way, including the most fundamentally human way, which is to turn toward relationships. She eventually met her need for relationship at a spiritual center she connected with, which allowed her to participate as an informal counselor and spiritual sponsor for addicts in recovery. "It's a godsend," she told me. "The people there, well, they are my family."

Pick Your Poison

The paradox at the heart of addiction, especially in its most severe forms, is that it is simultaneously an act of self-care and self-destruction. At the time of its inception, it serves a vital purpose that saves the Big T survivor from psychological torment. Riley survived the abuse of her early life through dissociation. She has little memory of her childhood other than being alone a lot, hiding under her bed, and losing herself in TV shows about "normal" families. Adolescence pushed the envelope of her coping skills. She didn't know how to act with peers and at school, which had been a struggle from the beginning due to her dissociation and lack of normative childhood experiences.

Identity formation is the crucial developmental challenge of adolescence. Ideally a young person has some sense of their strengths and weaknesses, values and goals, and a general sense of direction. Parents not only model a coherent way of living but also help the young person plan a future, pick activities, and provide a container to help the child deal with inevitable setbacks. Riley had none of these benefits. Diffuse identity formation is the negative outcome of teen identity formation, wherein the young person lacks the support to help them develop a coherent sense of what their values are, how they enjoy spending their time, and what kind of people they like. Riley's diffuse identity left her subject to the whims of peer pressure, her biology, and circumstance.

Alcohol gave Riley a needed point of connection with peers and also numbed the internal turmoil that was a constant gnaw when she was not in a dissociated state. Adding to Riley's attraction to substances was the early modeling in her family. She realized during therapy the impact that both her parents' daily drinking habits had on her. Her father, in particular, drank quite a bit, though she had never thought of him as an alcoholic since he didn't fit the picture of a drunk that she had in her mind. She later realized that his use of alcohol, in addition to prescription pain medication, kept him in a perpetually numb state and modeled addictive behavior as normal. Her mother, whom she had just thought of as overweight, she later realized relied on food to self-soothe. Her mother had gone through gastric bypass surgery when Riley was twelve and lost over a hundred pounds. Unfortunately, this weight loss lasted only a few years and her body expanded again under the weight of the grim, resigned mask that had long ago taken over her face.

Therapy allowed Riley to see the stark reality right beneath her addiction. Due to the lack of safety in her childhood, she learned early on that people were dangerous. Furthermore, she had never been exposed to the joy, laughter, and play that make people wonderful and life worth living. As a young person, she decided to pick the poison of alcohol over the painful poison of cruel, toxic relationships. When she decided to give up alcohol, following her last suicide attempt and hospitalization, she literally had no coping skills. This is where AA was a godsend for her. It gave her a structure and format to engage with people in a more real, honest way than she ever had before. She developed a social life and a community and even became involved in chairing AA meetings and sharing her story.

Problems occurred later that threatened her recovery and forced her to confront her early attachment wounds. Many people in recovery, and in this case her sponsor, are quite wounded and, because of this, can end up being hurtful. Riley and her sponsor had a falling-out after Riley did not follow her sponsor's advice to cut off her family, which she was not ready to do at that time. When her sponsor told her she could no longer work with her, Riley felt angry and abandoned. This was a crisis point for her, where she was essentially confronted with the question of whether she should live or die. "If people always let you down, then what's the point?" She did begin drinking again for a brief period. Interestingly, as much as she longed to check out and go into oblivion, she had established a long-enough period in recovery that she couldn't fully give herself over to the alcohol. As she later told me, echoing the words of her therapist, "I knew too much." Essentially, she realized there was no getting out of it. "Life is coming for you, one way or another. You might as well turn around and meet it." She looked sober as she said this, even with a wry smile on her face.

Riley had to choose between the poison of alcohol, which was a sure path to self-destruction, or the poison that she had so often encountered in her relationships with others. She decided to stay in the world, and although she had pulled away from many of her relationships in her recovery groups, she was still hopeful that she could learn better skills to stay safe with others she connected with in her life. She realized that she unconsciously gravitated toward people who were also very wounded. She became more discerning in her choice of the people she spent time with and was able to find people in a spiritual community that she felt safe and supported in. She continued to be mindful of her own boundaries with others and not allow herself to get lazy with her own self-care and become over-reliant on someone else to fill in for this. "At the end of the day, I need to be my own best friend," she summed up. "It's hard work, but it's the most important thing."

Riley's story is a poignant example of how Big T can make it nearly inevitable that an individual will become addicted to a substance. Riley entered the social world lacking the capacity to connect meaningfully with others and was already predisposed to be highly tense and suspicious. Substances provided a welcome crutch to help her through the difficult developmental phase of early adolescence. Since Riley lacked basic self-regulation skills, it is easy to see how she later resorted to substances to soothe her hyper-aroused system and then became dependent on them. Riley's story is also a testament to an individual's capacity to change. Next you will learn how root chakra addictions can also take hold in individuals with less severe trauma backgrounds but who find themselves overwhelmed by life's demands nonetheless.

Riley at a Glance

Big T: Physical and sexual abuse perpetrated by her brother and school personnel (physical)

Little t: Having her parents and teachers ignore or collude with the abuse; lack of attention to Riley's needs for play, stimulation, learning, and affection

Legacy Trauma: Marriage by young parents unprepared for child-rearing; father and mother both turned away from challenge and relied on root chakra addictions to cope; joyless and hopeless environment lacking the opportunity for learning, pleasure, and possibility; little known about parents' family of origin, though both grew up poor and Riley's mother was sexually abused by Riley's grandfather, who was alcoholic; father supported family from age fifteen, when his own father passed in a work accident.

The Download

Relationship to Body: The body, and its needs, is a source of stress and burden; lack of pleasure in meeting and tending to the body's needs; lack of experience in early childhood mastering physical skills and experiencing sensual enjoyment

Relationship to Self: Sense of being bad, wrong, and lost; lack of trust in own instincts; self-rejection devolving into self-hatred at times

Relationship to Others: Isolation and avoidance; lack of experience in the pleasure of connection with others; tendency to force and coerce self to comply with standards imposed by others, followed by rebellion; pattern of isolation or clinging

Root Chakra Addictions: Include food, cigarettes, and alcohol; need to soothe internal tension and lack of alternative coping skills; abuse of self through the substance; acting out inner self-rejection that confirms her belief that she is bad, hopeless, and out of control

Mental Health Disorders: Borderline personality disorder, dissociative identity disorder, complex post-traumatic stress disorder, attention deficit hyperactivity disorder, bipolar II disorder

Chapter 3

Little t and the Root Chakra

In this chapter you will learn more about root chakra addiction and Little t. In a prelude to what you will learn about the sacral chakra in part II, we will discuss the important role early caregivers play in helping a child express their feelings and how this impacts the child's relationship to themselves. You will then be introduced to Joe, who, like Belle, grew up in an ordinary, upper-middle-class American household. Through both Joe's and Belle's stories, you will further understand how Little t, or emotional invalidation, impacts a person's ability to name and regulate their feelings, resulting in symptoms that can later lead to substance use. Both Belle and Joe will demonstrate how a tense body reveals what cannot be named through language, resulting in physical symptoms that feel mysterious and random. Root chakra addictions can then develop as a way to manage these symptoms.

Little t and the Language of Emotion

Whereas Riley experienced stark Little t, which occurs when there is complicity with abuse and no attention at all is given to the child's emotional and cognitive needs, subtle Little t often falls under the guise of "good parenting" and refers to emotionally flat, repressive environments where appearance and performance are given priority over a child's internal experience. Experiencing subtle Little t sets the stage for addiction that is usually less severe than addiction linked to Big T but can still siphon energy and reduce quality of life

Your first experiences in your family teach you what feelings are acceptable and how to express those feelings. The importance of having an awareness of your feelings, and the capacity to put your internal experience into words, cannot be overemphasized. This is what provides the underpinnings of a self and bridges the gap between you and other people. You can think of this as learning a language that then serves as a reference point and lexicon to create a narrative of self. British psychiatrist John Bowlby, who researched attachment, captured this eloquently when he stated, "What cannot be communicated to the mother cannot be communicated to the self."[3]

The feelings that your family encourages become a reference point for who you are, while the feelings that are discouraged or censored get deleted from your narrative of self. The interior lexicon you develop has a direct impact on how you relate to others and the quality of your attachments. "Feeling felt" is a phrase coined by Daniel Siegel, a renowned researcher, writer, and clinician.[4] He uses this phrase to describe the invisible but very real bond that exists between people and their loved ones, even when they are not in physical proximity. Feeling felt is what allows some lucky individuals to be physically alone but not feel alone. Feeling felt is a building block in a child's ability to establish a relationship to the self. When an internal relationship to self is lacking, and when little value is given to the interior world of feeling, the child learns to be externally referential and becomes dependent on other people and material reference points to tell them what to do and when to do it and ultimately to validate their worth. This is how numbers on a scale, rank and status, and zeros in a bank account can take primacy in a person's priorities and sense of self. Measuring one's value through external referencing and relying on material supports to prove one's worth creates a subtle but pervasive anxiety that can then lead to root chakra addiction.

---

3. Ainsworth and Bowlby, "An Ethological Approach to Personality Development."

4. Siegel, *Mindsight: The New Science of Personal Transformation.*

You are now going to meet Joe, who illustrates the dilemma of being a good, hardworking person who nonetheless feels empty and lost inside and who finds himself drawn to alcohol to fill this void. He illustrates the plight of an individual who was not encouraged to develop a nuanced narrative of self and thus found himself lost and without a reference point when achievement in the world failed to fill the interior void.

Joe: My Body, Myself

When I first met Joe, I was struck by how handsome he was. He fit a cultural male ideal, presenting with a tall, lean, and athletic build. He carried himself well, like a man used to second looks, and he often wore suits to therapy, sitting formally with legs crossed and sporting expensive-looking, always polished leather shoes. Clearly he had an eye for fashion and sought to make a good impression. Sometimes he showed up with playful though always color-coordinated socks adorned with bright balloons or puppies to celebrate his much beloved dog. These little gestures were touching and contrasted with his overall heavy presence. You see, in spite of Joe's striking physical appearance, he seemed self-conscious and formal in a way that made it hard to engage him in a free exchange. He was stiff, appearing to measure every word before he said it to see if it was appropriate or smart. He even wore his body as if he had rented it from an expensive vendor and had to be very careful lest he return it with a dent or stain.

I started working with Joe when he was forty-six. He was an upper-level manager in a large corporation and by all accounts was quite successful in his role there. But from the beginning of our work together he expressed a mild yet pervasive dissatisfaction with his job and his life. He made good money and was the primary earner in his household, which consisted of his wife, two children, and the family dog. But there was something missing. "I don't know what it is," he said almost apologetically during one of our early sessions. He seemed uncomfortable with not having a clear answer when I probed the dimensions of his unhappiness. "I mean, I have everything I thought I wanted. Things are really good. I just don't know what it is," he repeated helplessly, sighing heavily as he leaned back in his chair, waiting for direction or clarification.

Joe was a man who enjoyed having and, I came to learn, needed straightforward answers. He'd thought about medication and wanted to know what I thought. I hesitated before offering a fix for his malaise, partly because I knew that the actual results of the medication often did not meet expectations, and also because I wanted to get a better sense of Joe's emotional landscape before suggesting solutions. I soon learned that he could recite facts about various landmarks in the area and give blow-by-blow details about the sports figures he revered, but when it came to understanding himself, he came up short

"Maybe I should have pursued a different career," he mused during one session soon after we had begun therapy. His dream had been to become a sports journalist or college coach, but he had never really pursued it. "I don't know, I doubt I could have made it. I mean, everyone wants a job like that, you know, the big-time positions. Things in my life are generally okay," he said, defending the status quo and minimizing his feelings. "I make good money. I really shouldn't complain." His self-disapproval reared up again as he reduced his feelings to merely being complaining or, even worse, just plain wrong.

I sat wondering about his childhood and was waiting for the right time to ask about it. Instead I took a different tack. "Joe," I began, "as your listener, it almost seems like you feel that you shouldn't feel what you feel, like somehow you're complaining instead of expressing very common struggles people your age have. You know, in their twenties, many people are filled with bright expectations of the future and reaching the top of the ladder, and, well, you get there and look around, and it's not unusual to feel, 'Is this it? Really?'"

In response, Joe looked mildly interested, perhaps comforted. "It does all just seem kinda flat," he responded, "anticlimactic somehow. I guess it's a midlife thing." He chuckled in the rather canned, forced way he often did. He seemed mollified by the cliché explanation for his unhappiness, perhaps comforted by the idea that he wasn't alone in it. I had noted his emphasis on "big-time positions" when discussing various job options. I wondered if this had to do with making his father proud by living up to his expectations.

It appeared that Joe compensated for his lack of emotional fluency by relying on his body and other material supports, like nice things, to provide validation and an inward sense of stability. He had been a somewhat gifted athlete in his youth and stated that he still worked out regularly. Similarly, he emphasized his title at his job and was very proud of the Mercedes he drove. In essence, he defined himself, his worthiness, by virtue of numbers, facts, figures, and appearances. He worshiped at the altar of the material world, the domain of the root chakra. His looks, status, and material possessions compensated for his lack of confidence and emotional fluency, which are capacities governed by the sacral chakra and allow one a sense of comfort and intimacy with one's self.

Walls Closing In

Joe's reliance on the material domain to feel worthy left him feeling perpetually unsafe, because as we all know, material things come and go. Besides that, even when everything is lined up on the material plane, that doesn't mean that things line up internally. Ever-present and unavoidable, the scarcity of Joe's internal space was beginning to haunt him, especially as time marched on and the boxes of "I'll be happy when . . ." were gradually being checked off. In addition, Joe was beginning to feel the gradual atrophy of his body's resilience and capacity. Being taller, stronger, and faster than others had been a cornerstone of his self-esteem, giving him a literal leg up on others. His body's natural decline with age threatened to strip him of his implicitly felt dominance. I was not sure how much of this was conscious for Joe, though he spoke often and regretfully about getting older and the physical changes he was noticing. I took note, strategizing a gentle way to discuss this bulwark of his identity without judgment or accusation. I wanted to get a better sense of his developmental history and the origins of his strong identification with his body, athleticism, and financial success.

The initial focus of therapy was helping Joe articulate his diffuse unhappiness, as well as getting a sense of the rhythm of the days he lived, his relationship with his wife and children, and his sources of pleasure and comfort. This kind of exploration can serve as a gateway into deeper conversations, especially with individuals like Joe who have difficulty finding words to describe their interior life.

I learned that Joe was highly structured. He rose early and worked out hard at the gym if sleep and energy cooperated. He then went to work, which he described as highly stressful, "putting out fires." He was distressed to see his blood pressure rising and starting to raise a red flag with his primary care doctor. He stated that he was prone to ignore his health and relied on his wife to cajole him into keeping his annual appointments and checking his blood pressure daily, which he was loath to do. "I have white coat hypertension," he quipped sheepishly. I asked him what he did to relax, and he reported usually having a few drinks to unwind and watching sports. It seemed his wife handled most of the homework and transportation for their children, who were just entering their teen years. I reflected silently that he fit an old-fashioned male pattern of leaving the behind-the-scenes stuff of the household, including his own medical care, to his wife. This fit a pattern of living life on the surface, without addressing what was under his own hood.

Softening Hard Edges: The Male Dilemma

It took several months of therapy to begin addressing Joe's alcohol use. I had asked him initially about his drinking patterns and he reported being a moderate drinker, stating that he enjoyed wine greatly. He then regaled me with his exploration of various vineyards and vintages that met his approval. Joe highly valued quality and craftsmanship and prided himself on looking beyond the labels and evaluating the real value beneath the brand. "Some of the big-name vineyards, well, a lot of it is a halo effect. I do my due diligence!" he added enthusiastically, laughing a bit due to knowing that he was humorously calling himself out, reinforcing my suspicion that he might be masking his alcohol use under the veneer of being a connoisseur. I needed to explore further what "a few drinks" in the evening "to unwind" meant, but first it was important to establish more of a therapeutic alliance.

Like many people, particularly men, raised in an emotionally repressive, performance-based household, Joe lacked both the language and the context to understand what he felt. Men are traditionally raised to perform, achieve, and bond with guys doing guy things. Men who don't easily fit this norm often feel isolated and inadequate. Joe never felt very comfortable socially, so he didn't have many friends. Try as he might to perfect the exterior, complete with a nice house, pretty wife, and children, all was not well and he knew it, though he was hard-pressed to explain why. The inner terrain of his body expressed the reality of what he could not yet put into words. Tense shoulders and neck, chronic sleep issues, and rising blood pressure told the story of a man overwhelmed by the demands of the world and exhausted by the ongoing performance that was required. He attempted to comfort himself with old habits and pastimes like working out and watching sports, but these props were no longer sufficient. A sense of deeper purpose and the joy of connection were missing. I wondered if his drinking was increasing in response to his disorientation. I wanted to learn more without triggering defensiveness or shame.

During a session that occurred further into his therapy, Joe was exhausted due to being awake much of the night tossing and turning. I decided to broach the subject of alcohol and inquired whether he was aware of the fact that alcohol directly interferes with sleep, particularly REM sleep. He said that he knew it wasn't great for sleep and that he was trying to moderate his drinking. I asked how his efforts were going. "Okay, I guess," he replied. He elaborated but remained vague. "I mean, during the week I try to only drink wine, though sometimes I'll have something a little stronger after work. I started exploring malt whiskey recently. I know it's probably not the best thing for me, so I try to only have that on the weekends." I felt strongly that he was minimizing and shrouding his need for a stronger buzz with a sophisticated alibi. Drinking more on the weekends was also a red flag, indicating the need to take cover in the conventionally accepted habit of the weekend being a time to loosen the grip of restraint. I asked if his wife drank as well. "Not so much. I mean, she'll have some wine occasionally, but actually she's been on me to cut back. It's kind of a thing between us." This confirmed my hunch that his alcohol use was raising red flags with his wife and beginning to interfere with his relationships.

Moderate Addiction: A Silent Saboteur

Alcohol use for people like Joe is insidious because it does not raise any particularly noticeable red flags. After all, a few drinks at the end of the day is an acceptable tradition in American culture. Alcohol's function, however, which is to numb and soothe, can gradually shave away a person's physical and emotional vitality. A common understanding in addiction therapy is that a person's emotional growth stops at the time an addiction takes hold. This is because addiction interferes with developing other skills and interests that kindle emotional growth and move an individual out of their habitual comfort zones. Addiction also interferes with a person's capacity to feel and tolerate necessary emotional pain. For example, if booze hadn't been providing a warm blanket of comfort, Joe might have realized more pointedly just how bored and empty he felt. If he had been able to stay with those feelings and bring them up in therapy, he would have been able to face his internal agitation and address what was underlying his unhappiness. This would have been painful, but it is only through facing pain that we grow. Because Joe continually numbed himself, the pain remained unnamed and free-floating and therefore did not galvanize meaningful change.

Joe was a challenging client, though not in the sense that he was resistant in any outward way. He genuinely wanted help for his depression and anxiety. The difficulty working with him lay in finding a way to help someone with little self-awareness describe an inner landscape that was uncharted and didn't seem that worthy of investigation. He was feeling around in the dark, struggling for language to make sense of things, but his need for approval, and likely feelings of shame about this, stood in the way, not just with me but, more importantly, with himself as well.

For individuals mired in psychological pain that remains unnamed and lacking apparent cause, root chakra addictions are a grounding tool and a numbing agent, as well as a means to induce sleep and a softening of the energetic body. Joe had a history of self-discipline and success. These qualities allowed him to moderate his drinking so that it never directly interfered with his health or functioning. His drinking habits, however, had also blocked development of alternative ways of coping with stress and emotional discomfort. These avenues of growth remained unrecognized and untapped because he was habitually taking the edge off his discomfort and blunting his awareness with a substance.

Joe at a Glance

Little t: Lack of empathic mirroring in childhood leading to a dearth of emotional language and limited self-expression; lack of humor or capacity for joy and strong emphasis on performance in family of origin; unmet need for attention and shame and denial about this; sense of being conditionally loved

Legacy Trauma: Parents highly image- and rule-based; stress on achievement and climbing the social ladder; high value on status, titles, and possessions; working valued over playing, imagining, or creating

The Download

Relationship to Body: The body as a tool to perform; physical prowess, beauty, strength, and capacity measure a person's value; body as a status symbol to dress and groom in order to garner attention and admiration

Relationship to Self: Self-regard is precarious and always in relation to how one is esteemed and judged by others; internal experience is not recognized as important; lack of language for or attention to internal experience; disowned shame around perceived failures and inadequacies; need to hide inner fragility; contempt for self for this fragility

Relationship to Others: Others perceived as better or worse than oneself; feel safe with those to whom one deems self to be superior and insecure with those one deems to be superior to self; need to please and impress the superior others through looks, status, and competence

Root Chakra Addictions: Dependence on food and alcohol to self-soothe and ease internal tension; pride in restraint of these habits and successful maintenance of external appearance that belies inner dependence

Mental Health Concerns: Dysthymia and low-level anxiety that can manifest in panic attacks

Belle: Stoking a Dwindling Fire

Belle's addictions were similar to Joe's in that they were low-level and, some would argue, did not fit the definition of addiction at all. She was also similar to Joe in that the emphasis in her family was on performance and appearance. How things looked on the outside trumped what was going on in the less visible inside. In keeping with this, Belle had inherited her parents' concern with weight and appearance, which was modeled by both of them. Belle recalled how her mother was always trying to lose weight and bemoaning the calories in things. She also recalled her father criticizing her mother for gaining a few pounds. This early modeling left a mark on Belle, and she found herself highly focused on maintaining her own weight beginning in her teens.

Through therapy, Belle was able to explore how her family's focus on weight and appearance had affected her and caused a lot of rigidity and focus on self-control around food. She was also recognizing that her own life had gotten reduced to a grinding routine that left little room for play, exploration, or creativity. "It's like all it is now is work, work, work, and then we unwind with a dinner and a few drinks. God," she moaned, "I've become my parents." She went on to discuss her younger years, when she'd had a more vibrant social life and participated in a lot of dance classes. She expressed feeling saddened by the changes she saw in herself. "It's like I know I'm in there, but it's a flickering flame."

The above exchange occurred several months after Belle began therapy. Her anxiety had reduced soon after starting therapy. For her, having a place to express her feelings and receiving gentle encouragement to attend to her own needs was immediately beneficial. Given the opportunity to take a step back and take a more objective view of her life, she realized how routinized and dull her life had become. Without my prompting, she decided to reduce her daily drinking. She saw that it had a numbing effect and was getting in the way of using her evenings in a more productive manner. She joined a book club in her neighborhood and established a walking routine with a friend. These small changes had an energizing effect on her, and her overall mood and energy level immediately improved. "I feel like I'm taking charge of myself," she reported. "Like, I knew that my habits weren't that great, but I guess I got so used to them I just was on autopilot. It's weird, as soon as I decided not to drink in the evening, well, the rest followed from there."

"That's called momentum, Belle," I responded. "It's a curious phenomenon that I've noticed in myself too. It's like you make one small change and the next one presents itself and it just feels right." Belle nodded in agreement.

As Belle made changes in her day-to-day patterns, space was opened in therapy to explore how she had fallen into such routinized, deadening patterns in the first place. In our discussions it became apparent that she had used a strategy of force and self-coercion as a method to override her needs and feelings so that she could function according to others' expectations of her. This mirrored exactly how her early environment had encouraged and coerced acceptable behavior from her.

Recall the principle expressed with regard to Riley in chapter 1: *We treat ourselves as we were treated.* Belle had been raised to conform to the standards of others regardless of how she felt about them. As an adult, this pattern of rigid, forced behavior began to take a toll on her. As her energy wore down, Belle turned to substances such as caffeine and sugar as a means to get her through her days. This left her system amped-up and seized, making it hard for her to come down at the end of the day. This is how she became reliant on the alcohol that she and her husband shared together as part of their nightly routine. Over time, due to the chronic stress she was under, she had also turned to pills like Valium and sleep aids to help her let go and fall sleep.

Belle's use of substances provides an example, in addition to Joe's, of how individuals who did not endure severe trauma in childhood are still liable to dial down to the root chakra and rely on passive application of substances in order to calm the unnameable and unmanageable energies that inhabit, and then threaten to overrun, the body. Not being able to sleep and lacking energy to get through the day contributes to an individual's sense of overwhelm and lack of mastery. Not only is the world constantly demanding its due, but now the body is adding an interior sense of stress and also demanding its due, like a hit of sugar, caffeine, or booze. Substances offer a quick and easy, as well as socially condoned, way to manage the unnamed, rogue forces that live within. They exact a toll, however, and Belle was beginning to recognize this.

Comfort and Control

It took Belle more than a year in therapy to identify the low-level addictions that had plagued her since adolescence. She told me she had never really questioned her food behaviors because all her girlfriends were weight conscious and restricted their food as well. When she first started therapy, she was candid about her dissatisfaction with her weight, but at the time she considered it a cosmetic problem that merely needed the application of more willpower. Later she came to realize just how much food meant to her and became aware of the shenanigans, as she referred to her habits, she went through to maintain her slim physique. She often used caffeine and sugar to get through the day and then would eat too much at night. She had thought her intestinal distress was an inherited problem but was realizing now that it was caused by her frantic lifestyle and poor eating habits. This was eye-opening to her and gave her an enhanced sense of empowerment over her health. "It's amazing how resigned I had become to just not feeling well," she said as she reflected on her former attitudes about her health and lifestyle. This allowed her to recognize her unconscious dependence on food and alcohol for comfort.

As Belle unraveled her conflicted relationship to food, she realized that she was always thinking about it, wanting more of it, and feeling guilty after she finished a meal. She realized how much energy she was wasting trying to control and manipulate her eating habits. She also realized that while she habitually used food for comfort, it rarely delivered what she was seeking. She reported that she usually felt very tense after eating and drinking and often needed a sleeping pill before going to bed. "It's embarrassing, really," she confided, "how much it rules me and I never even realized it." I explained to Belle that often our patterns sneak around just under the level of consciousness and her ability to come to terms with hers was an extraordinary step in self-awareness. I also explained that she was coming to terms with what is the hallmark of all addictions: The feeling you are chasing is never delivered by the substance or behavior. Instead, the substance leaves you as tense, destitute, and distraught as ever, as much as it may promise a coveted respite.

The unconscious reliance on substances like food, cigarettes, and alcohol to structure time and offer reward and comfort is not at all unusual. The dependency is deeply woven into the fabric of an individual's daily life and, similar to Belle's experience, often flies beneath the radar of conscious awareness so that the dependency is not even recognized. As frustrating and even tormenting as root chakra addictions can be, the thought of giving the substances up can send many otherwise highly rational individuals into full-on resistance. This is because the substances, and even the problems that come along with them, serve to bind the anxiety that lies at the root, and facing this would require changes in lifestyle and priorities. These changes are often resisted, as you witnessed through Joe's story.

Charting a New Course

The problem with prioritizing comfort and control is that it leads to boredom and emptiness. This vacuum lies beneath the routine, and its downward gravitational pull intensifies the more you ignore it. Due to her breakdown, Belle was motivated to make changes and face the issues that had led to her unhappiness.

Since Belle's addictions were not as severe as Riley's, she did not have to do a major life overhaul in order to begin a recovery process. Her relatively easier path of recovery was due to the fact that she had more resources and positive experiences to draw from as she created changes in her life. Belle had a few solid friendships and latent interests to sustain her as she began making lifestyle changes. She also had the capacity to self-structure and suffered less of the diffuse, nameless anxiety that Riley suffered from. In essence, Belle's problems were not woven into her mind-body system in the same way that Riley's were. Instead of having an embedded dysregulated nervous system that was wired for adaptation and survival in a dangerous world, Belle had patterns of behavior that stemmed from her long-term efforts to control her feelings and needs in order to meet an expected standard imposed by others. This boded well for her recovery because she had resources to draw from and none of the changes she needed to make required extreme measures or removal from her environment.

Belle decided to embark on a whole-body course correction, eliminating processed food and sugar, eating more vegetables, and eventually, due to her digestive issues, removing gluten and dairy. It took her a while to embrace this approach, and she first had to recognize and address the fantasy of a short-term fix that would eliminate the problems. She resonated with the idea of eating to enhance her energy, functioning, and vitality, and this new perspective began to gain traction in her psyche. She liked the idea of adopting a food plan that would improve her overall health and digestion and felt very motivated. "It feels different this time," she later elaborated. "In the past, a diet was always accompanied by dread. This time, well, I know it will be hard to give up the cookies and pasta and the alcohol," she said as she rolled her eyes wistfully, "but it feels kinda right.

Like, I also know that this is good for me, and it doesn't need to be all or nothing. Like, if I want a glass of wine or a dessert sometimes, I'll have it. The main thing is that I am trying to be more present when I eat. I never realized before how anxious I am when I eat. It's kinda sad, almost embarrassing. I mean, eating is so basic and somehow I can't even do that. I guess it's good to recognize it."

I responded to Belle by telling her that she was exactly where she needed to be and that coming to terms with her basic distrust of her own needs would eventually free her from the anxiety. I also reminded her that her condition made sense. After all, her mother had downloaded her own discomfort with the body straight onto Belle's mind-body hard drive. The feeling of intuitive rightness and exploratory curiosity that she was now accessing in relation to her most basic appetites was her most sturdy guide. By reaching back to her root chakra and making a change in the material domain involving how she fed her body, she was accessing her sacral chakra, the world of energy and feeling, which would in turn enhance her felt sense of safety residing in her physical incarnation. A positive feedback loop was being established and galvanizing a new balance in her root and sacral chakras.

There is a synergistic momentum that healing creates in the mind-body system. Changes in her root chakra (how Belle ate) required participation from her sacral chakra, the source of feeling and intuitive awareness. The involvement of her sacral chakra galvanized increased trust and communication between both chakras, leading to an increase in self-trust and intuitive awareness. This freed energy from her anxious preoccupation with her body so that she could channel it into more productive pursuits. Since her weight was no longer of such fundamental concern and she had more energy, she decided to take up sewing again. "Not to brag," Belle said with a twinkle in her eye, "but I actually was pretty good at it in my teens. My mother, bless her, was quite a seamstress and it gives me a way to connect with her now. I am actually sewing in the evenings over Zoom with her and my aunt. It's really cool."

Healing has a ripple effect that creates a swath of energy that extends to others and brings about an unexpected bounty one might never have imagined. Sewing with her mother and aunt allowed a new ease and warmth to grow between them, softening Belle's feelings toward her mother and easing her own discomfort with herself.

Belle at a Glance

Little t: Emphasis on appearance and performance in family of origin; need to conform to the status quo and fit in with others; high degree of control over the body and suppressed shame around biological functions; strong messages about being female and the necessity of behaving in a way that pleases others

Legacy Trauma: Both parents grew up in rigid, upwardly mobile households that prioritized status; emphasis on rules and obtaining status based on looks, money, and achievement; mother very conscious of femininity and rules of behavior associated with this, including an emphasis on physical appearance and self control

The Download

Relationship to Body: Self-consciousness and acute awareness of being seen and evaluated by others; fear of being out of control; shame around her body's functioning and structuring her life to avoid this shame; drive for comfort sabotaging the need to appear a certain way, e.g., eating and drinking too much threatened her need to be thin, creating inner conflict.

Relationship to Self: Ongoing self-criticism and disappointment with regard to not controlling impulses and living up to internal standards; chronic attitude of distrust and criticism toward self; preoccupations interfered with ability to take pleasure in more creative pursuits that did not involve oral gratification, adding to sense of failure and inadequacy.

Relationship to Others: Lack of energy to reach out to and connect with others; shame about social avoidance and low self-esteem furthered by chronic inertia; suppression of shame and disappointment with self interfering with ability to be honest and genuine with others

Root Chakra Addictions: Chronic use of food, alcohol, and sleep medications to self-regulate and self-soothe; usage not a direct threat to health but undermined health and happiness in a subtle way

Mental Health Issues: Chronic anxiety and mild depression

Chapter 4

Mental Health Disorders and Root Chakra Trauma

When I was in graduate school, psychiatric diagnoses carried an aura of profundity and certainty for me, as if they defined something essential about a person that only a well-trained eye could identify. I remember comparing personal diagnoses with classmates who, like me, were also seeing therapists. "What did you get?" we would query one another, titillated to compare our afflictions. The diagnosis carried more gravity than an astrological sign because it was bequeathed with white coat authority and symbolized what we were all striving to become. But I also remember being mildly disappointed. Generalized anxiety disorder? "Hmm," I thought to myself, "doesn't that just mean you're gnarled with worry all the time and obsessed with what others think and all the things that could go wrong? Well, I already knew that."

Then there was the subtle violence done to one another with our newly acquired knowledge. "Do you think she's a borderline?" we would whisper among ourselves. This diagnosis, especially in the 1980s, carried a terrible stigma and was sometimes used among professionals as a means to blame clients for not getting better. Our professor, a patient and creative woman, told us that essentially diagnoses were shorthand ways for clinicians to communicate with one another about a client's primary patterns of dysfunction. That made sense, though it took years for me to fully appreciate her wisdom as I agonized over what label to anoint a client's brow with.

In this chapter I will attempt to demystify serious mental health diagnoses and help you see how these diagnoses are related to trauma and development. I will use Riley to illustrate how a traumatizing early environment can impact personality formation and lead to incomplete personality development that is later medicalized and diagnosed. I will not address bipolar I disorder or psychotic disorders, including schizophrenia or schizoaffective disorder, because these disorders have a more discernible genetic component and are not as clearly linked to trauma.

Riley's mental health file included three serious diagnoses: borderline personality disorder, dissociative identity disorder, and complex post-traumatic stress disorder. These diagnoses were all accurate, albeit incomplete, labels by which to understand the patterns that she relied on to navigate the world. We shall work through these diagnoses one by one to help you understand how they developed and unfolded in Riley's life and how she eventually learned to manage her symptoms.

Borderline Personality Disorder (BPD)

Borderline personality disorder is a constellation of symptoms that essentially describe an unformed, immature personality. If you suffered ongoing physical or sexual abuse, or physical neglect, as a child, you experienced frantic states of arousal coupled with a developmentally determined inability to self-soothe. Terror and helplessness overwhelmed your unformed psyche and caused you to dissociate, resulting in a biologically adaptive response of emotional numbing and withdrawal into your own world. If this was a frequent occurrence in your childhood and existed in the absence of consistent, loving care and repair efforts by your caregivers, then your root chakra formed itself around the anticipation of danger and the need to self-protect. This established a core instability at the root of your being, which unfortunately interfered with the development of your ascending chakras.

Individuals who later end up being diagnosed with BPD also come from homes with chronic emotional invalidation. When a child's feelings and sense of reality are continually undermined by caregivers, the child's core self is not able to develop fully. This leaves the child without a reliable internal compass that they can trust. Furthermore, if messages from caregivers are inconsistent or gaslight the child (essentially telling the child their feelings and perceptions are wrong), the child will forsake the self in the interest of maintaining the relationships upon which their life depends. This is a common problem for individuals who grew up under the care of a narcissistic person who demands conformity to their pronouncement of what is true.

Treating individuals with BPD can be difficult if the trauma they experienced was severe and if the home was depriving. This is because the person lacks an internal reference point for the good feelings that connection with others, learning new things, and mastering skills provides. When there is no reference point for good feelings, it is hard to ignite hope that things can get better. In spite of this, treatment for BPD can be effective, because many of the skills that contribute to a mature personality can be taught. The capacity to self-soothe, manage impulses, regulate behavior in relation to an anticipated future, and integrate the needs of others with one's own needs are all adult skills that are evident in a mature personality. Someone with these skills likely learned them in childhood through the modeling of caregivers. Individuals like Riley, who did not experience this, can acquire these skills later in life. This is the premise of *dialectical behavior therapy*, the preferred method of treatment for BPD, which provides a hopeful, life-affirming method for helping traumatized individuals.

The following sections describe symptoms of borderline personality disorder using Riley's story to help concretize the lived experience of individuals with this disorder.

Not Okay for No Reason

A common complaint of individuals on the borderline spectrum is a feeling of emptiness or being lost in space. The vagueness of these descriptors derives from the difficulty describing what emptiness feels like. It can range from feeling agitated and aimless to feeling downright terrified. Riley was not experiencing these diffuse states when she was working with me, but she certainly remembered them and never wanted to feel that way again. "It was awful," she recalled. "Some days I would wake up, especially when I didn't have to work, and I would just feel so, I don't know, empty. Like I had no one, there was nothing for me, nothing I wanted to do or could do. It was scary, almost like I wasn't real. If I could, especially when I was in therapy, I would try to go to the store or something just to feel normal, but sometimes that didn't work or even made it worse. It was like I was in slow motion or seeing everything through a thick glass. That's when I used to binge, or sometimes I would cut myself. I would feel bad afterward, but at least I felt something. At least I felt real."

Riley's description of this state is poignant and tragic. The technical terms for this state are *derealization* and *depersonalization*. These terms describe the plight of those who are not tethered to the world of other people, to any prevailing culture, to any type of routine, or even to the routine rituals of eating, sleeping, and grooming oneself. The rhythms of the body, and of the world, are lost to them, and this is deeply unsettling. Riley's use of self-injury to ground herself is indicative of the function these very dysfunctional behaviors have. When you suffer from BPD, cutting or bingeing essentially brings you back into your body, back into time, and back into the world. In a strange, sad way, these behaviors provide form and structure, even if it's of an unpleasant nature that requires cleaning up blood and bandaging wounds or getting rid of the evidence of a purge. Cutting and bingeing also have a calming chemical effect on the body, unleashing the inner pharmacy in a palliative way.

Fear of Abandonment

A longing for relief from the interior terrors of emptiness creates a strong need to be loved and a desire for someone to take away the pain and provide the care that was never experienced. This longing is coupled with a terror of rejection and punishment, or even engulfment, which has been integral to the person's most intimate connections. *Engulfment* refers to having one's own needs and feelings subsumed by another person, making it hard to identify what is true and real for oneself. This is an artifact of chronic emotional invalidation and occurs frequently in adult children of narcissistic parents. The conflict of both needing and fearing relationships leaves you with an unsolvable problem: While you desperately long to be cared for, this care is also threatening and comes with a looming threat of backlash. There is also a fear of being seen for who one truly is, which one fears is worthless and damaged.

Individuals with borderline personality syndrome often don't have the resources or stability to have developed socially affirmed skills and identities. Lack of education, a job, or life skills contributes to feelings of inadequacy and inferiority to others. This lack of self-regard ups the ante relationally, making the person all the more dependent on acceptance from others. Before Riley was working, going to the gym, and developing community with others, she felt like she had nothing of interest to offer to others, which led her to be socially avoidant and cling even more to her abusive boyfriend.

A History of Volatile, Broken Relationships

In the past Riley had dealt with her fears of abandonment by being in an extremely abusive eight-year relationship that ended up becoming life-threatening. She described it like this: "When I was with Rick, I was so desperate. I would freak out if he didn't want to hang out. And I thought he was cheating on me the whole time. And he probably was. I just never knew for sure. He would flirt with other women all the time, really just to get a rise out of me, I think. I probably chose him because he was just as insecure as I was. I never did cheat on him, but he was so paranoid. He would beat the hell out of me if I was talking to a guy at a party or something." Riley paused, looking reflective. "You know the weird thing that I'm literally just realizing now? Man . . .," she paused for an even longer time. "It's just so sad. I'm realizing that I knew he would beat me up and that's partly why I would do it—flirt, I mean. It's like I needed it somehow. Somehow when he beat me, it's like I knew that he loved me and needed me. He was careful to hit me in places others wouldn't see. Like, he never broke my nose or anything. It was our secret."

Riley was still trying to work through why she had stayed in the relationship for so long and was processing the trauma she had endured living with the chronic threat of physical violence. She saw that by intentionally creating conflict, she would gain a false sense of control that temporarily relieved the anxiety of abandonment and solidified their bond. "He would be sorry afterward and we would have a few days of peace," she mused. "Those were the good times."

Poor Impulse Control

In a parentally adequate family, children are offered structure that helps them manage their needs within a safe environment. "Do your homework and then you can play." "Eat your dinner and then we can have dessert." Children are taught within safe constructs to manage their immediate needs in anticipation of something more pleasant in the future. This structure helps the child learn to delay gratification and manage impulses. Riley was not gifted this kind of environment, which impaired the basic hardwiring of her nervous system. She never internalized skills to manage her needs, monitor her impulses, or delay gratification for a promised future that she could count on.

Riley's difficulty managing her impulses had put her in perilous situations and set her up for alcoholism and food addiction. She used to binge and purge to the point that she threw up blood. Her alcoholism landed her in the hospital several times. "It was a nightmare," she told me. "I know I've said this before, but Christians who think hell is somewhere that you go, well, I have news for them. It's right here inside." She rubbed her stomach and chest. "It lives inside and it's a torment. It almost killed me." She had expressed this sentiment to me before, and I knew she needed to repeat it to reinforce the fact that her early childhood programming in the church her family attended was wrong. I nodded in agreement, knowing that the inability to self-structure and manage the tide of impulses, feelings, discomforts, and longings that ebb and flow within is a terrible condition. In Riley's words, "It's borderline hell at its worst."

Black-and-White Thinking

Rigid thinking is the hallmark of immature personality development. A small child does not have the cognitive skills or experience to make sense of a complex and nuanced world. In an effort to make sense of things and establish control, the child puts things into binary categories of "good" and "bad." When you have borderline personality disorder, you never outgrow this binary worldview and seek to avoid the hell of impulses run rampant, and the anxiety of relationship ambiguity, by categorizing things into stark, either-or silos. Hence, a bite of cake means the diet is ruined. Not going to the gym one day throws the commitment to work out into the trash can. The friend not being available to hang out means they don't care. It is also common for someone with BPD to idealize or demonize other people. Learning to see relationships in a nuanced way is one of the primary goals of therapy.

For Riley, black-and-white thinking manifested in rigid behavior that marked a "good" day and her utter collapse if she wasn't able to fulfill her strict expectations. This personality trait lasted far after she began her recovery process because it was such an embedded way that she maintained a sense of control over herself and her world. She still struggled with this tendency in response to difficult situations, and our therapy was often oriented to help her gain a more nuanced view of obstacles in her life.

Starting and Stopping Projects or Endeavors

One consequence of black-and-white thinking and poor impulse control is the inability to sustain a trajectory of interest over time. It is easy to fantasize about a goal, such as starting an innovative business or learning to scuba dive, belly dance, or cook. The excitement of the initial commitment lends a rosy glow to the endeavor. You imagine how good it will feel when you've mastered the skill and are enjoying the rewards you've reaped. In your mind, it is a fait accompli. Then, inevitably, the commitment grows difficult. Unanticipated obstacles appear. It's frustrating. Fatigue and defeatism crowd out the inspiration and you default into rigid thinking. Self-defeating thoughts win the day and the goal is abandoned. When too many of these foreclosed projects stack up in your life, it creates a deficit of self-respect and self-esteem, in addition to a deficit of enjoyable, skill-based activities that are pleasurable.

With awareness and persistence, this pattern can be interrupted, and Riley provides a wonderful example of this. Her newfound pleasure in cooking and hiking added vitality to both her inner life and her social network, though she had to work hard to continue to push herself to do these activities, particularly at the beginning, when she was new to them.

Self-Hatred Leading to Self-Injury

Self-hatred is the most noxious aspect of borderline personality syndrome and points directly to the environmental deficiencies in the person's developmental history. Due to a lack of a stable identity, loving relationships, and sustained interest in productive activities, people on the BPD spectrum are vulnerable to feelings of intense inadequacy and self-hatred. During these self-hatred attacks, which often follow perceived rejection from others or falling short of one's own rigid expectations, the suppressed litany of all one's real and made-up failings comes to the surface. Unfavorable comparisons to others are made, and a litany of ruined relationships and foreclosed projects run rampant in the mind. This leads to an avalanche of intense feelings of failure, inadequacy, and self-hatred that can result in bingeing, cutting, and even suicidal ideation or behavior.

Learning to nurture self-compassion in the face of your failings is an initial step to healing for those who suffer from this ghastly tendency to turn against the self. Riley learned that self-compassion was not a free pass to do whatever she wished without consequence, but rather was an affirmation of both her pain and her inherent value. "I know that I love myself now," she stated in a session nearing the end of her therapy with me. "I can't really describe it and it's not based on anything in particular. I just know that I'm good. I know that I've faced up to my work."

Strong but Vacillating Attachment to Varying Ideas or Groups

The emptiness of the self, inability to manage feelings and impulses, and terror of being alone in this morass can result in a compulsive craving for identity and affiliation no matter the cost. This renders an individual with borderline personality disorder vulnerable to extreme spiritual or political affiliations and even cults that offer an explanation for their feelings, as well as a cohort to immediately bond with. Identification with a group and the certainty of the values that are promulgated provide a scaffolding for the fragile, yearning self to attach to. This allows a person an immediate, albeit false, sense of community and acceptance, while also opening them up to predatory behavior by others. It is not uncommon for systemic abuse to be perpetrated and normalized among members of these groups. Predators are skilled at sniffing out individuals who are not strong in their boundaries and do not have contact with their own intrinsic sense of what is right and wrong. Hence, individuals who were raised in traumatic households are at great risk of being further manipulated and abused in the larger world.

Borderline Personality Disorder (BPD) at a Glance

History: When first identified in 1938 by Adolph Stern, the term *borderline personality* referred to mental disorders resembling mild states of schizophrenia. In the 1940s psychoanalyst Helene Deutsch described such individuals as having an "as if" personality. In the 1960s Otto Kernberg identified borderline states as being on a continuum between psychotic and neurotic disorders. Psychotic disorders refer to when an individual has lost contact with reality. Neurotic disorders describe individuals who have contact with reality but are embroiled in internal psychological conflict. In the 1970s more research on the disorder was conducted identifying diagnostic criteria. The disorder was included in the *Diagnostic and Statistical Manual of Mental Disorders, Third Edition (DSM-III)*, published in 1980.

Etiology: Borderline personality syndrome is strongly related to abuse and neglect in the early childhood environment, with twin studies indicating a 40 percent heritability rate.[5] Keep in mind that inheriting a more sensitive temperament can look very different in different developmental environments, e.g., a sensitive child raised in a loving home could grow up to be artistic and creative but be more prone to developing borderline personality if raised in a traumatic home.

Prevalence: Borderline personality disorder is thought to affect 1.4 percent of the population (gender specific data not available).[6]

Treatment: The most effective treatment of BPD is dialectical behavior therapy, developed by Marsha Linehan in 1993.[7] This is an intensive form of therapy providing both group and individual therapy on a multi-session-a-week basis. Self-regulation skills are emphasized, as well as reinforcement of appropriate boundaries and firm limits to discourage self-harm and manipulative behavior. Medication is often used to regulate depression and anxiety and to treat comorbid disorders.

Current Understanding of BPD: Borderline personality disorder is thought to be caused by a combination of genetic and environmental factors that are treatable through skills-based therapy and medication aimed to downshift and stabilize the nervous system.

Controversies: Some researchers and clinicians believe that childhood trauma and complex PTSD are causative factors of the disorder and outweigh the influence of genetic factors.

DSM-5 Diagnostic Criteria: BPD is included in the DSM-5 and is a cluster B personality disorder. It includes nine symptoms, five of

5. Amad et al., "Genetics of Borderline Personality Disorder."

6. Lenzenweger et al., "DSM-IV Personality Disorders in the National Comorbidity Survey Replication."

7. Linehan, *Cognitive-Behavioral Treatment of Borderline Personality Disorder*.

which are required to make the diagnosis: (1) frantic efforts to avoid abandonment, (2) pattern of unstable and intense relationships, (3) unstable identity, (4) impulsivity that can lead to self-harm, (5) suicidal behavior, (6) unstable moods, (7) feelings of emptiness, (8) inappropriate and intense anger, and (9) transient paranoid ideation or severe dissociation.

Dissociative Identity Disorder (DID)

Dissociation is a psychological defense that is designed to be protective in the face of unpleasant or terrifying events. Dissociation occurs on a continuum, with dissociative identity disorder (DID) at the most extreme end of the spectrum and normal forms on the other end. Normal forms include spacing out, a common and unremarkable experience that occurs when you are seeking refuge from the task at hand. If you have ever driven past your exit on the freeway only to wake up (not literally) and realize you were lost in thought, you were mildly dissociated. More extreme forms of dissociation are derealization, which is a sense that things around you are not real, and depersonalization, which is a feeling that you yourself are not real. For people with dissociative tendencies, these experiences are common and occur for no apparent reason, as mentioned in the section on borderline personality disorder. For most people, depersonalization and derealization happen only during disturbing or life-threatening events, such as a car accident or a rape or assault, or after the sudden shock of hearing bad news, such as finding out a loved one is in harm's way or has died.

If trauma in childhood is frequent and severe, dissociation can become an embedded psychological defense that is relied upon routinely in order to cope. This can result in dissociative identity disorder (DID), formerly known as multiple personality disorder. DID is diagnosed when there are two or more distinct self-parts that have an independent sense of awareness, perception, and motivation. In extreme cases there is no awareness between the parts, and different clothes and personae are donned for the different parts, which can range in number from two to one hundred. The afflicted person suffers from large gaps in memory and a lost sense of their own continuity in time. Consequently, their internal narrative is spotty and fragmented, and they possess little insight into their actions, feelings, or motivations. When the anxiety of this disorientation becomes too great, a switch in personality becomes a coping mechanism.

DID is most problematic when the multiple selves are not aware of one another and act out distinctly different, even contradictory, aspects of the personality. Moderate forms of the condition occur when a person has different names for different parts or functions of their self-system, for example, naming an angry part Jezebel while maintaining conscious awareness of Jezebel's feelings and behaviors. The defining difference between severe presentations of the disorder and milder expressions has to do with how strong the core personality of the individual is and how much awareness the core self is able to maintain regarding the functions that the different self-parts have and the origin of the impulses they are expressing.

Symptoms of dissociative identity disorder resemble those frequently found in borderline personality disorder. This is because both syndromes stem from dysfunction of the core self and identity; hence, some of the coping mechanisms and symptoms are the same.

Poor Memory

One of the most difficult issues people with DID tendencies experience is the lack of a coherent storyline linking their past self to their present self. Riley struggled mightily with this and had a difficult time when I asked her questions about the past. "I don't know. There's just not much there," she would say in a resigned way. Riley had absolutely no memory of her seventh grade year, and eighth grade was very spotty. Her early life before age ten was all but gone.

It is disorienting for individuals who lack contact with their own past, and many trauma survivors complain of friends mentioning events of which they have little or no recall. "It makes me feel like something is really wrong with me," Riley told me once. "Like, do I have early dementia or something? Even now I can blank things out and have trouble remembering plot lines of a movie I've seen. It worries me." I did my best to reassure

Riley and explained to her that in order for a person to have explicit recall of events, the memory has to be encoded in the hippocampus, a part of the brain associated with conscious recall. If you're not paying attention, the memory isn't encoded and hence the memory is not laid down for later recall. This is a terrible problem for traumatized and dissociated young people, who end up questioning their basic intelligence or brain health. If a child is not paying attention in class and is habitually in fantasyland and then fails a test, the child can easily believe they are stupid. The real culprit is that the child isn't attending to what is happening in the present. The lack of a coherent life storyline, coupled with erroneous beliefs regarding native intelligence, are both tragic outcomes of a life spent somewhere else.

Spacing Out

The tendency to drift off while driving or reading or even while talking to someone is a symptom of habitual dissociation, leading to the lack of memory described above. Habitual use of this coping style creates social problems, disorganization, poor recall, and an overall sense of disorientation and low self-esteem. The ability to attend to details, read and retain information, remember important chores, and sustain interest in things suffers when you are not attending to the present. During therapy, Riley would frequently ask me to repeat myself because she was thinking about something else while I was speaking. Her ability to call it out when it happened marked significant improvement, because now she knew it was happening and felt less shame, which allowed her to circle back and absorb the information that had initially passed over her. This improved her self-esteem and gave her hope that she could gradually practice paying attention and strengthen the neural connections involved in maintaining concentration.

Different Sides of the Personality Are Vastly Dissimilar

Another symptom of dissociative identity disorder is the tendency to act in ways that are contrary to your values. Riley suffered more from this symptom in the past, when she felt that someone else had taken hold of the controls of her personality. This occurred during rage episodes in her twenties and could still happen when she got angry or felt threatened in her current relationship.

Other examples of severe lack of integration are acting out in sexually explicit ways that are contrary to your religious or moral values or shoplifting when you consciously consider yourself to be a law-abiding person. Riley had had affairs in the past when she was in a relationship that she thought she was happy in. She would then feel very guilty about the behavior and swear to maintain fidelity, only to repeat the behavior again. When discovered by her partner, she found herself hard-pressed to explain what she had done and was suffused in shame. She later realized that her behavior had to do with repressed feelings about the relationship and fears of intimacy that she had not allowed herself to acknowledge. She learned that having sex with someone else was a way to exert control, although, as with all unconscious and unskillful behavior, it left her less in control. As she allowed herself to touch more deeply into the feelings associated with having been abused and helpless in the past, she gradually learned to understand and express her needs and feelings to her partner before they became toxic and led to acting out.

Dissociative Identity Disorder (DID) at a Glance

History: Cases of individuals with strange symptoms indicating different personalities were recorded as early as 1591. In 1791 a woman shifted between a German and a French identity and was referred to as having an "exchanged personality." Other cases have been noted and were at times attributed to demonic possession or hysteria. The first officially diagnosed case, Louis Vivet in 1885, was extensively studied. The diagnosis became more common in the 1980s following the publication of Flora Rheta Schreiber's 1973 novel *Sybil* and the release of the 1976 TV film based on the book. The surge in diagnosis decreased in the 1990s when the validity of the diagnosis was widely challenged. Some believe that the prevalence was due to iatrogenic causes, meaning the treatment of hypnosis, age regression, and therapeutic suggestion actually caused, rather than ameliorated, the symptoms.

Etiology: Dissociative identity disorder has been linked to childhood trauma, particularly sexual abuse, since it was first identified. Fragmentation of the personality is attributed to the child's vulnerable psyche not being able to handle the abuse. The fragmented parts then form into separate entities designed to cope with the traumatic environment that requires them to "forget" and act as if everything is fine.

Prevalence: The current global estimate of prevalence of DID is 1.4 percent of the population, with no gender predominance specified.[8]

Treatment: Treatment approaches for DID include long-term psychodynamic therapy aimed to work through childhood trauma and abuse and dialectical behavior therapy, also used with BPD. Hypnotic age regression is still used for DID, though it's becoming less common. Internal family systems (IFS) therapy is the most current approach. This form of therapy aims to integrate different self parts by naming them and establishing their functions, while also identifying and strengthening a core, overseeing self.

Current Understanding of DID: The name of this disorder was officially changed from multiple personality disorder to dissociative identity disorder in 1994. This represented an attempt to more accurately describe the condition and cover a broader spectrum of the disorder, including patients manifesting a splintered identity rather than an identity composed of several fully developed personalities.

8. Mitra and Jain, "Dissociative Identity Disorder."

Controversies Surrounding DID: There is concern that social contagion has led to more diagnoses of dissociative identity disorder and that iatrogenic factors, wherein the treatment can encourage the problem, is a high risk due to individuals with a weak core self being highly suggestible. There are also concerns about patients malingering in order to escape criminal prosecution.

DSM-5 Diagnostic Criteria for Dissociative Identity Disorder: The DSM-5 lists the following diagnostic criteria for DID: (A) a disruption in identity caused by the existence of two or more personality states; interruption in sense of self, agency, affect, memory, perception, cognition, behavior, and sensory-motor functions; (B) recurrent gaps in memory; (C) symptoms cause impairment in functioning; (D) symptoms are not related to culturally accepted religious practices; and (E) symptoms cannot be attributed to the effects of a substance.

Complex Post-Traumatic Stress Disorder (C-PTSD)

PTSD is diagnosed when you either experience a traumatic event that is life-threatening or witness another person in an imperiling situation. Your bodily integrity may be threatened and the order of things in the familiar world is turned upside down. During the event, you experience a sense of helplessness and terror coupled with an inability to cope that imprints a felt experience of horror upon your body-psyche. This helplessness is the most pernicious part of the experience because it leaves your biological survival instinct unable to complete a positive coping response. Since your natural human/animal survival mechanism is thwarted, you are unable to move on in your mind and therefore continue to reexperience the trauma, in the form of flashbacks or dreams, or even in seemingly bizarre, deliberate efforts to re-create the trauma and thus complete an effective coping response. This is a misguided effort to repair the psychic injury. Examples of repetition of the trauma range from staying in an abusive relationship to recurrent dreams and flashbacks. Unfortunately, these reparative efforts merely serve to reinforce the trauma and keep it alive in your psyche.

PTSD can occur even if you had a previously well-developed root chakra. Due to the enormity of the crisis you endured, your previous sense of safety is shattered. War veterans, survivors of rape and violent crime, and survivors of natural disasters, car accidents, and terrorist attacks fall into this category. When the childhood environment was adequate and if your current environment is supportive, the prognosis for recovery and integration of the trauma is good. People who are able to cope effectively with a traumatic situation and are supported by others often have an acute reaction to the event but don't develop long-term PTSD.

Complex PTSD (C-PTSD) is diagnosed when you have endured or witnessed ongoing violence of a sexual or physical nature or have been subjected to ongoing neglect. This diagnosis can be applied to individuals who were raised in an abusive home, such as Riley, and also to those who were exposed to ongoing racism, homophobia, or sexism during their early years. In these cases, symptoms are less acute and may be present as an unconscious armoring of the personality that the person is largely unaware of or considers to be appropriate. An example of this is a person who carries a gun even in relatively safe environments.

C-PTSD is often the most accurate diagnosis for those with severe personality disorders, such as borderline conditions and dissociative identity disorder, due to the lack of safety and nurture during the individual's developmentally sensitive years of childhood. As indicated, the symptoms of C-PTSD are chronic rather than acute and involve a structuring of the self around dangers that were relevant to the family of origin. This causes the individual to perceive the current environment through a lens informed by the traumatic past, which skews the person's interpretation of the present. A negative bias in the person's perception interferes with the capacity for new learning and corrective emotional experiences. A tragic self-fulfilling prophecy is put in place where the world is believed to be unsafe and opportunities to experience something different are bypassed.

The following material applies to individuals suffering from complex rather than acute PTSD. Complex PTSD has a more insidious impact on the nervous system and identity formation than acute PTSD does because the whole mind-body system has formed itself around the need to survive in an inherently dangerous environment. Features of this condition are highlighted below.

Lack of Trust in Self

The work with Riley involved helping her understand more deeply how her sense of herself and her lack of belief in her own goodness and worthiness were shaped by her earliest experiences in the world. "Yeah, I've heard of Freud and all that oral, anal, oedipal stuff, but I don't buy it," she said dismissively during an early session of our work.

"Riley," I responded, "it's not necessarily a literal thing, like you were sexually aroused by pooping or you were in love with your father. What I think Freud understood and gave language to is that when we are children, we have raw feelings of pleasure associated with our bodies and the way our caregivers interacted with us and responded to our pleasure and discomfort shapes how we relate to our bodies and our basic impulses. From what I know about your parents, I don't think they had the resources or energy to relate to you in a tender, consistent way. Your mom must have been overwhelmed by a second child that it sounds like your father didn't want. And she was also likely experiencing the fallout from his alcoholism and irritation with having small children and being a primary breadwinner. This doesn't even touch on the sexual abuse by your brother that started when you were very young."

Riley nodded her head and was silent for a bit. Finally she said, "I guess it's kind of scary to me, because what am I supposed to do with that? I mean, it goes back so far and down so deep. In a way it feels hopeless, so I just don't think about it."

Lack of Trust in the World

As a result of early and ongoing trauma, Riley never developed trust in her capacity to stand up to and cope with threats in the world. This resulted in avoidance patterns and hypervigilance, both of which are classic markers of PTSD. Although Riley was currently able to function in the outside world, she was still very aware of the potential for danger and always kept a lookout for nearby escape routes. She once considered getting a gun but changed her mind due to not wanting to walk through the world armed to fight. In the past she purposely maintained a heavier body weight in order to be able to fight off potential assailants, and she also perused the news to alert her to the bad things happening in the world. This reinforced her vigilance and need to be prepared for attack. I would remind her that violent events, though too frequent, are still thankfully rare. She was aware now that her early history had primed her to be hypervigilant around danger. "I try to push myself now to be more 'normal,' you know, to go to crowded places or take the train. It's hard for me because I used to pride myself on being more realistic than other people. But that doesn't mean so much to me anymore."

Lack of Trust in Others

Riley had a particularly hard time establishing trusting bonds with other people. It was only through her early relationship with a gifted therapist that she experienced a reciprocal and trusting relationship. She was then able to build on this in her recovery groups and later at the spiritual center she joined. Her biggest challenge was integrating the negative and positive characteristics of another person without succumbing to black-and-white thinking and sabotaging of the relationship.

Riley's difficulty with relationships is pervasive among trauma survivors. Bessel van der Kolk gives language to this in his seminal work *The Body Keeps the Score*. He describes the unsolvable dilemma the abused child faces when the child's survival depends on the individuals who are also perpetrators of torment. How this dilemma plays out in future relationships spawns further suffering for all. This is because the survivor inadvertently chooses others who reinforce the abuse. Although this defies common sense, choosing a partner who reinforces the abuse is partly an effort to master the situation. It is fueled by the fantasy that if you can just get it right this time and somehow learn to navigate the treacherous terrain of the other's volatile emotions, the abuse won't recur.

Loss of Body Integrity

Riley suffered from severe dysregulation in her nervous system leading to over-reactive responses to small, relatively innocuous stimuli, like a loud vehicle or even a leaf blower. This was very disruptive to her daily functioning. When you respond to the ordinary impingements of daily life as if they are five-alarm fires, it makes it hard to get through the day. It's no wonder Riley suffered severe exhaustion and eventually physically broke down.

This problem is not unique to Riley. Individuals with C-PTSD often suffer from fluctuations in sleep and appetite as well as bowel dysregulation, leading to loss of the homeostasis and rhythm so necessary for inner safety and so vital to physical health and emotional well-being. Poor breathing, due to the natural tendency to restrict the breath when under threat, becomes a habitual pattern, which also has a deleterious impact on long-term health. You never feel at home because you are not at home in your own body. When you are an uncomfortable visitor in your own body, without a sense of predictability and coherence in relation to your own natural rhythms, you are truly homeless.

Encroachment of Past upon Present

Riley had suffered from nightmares and flashbacks since she was a child. Her nightmares were often dark and violent and she had a hard time making sense of the vivid and often gruesome scenes she endured in her sleep. It was not unusual for her to writhe in her sleep, and her partners, too often without kindness, told her that she was disturbing them due to her strangled cries and sudden movements.

Riley realized soon into her first therapy experience that her dreams were visitations from the past transposed upon the present. "It was as if I tried to build this steel barricade between me and the nightmare of my childhood, but the nightmare kept breaking through the dam," she said. She realized that even if it was not a vivid dream or memory, the feelings of dread and terror she so often experienced in her day-to-day waking hours were also visitations from the past. "Sometimes just a smell or a sound sends a shudder of dread through me. Now I can name it for what it is—'It's just the past'—and this helps me release it." She shrugged with a rueful smile. "It's an improvement, but sometimes I wish it could just go away."

Post-Traumatic Stress Disorder (PTSD) at a Glance

History: Formal recognition of the impact of trauma reaches back to 1861, during the American Civil War, and to 1870, during the Franco-Prussian War. At that time, "soldier's heart," or "irritable heart," was noted among war veterans. Symptoms included rapid pulse, trouble breathing, and anxiety. In 1919, following World War I, "shell shock" was the term given to soldiers exhibiting anxiety and sleep issues and was attributed to invisible damage to the brain caused by combat injury. During World War II, combat stress reaction (CSR) was identified in soldiers with strong reactions to combat, and half of military discharges were deemed to be due to CSR. Of note, General George S. Patton did not believe CSR was real. In the first edition of the DSM in 1952, what is now PTSD was called gross stress reaction. In the second edition of the DSM in 1968, it was redefined as an adjustment reaction to adult life. In 1980 PTSD was added to the DSM-III and the diagnosis was backed by research into Vietnam War veterans, Holocaust survivors, and survivors of sexual abuse. The DSM-5 has reclassified it from an anxiety disorder to a trauma-based disorder.

Etiology: Distinct from other diagnoses, PTSD requires the occurrence of an external event that is outside the purview of common human experience in order to warrant the diagnosis. Not everyone develops PTSD after an untoward event, and the reasons for this are not clearly understood, though it likely involves the interaction of genes with the environment.

Prevalence: Approximately 5 percent of the US population has PTSD in any given year, with lifetime rates estimated at 6 percent.[9] Women are approximately twice as likely as men to experience PTSD.[10]

Treatment: Early treatment of PTSD focused on getting war veterans back into battle as quickly as possible. In 1952 gross stress reaction assumed a six-month recovery. Immediacy, proximity, and expectancy were the guiding principles aimed to get the soldier back to the front. Techniques utilized were exposure therapy through movies and memory recall. Similar techniques are used now through desensitization techniques involving exposure and cognitive interventions. Cognitive processing therapy (CPT) involves education, challenging thought distortions and beliefs, processing painful memories, and building skills to reduce avoidance. Eye movement desensitization and reprocessing (EMDR) is an alternative treatment involving recall of the event coupled with bilateral stimulation through eye movements or rhythmically stimulating the right and left sides of the body. Group therapy has been a common therapeutic intervention for PTSD since World War II. Psychopharmacology has been used since the Civil War, when barbiturates (sodium pentanol) were utilized to support recall with hypnosis. Selective serotonin reuptake inhibitors (SSRIs) to downshift nervous system reactivity are currently the psychopharmacological treatment of choice.

Controversies: There was a movement led most notably by Bessel van der Kolk to include C-PTSD due to childhood trauma as a separate diagnosis in the DSM-5. This was voted down due to there not being enough empirical evidence to support the diag-

9. "How Common Is PTSD in Adults?" PTSD: National Center for PTSD.

10. Kessler et al., "Lifetime Prevalence and Age-of-Onset Distributions of DSM-IV Disorders in the National Comorbidity Survey Replication."

nosis. This is related to the larger controversy around PTSD, which is how to define trauma and how to understand the cultural factors that play into an individual's understanding of and response to trauma. It has also been posited that distress after trauma is a normal reaction and it is not accurate to deem it a mental health disorder.

DSM-5 Diagnostic Criteria: The DSM-5 diagnostic criteria for PTSD are as follows: (A) exposure to an event that threatens death or serious injury, including sexual violence; exposure can be directly experienced, can be witnessed, or can happen to a family member or loved one; repeated exposure to victims of trauma also qualifies and is called vicarious traumatization; (B) recurrent memories, dreams, or flashbacks, dissociation, or an extreme stress response to reminders of the trauma; (C) avoidance behaviors precluding engagement in normative activities; (D) negative alterations in mood and distorted beliefs associated with the event; (E) marked nervous system reactivity interfering with sleep, relaxation, digestion, and appetite; (F) duration of the disturbance longer than a month; (G) marked interference of symptoms with normative functioning, such as attending to a job or family; and (H) symptoms are not attributed to a drug.

In conclusion, there is a clear link between childhood trauma and severe mental health disorders that involve a lack of coherence in the personality and an inability to cope with life in a functional way. Riley's story vividly conveys that predicament faced by survivors of trauma, who were not afforded the safety or teaching that enables development of healthy coping skills and a coherent sense of self. On a hopeful note, these disorders can be treated successfully when there is a comprehensive understanding of the disorder's origins and a compassionate approach to treatment is implemented.

Chapter 5

The Legacy Download

This chapter reinforces concepts of legacy trauma through Riley's story. Coming to terms with the fact that her parents were merely repeating their own histories with her helped Riley in her intention to move beyond her anger at them. In this chapter you will learn about the importance of early modeling, how people act from the level of consciousness they have at the present time, and how abuse is passed down through generations. Riley demonstrates the possibility of coming to terms with one's own trauma and moving beyond it.

Before I began working with Riley, she had participated in extensive therapy unpacking the abuse from her early life and understanding how severe trauma and neglect had affected her. During her work with me, she expressed a desire to move beyond the past. "You know," she said wearily, "I get it now. I know why I am the way I am, and frankly sometimes I'm sick of talking about it and thinking about it. And it bugs me that I'm still angry. I mean, I know my brother's an asshole, and shit, my folks are dead. I just don't want to hold this anger anymore."

At one time Riley's anger served an important role in her differentiation from her family. It allowed her to name the abuse and feel the outrage of having been deprived of the love and nurturance human beings require to develop properly. Now, however, she just felt weighed down by it. "How do I move forward without the anger but also knowing where I come from and why I am the way I am?" she queried during one session.

I introduced Riley to the concept of legacy trauma, which refers to how the unprocessed trauma carried by our parents and ancestors is passed on to us. "I mean, think about it, Riley," I said. "You know that both your parents came from hardscrabble families and their basic needs weren't met. And your brother, well, he was raised in the same family you were. I'm not excusing his behavior, so please don't take it that way, but people respond to deprivation and humiliation in their own way. Your brother chose, unconsciously of course, to perpetrate abuse as a means to cope with the humiliation and rejection he likely endured at the hands of your father. I'm not sure this will help you fully forgive them, Riley, but I do believe that understanding that your parents behaved the only way they knew how could help you move forward. At the very least my hope is for you to internalize that they just didn't have the capacity or consciousness to do better than they did. Perhaps this could reinforce your own sense of integrity and self-respect for doing the work and gathering the tools to choose differently.

Living Your Parents from the Inside Out

Entrenched patterns of stress and dis-ease related to living in and caring for your body directly mirror the unprocessed trauma of those who cared for you. What this means is that you serve as a container for what your parents did not recognize or have the capacity to process in their own psyche. For example, Riley had difficulty recognizing and meeting her basic needs. Her mother had had trouble recognizing and caring for Riley's needs, as demonstrated by the severe neglect she perpetrated when Riley was a child. The source of her neglect of Riley was her own dissociation from her body and inability to deal with her own needs, as evidenced by her addiction to food. Riley's mother had never had the opportunity or awareness to acknowledge, let alone come to terms with, the abuse and neglect she had endured as a child. Hence, it was inevitable that she would pass this on to her offspring. This inheritance of unconscious patterns related to trauma is as significant as the genes one inherits for eye color.

The concept of modeling to shape behavior, though understood at a superficial level, is underestimated with regard to its power to permanently shape behavior. We are such a mind-based culture that we imagine people should be able to overcome their early conditioning through the power of acquired knowledge. After all, what's so hard about going shopping and cooking a nutritious meal or setting an alarm clock, let alone putting on a sweater when you're cold? But the volition to do it is lacking when the download shaping behavior favors inertia and self-neglect, as Riley's did. You simply do not know what you don't know. Hence, in theory eating healthful food and caring for your body is quite simple; however, in your lived mind it's something that other people do but you are incapable of doing or don't deserve.

Along with behavior, the psyche also forms itself around early modeling. The following quote, often attributed to Carl Jung, captures the subtle potency of the parent's legacy: "The greatest tragedy of the family is the unlived lives of the parents."[11] The content of one's early modeling is not necessarily conscious, but it creates a network of habit, expectation, and experience that is familiar and becomes identified with the self that you know yourself to be. So although you may want to take better care of yourself at a conscious level, unconsciously you do not believe you are worthy of it and you feel invisibly barred from it. Alternatively, you may have even learned to make self-neglect into a virtue. Cooking and eating vegetables is something pampered, overprivileged, finicky people do, and sleeping for eight hours is for weaklings.

If these beliefs look and sound absurd, it's because they are. However, they are also very real. You might be surprised to peek under your own hood and find some of them nestled inside. I've had individuals with chronic health issues related to a heavy body weight and inactivity admit a secret pride in eschewing "rabbit food." When your basic physical and

---

11. This popularized version is paraphrased from Jung's quote "Nothing exerts a stronger psychic effect upon the human environment, and especially upon children, than the life which the parents have not lived," in Jung, "Paracelsus," *The Spirit in Man, Art, and Literature*, paragraph 4.

emotional needs were neglected by your caregivers, or even mocked, you learned to block out your physical organism's needs and now carry a secret shame about them. Consequently, it feels weak, forced, or indulgent to eat regular meals, ensure an adequate amount of sleep, or shower daily. Because such simple gestures of respectful care were never bestowed upon you, it takes a leap of faith, usually assisted by a caring relationship with at least one other person, to help you overcome inner resistance to a gentler, more responsive orientation to your basic needs.

Generational Trauma

Trauma is usually, if not always, multigenerational. Most often when parents perpetrate abuse, it is not calculated and occurs despite their better intentions. People usually create a family and embark upon the role of becoming a parent with excitement, and if not that, then at least an intention to meet the situation with their best selves. And then life happens and takes a toll. More children, less money, marital disappointments, addiction, unexpected losses, and innumerable other life events converge and exceed an individual's coping skills. When the demands of the environment overwhelm the resources of the individual, the system weakens and the person dials down from an aspirational mode to a survival mode, the root chakra. Individuals who do not have a strong foundation of self-care, the ability to self-regulate, and adequate emotional and financial support resort to primitive coping methods when faced with too many demands. Hence, patterns of dissociation, externalization (often enacted in abuse), addiction, and comfort seeking are adopted and the higher ideals of parenthood are abandoned with scant reflection.

When you are born to parents who have not had the opportunity to understand and come to terms with their own trauma, they will have no choice but to pass on the only thing they know. Thankfully, this is not game over for you, as it was not for Riley either. By coming to terms with the legacy of your own trauma, feeling the pain of it and acknowledging your anger about it, you are afforded the capacity of moving beyond it. Riley was still in the process of doing this, and her wish to move past her anger harkened a new level of growth for her. The next chapter elaborates on healing from root chakra trauma and subsequent addictions. This is not easy work, but it is good work, and the rewards, as demonstrated by Riley, extend far beyond the self.

Chapter 6
Healing Your Root Chakra

This chapter provides guidance for healing your root chakra. The suggestions you will find are jumping-off places to begin setting a different track for how you relate to your physical self and your deep programming. This chapter is intentionally general and suggestive rather than prescriptive. A strict regimen imposed by another person is not going to fix your relationship to your root chakra. That is because healing at the root is a process of reconnecting with your organic intelligence and establishing a more trusting relationship with yourself. With that in mind, the following suggestions and options guide you to name and then gradually reset dysfunctional habits and attitudes that you have internalized from your family of origin and cultural inheritance. The overall intent of the following material is to help you find comfortable and sustainable ways to maximize, and even enjoy, the health and innate wisdom of your body.

Insight: Necessary but Not Sufficient

Insight is a good thing. It refers to having an intellectual understanding of your issues and how you came to have them. Many therapy techniques are aimed to identify the origins of your patterns of thought and behavior and develop an understanding of how they function in your life. This is done by exploring your developmental history, recognizing distorted patterns of thinking and behaving, and examining how your behavior affects others. Insight, however, does not create change. Change comes about only through doing something different. You must act your way into change.

With this in mind, journaling is an extremely helpful tool for processing insight and exploring pathways for new behavior. You must be able to imagine something different in order to enact it. Journaling kindles both insight and imagination. The following exercises include journaling prompts and behavioral suggestions. The first set of prompts asks you to look at your developmental history in a clear-eyed, objective way. Recount what you know, including your memories, stories you have been told, pictures that you have, and what your family of origin has shared with you. Beware of your tendency to minimize or discount things because you do not have a clear memory of them. You must learn to trust your felt sense. You are not looking for historical accuracy; rather, you are plumbing for what feels true to you.

Your Download

1. What is your understanding of your first five years of life? Include significant memories, stories you have been told, and pictures from your early years that you have seen. Feel free to interview those who knew you as a baby, including parents, extended family, and older siblings.
2. Knowing what you know about your mother, imagine the climate of your prenatal environment. How did she take care of herself? Did she smoke? Was she working? Was she in a stable relationship with her family of origin? What do you imagine her relationship with your father was like? Did she have a network of support within her community?
3. What do you know about your birth and your first few months of life? How might these circumstances have impacted your first experiences in the world and shaped your general orientation to life?
4. How do you imagine your needs for nourishment, bathing, play, and affection were handled during your infancy and toddlerhood? Do you think you were on a schedule? From what you

know about your parents, was this rigidly enforced? Or were things more fluid, perhaps even haphazard and chaotic?

5. How much stress do you imagine your family was experiencing during your developing years?
6. Were you exposed to any traumas during your first eighteen years? This includes physical and sexual abuse, fighting, yelling, or physical altercations in the home. Consider how these things affected your sense of safety and security. Also consider how other issues, such as poverty, deaths, job loss, divorce, illness among family members, and emotional neglect, may have impacted you.
7. Now reflect on how these aspects of your history are downloaded onto your body-psyche. Reflect on both positive and negative aspects of your early experiences. Perhaps there was a steady routine in your care but a lack of play, or perhaps things were going well and then something untoward occurred in the family, like cancer, job loss, or an accident. Reflect on how these aspects of your development impact your current sense of safety and security in relation to your body, other people, and the world.
8. Looking over your answers, does it make sense that you struggle with the issues you have? Given what you were born into, could it be any other way? Does this enhance your compassion for yourself?
9. Consider how increased insight may lead to changes in your current behavioral patterns. Given your insights, are you inspired to make any changes in how you care for yourself?

Self-Care vs. Self-Neglect

The reflections above are designed to help you unpack your download. Now it is time to track how your download manifests in your current day-to-day living. The following prompts help you identify how the silent stress of managing your body from day to day can create an unnamed pressure that degrades your daily sense of well-being. This includes tracking and meeting your body's needs and dealing with the sometimes mysterious ailments that may shadow your everyday life. This stress can result in patterns of self-care that are less than optimal and are fueled by a misguided attempt to avoid or control the ever-present reality of your incarnate being.

1. What is your relationship to your health? Are you overly concerned and hypochondriacal or do you veer to the other end and ignore or minimize your basic health needs? Consider whether you get regular checkups with your doctor, complete recommended screening tests, visit your dentist regularly, and follow up on unusual symptoms when you have them. Are there changes you would like to make regarding your approach to your health care? What stands in the way of you making these changes?
2. Do you struggle with any of your basic bodily functions? This includes eating, elimination, sleep, breathing, and energy. How much of your emotional energy goes into worry and management of your symptoms? Do your issues get in the way of your basic functioning at home or work or interfere with your socialization and need for play?
3. How would you rate your physical self-confidence? Do you carry shame about your size, your level of conditioning, or your eating, smoking, or drinking habits? How does this shame impact your day-to-day life?
4. Consider whether specific physical concerns impede your willingness to travel or participate in certain events. These include concerns regarding sleep, bowels, eating habits, smoking, and other addictions. Concerns about body size or lack of conditioning may also interfere with your willingness to participate in activities that involve walking, dancing, or being in an unfamiliar place. Give an honest assessment of whether you avoid

activities to stay in your comfort zone. Then consider if you are willing to stretch this zone. What are some progressive steps you could take to increase your willingness to be uncomfortable?

5. Do you put a lot of energy into external self-care? This refers to grooming, cosmetic procedures, clothing and bling, pedicures and manicures, tanning, and hair coloring and removal. What level of importance does your physical appearance have for you? Conversely, are you someone who puts little energy into your external appearance? Have you always been this way? What are your reasons for minimizing this aspect of your being?
6. How much energy do you put into your internal body? This includes being mindful of sleep and nutrition and trying alternative treatments, such as acupuncture and chiropractic services, for health conditions. Reflect on whether you want to make changes in this area of your self-care.
7. What are some reasonable changes you could make that would move you toward a more mindful, balanced relationship with your body and its needs? List five changes you would like to make and then order them from easiest to hardest. Are you willing to start by implementing one change a week? There is no hurry, and it is advised that you take a wait-and-see attitude. You could opt for one change a month or implement one change for several months. If you don't know where to start, go to the basics. Start with your nutritional needs, sleep needs, organizational and cleanliness issues in your home, your need for medical screenings and dental care, or your need for appropriate movement.

Your Addictions

Root chakra addictions refer to patterns of passive self-soothing with a substance that impacts the nervous system. There is a broad spectrum of how these patterns can manifest, ranging from healthy to deleterious.

Healthy self-soothing is having a hard day at the office and going home for a comforting meal with your family. Individuals can also enjoy alcohol, for example having wine with dinner, in a pleasure-giving, sustainable way. If your behavior feels good, soothes your nervous system, and aligns with your overall health and functioning, it is a healthy form of self-soothing. Belle and Joe illustrate more rigid and problematic patterns of passive self-soothing that interfered with exploration of other activities and experiences. Riley exemplifies self-soothing run amok because her behaviors became highly self-destructive. This section will address the spectrum of addiction and give suggestions particular to the different levels.

Advanced Addiction

Advanced addiction is a pattern of substance use wherein the substance takes over your life. You frequently use more than you intend and prioritize the substance over your financial, relational, and physical health. When you are forced to go without your substance, you experience cravings and withdrawal and will go to lengthy measures to procure it regardless of the consequences. You continue to use it in spite of obvious deleterious effects, which become easier to ignore and minimize over time. It is a slippery slope wherein chaos gradually becomes the new normal. Often only something catastrophic and shocking, like a DUI, health issue, or loss of a relationship, can wake you from this treacherous slumber. Even then, you may briefly try to reform but then revert back to your former ways. This is because the road to recovery is difficult and filled with obstacles. These obstacles can be overcome, but it isn't easy and requires ongoing perseverance and readjustments. It is important to know this up front so you can prepare your mindset and strengthen your resolve. The following questions aim to help you prepare for the challenges of recovery from advanced addiction.

1. Reflect on the level of risk you are taking in relation to your current substance use. Are you procuring substances illegally or taking other risks with your physical or legal safety, e.g., driving while buzzed, using untested or possibly contaminated sub-

stances, or spending time with people whom you don't know well and who may not have your best interests at heart?

2. How is your substance use affecting your finances? Tally how much money you spend on your addiction. Have you considered other, more productive ways that money could be used?
3. How is your substance use affecting your job performance? Are you showing up late or missing days? Does it impair your focus and concentration because you are recovering from a hangover or distracted by cravings? Has anyone expressed concern about your job performance?
4. Reflect on how your substance use is impacting your relational health. Have people you're close to talked to you about your substance use? Have you regretted your behavior while under the influence? Have you lost relationships because of your use?
5. Now reflect on your future self. Where will you be in five years if you continue your current use pattern? Consider health, financial, and relational consequences.
6. List your reasons for your current usage and how you minimize or justify your behavior to yourself. Common defaults rely on the fact that others in your orbit do the same thing or that you plan to cut back eventually and will clean up your act when things in your life calm down. Dig into your denial system and list five of your rationalizations. Then counter these rationalizations from the point of view of your wiser, more objective self.
7. Reflect on what stops you from changing your current patterns. What measures have you tried before and why have you defaulted to the status quo?
8. Do you believe you can fix the problem on your own? What makes it hard to reach out for help?

Before leaving this section, it is important to reinforce that if you are in advanced addiction, you will need intensive support and a major lifestyle overhaul. This sounds intimidating, but the good news is you don't have to do it all at once. The first step is admitting that you have a problem. The second step is reaching out for help. If you can do this and drop your conviction that you can do it alone or that merely cutting back will be enough, then you are on your way.

If you are open to help, consider both individual psychotherapy and a 12-step program. When looking for a therapist, be persistent. It can take a while to find a good fit, so don't stop if your first attempt falls flat. Therapists are like snowflakes. We are all different and it can take time to find someone with whom you have the right chemistry. You should feel validated and understood by your therapist but also challenged. Be honest with your therapist if you don't feel that the sessions are helpful. See how the person responds and if they are able to shift course to meet your needs. Remember, addiction sets in where relationship fails, so you need to go back to the source to heal yourself. That means you will need to confront your hopelessness and suspicion regarding others' capacity to be there for you.

On the subject of 12-step programs, please do not let the objection that you aren't a joiner or aren't religious stand in your way. Many people object to the mandate that you turn your will over to a higher power of your choosing. A higher power does not refer to an almighty bearded fellow in the sky. That is a culturally informed, patriarchal image of God that is far from how many people conceive of their higher power. A higher power can merely mean that you accept that you are not the ultimate arbiter of reality and there are forces larger than yourself at play in your life. For example, your cell phone is powered by a force larger than you that you likely have little understanding of. So, too, can the earth spinning in space, the orchestra of cells in your body organizing themselves into you, and the countless other miracles unfolding around you serve as reminders that you are beholden to forces far beyond your limited understanding. Hopefully these obvious truths will be enough to allow you to overcome any suspicion of religion and give the program a chance. And remember to try several different groups before deciding that recovery is not for you.

Finally, consider whether you need a detox program and an intensive rehabilitation program. People who are physically dependent on alcohol need a monitored detox program to ensure medical safety and compliance. Following this with a structured recovery program that offers intensive individual and group therapy can provide the necessary scaffolding to support your ongoing recovery after you leave an inpatient setting. If you think you can't afford it or can't take time off from work, this is a valid concern but also an excuse. There are sliding fee programs available and many are covered by insurance. Jobs are real and important and not all allow for extended absences. It may be worth it, however, to take a hiatus, get clean, and have faith that new possibilities will emerge.

Mild/Moderate Addiction

Mild to moderate addiction encompasses habitual behaviors that, although they may not have a direct impact on your life, silently chip away at your health, well-being, and overall quality of life. This might look like a few glasses of wine daily that then affect the quality of your sleep, which then affects your attitude and well-being the next day, priming you to want the wine the next evening. Keep in mind that mild to moderate addiction can progress into severe addiction if untoward events occur in your life for which you lack adequate coping skills due to your habitual use.

The following journal prompts ask you to take an honest look at your habits and assess how they are affecting your current quality of life and the well-being of your future self.

1. Do you have habits or behaviors that you know aren't in your best interest but that you continue regardless? This could include eating too many sweets, drinking a few glasses of wine nightly, or imbibing too much caffeine. List these behaviors and how you rationalize them.
2. Reflect on how these behaviors leave you feeling. Be specific regarding the physical and emotional effects you experience.

3. Reflect on the downstream effects of your behaviors. For example, you may miss workouts because of drinking too much the night before. Eating too much sugar is contributing to rising blood sugar that has placed you in the prediabetic range.
4. Now reflect on what behaviors you would like to replace your less salutary habits with. For example, you might decide to stop snacking on sweets in the afternoon and instead go for a walk, or you might replace your daily wine with relaxation exercises at the end of the day. The brain does not like a "no," so it is more effective to focus on the positive thing that you are going to start doing rather than the negative thing that you are trying to stop doing.
5. Choose one change you can commit to making over the next week and the behavior you would like to replace it with. Get a notebook and note your progress and your feelings about the process daily. At the end of one week, commit to either continuing the current change or adding a new one. Remember to pace yourself and not to do too much too quickly. Also remember that it takes a minimum of twenty-one days for a new habit to crystallize and become part of your routine.
6. Reflect on the supports and reinforcements you will need to stay on the path. Don't minimize the need for this even if you deem your problem to be mild. Confide your goals to at least one person and consider if you could enlist anyone else in your life to join you in a similar endeavor.

Relationships with Others

Addiction begins where relationship fails. If you suffer from severe addiction, then at some point in your life you made a decision that other people were not trustworthy and the substance would never let you down. The pain was too much, your heart closed, and the armoring began. For individuals who suffer from more severe addictions, this decision was likely made early in their development. Passive, chemical soothing became a pseudo-solution to the problem of not having nurturing others to depend on. Riley discovered alcohol when she realized that it helped her connect with peers and gave her a sense of identity in a wasteland of isolation and fear.

For those experiencing milder forms of root chakra addiction, the failure of relationship is more subtle and falls under the rubric of emotional invalidation. Belle's and Joe's stories exemplify how this happens. As in their cases, milder addictions usually arise from the need to soothe a mind and body driven to appear a certain way and achieve in order to gain approval. The sense of having only conditional worth programs the mind and body with an unconscious fear of abandonment. The stress of this takes a toll and substances provide a seemingly easy fix for a mind and body that have lost their capacity to release.

The following reflections are designed to help you delve into your deep programming around other people and determine how and when your capacity to trust others was disrupted. This work can be painful, and you may find yourself not wanting to uncover the feelings of abandonment and hopelessness at the root of your distrust. Often what you find is a conviction that something is fundamentally wrong with you. It is important to touch this root so that you can feel the pain there and eventually learn to feel your own inherent worthiness. You then need to learn to give to yourself in a way that your parents were unable to, which creates a deep sense of self-empowerment.

1. Were people a source of comfort or pain when you were a child? Who was a source of comfort and who was a source of pain? This is a nuanced question, as one person may have been a source of both pleasure and pain, which becomes very confusing and creates a disorganized attachment style.
2. What beliefs about yourself do you carry related to the harm that others caused you? Write down those beliefs and the associated traumas or relationships that fostered them. Can you

associate your current substance use with these distorted beliefs about yourself?

3. Was there a point where you turned away from other people for comfort and enjoyment and instead turned to a substance? How did the substance help you at the time? Did you feel guilty, happy, or proud to have discovered your fix? Did it give you a sense of power and control at the time? When did the tide turn and it began to diminish your sense of yourself?
4. Describe the progression of your usage and how it became problematic in your life. Include when you first identified it as a problem.
5. Reflect on how failure of relationships was implicated in the inception and progression of your problem. If you have milder dependencies, describe how your usage is linked to a need to be a certain way so as to ensure your value.
6. Are you willing to attend a support group such as Alcoholics Anonymous or another 12-step program? Reflect on your resistance to and fears about this. Also consider whether you would consult a therapist and what might hold you back from doing so. If you have milder addictions, consider if you are willing to talk candidly with a friend or therapist about your struggle. How honest are you willing to be?

Legacy Trauma

The following questions encourage appreciation for the fact that your parents likely carried unprocessed traumas that impacted their ability to care for you in a mindful and nurturing way. Linking your difficulties to how you were cared for, while also understanding that your parents were suffering themselves, can reduce blame and encourage compassionate understanding for them as people.

1. Reflect on how your issues are related to your parents' issues. Do your behaviors either mirror theirs or reflect the opposite

of their patterns? It is not uncommon for overweight parents to have children who are overly fixated on weight or for miserly parents to have children who are careless with money. Too tight or too loose each reflect the same core problem related to a person's ability to mindfully balance pleasure with restraint.

2. Do your reflections about your legacy trauma help you understand your parents better and feel more compassion for them? Reflect on how their childhoods shaped them to have a problematic relationship to their own needs.
3. Reflect on the idea that you treat yourself as you were treated. How does this manifest in your life?
4. Reflect on your relationships with your parents. If they are living, reflect on your patterns of interaction with them and your feelings toward them. Do you hold resentments? If so, how do your resentments impact your interactions with them? How do your resentments impact your feelings about yourself? If your parents are deceased, reflect on how their deaths have affected you. Has their death changed your feelings about them? Do you feel that you still have a relationship with them even if they are deceased?
5. Consider writing a letter to each of your parents that you won't send. Express your feelings about them, how their parenting affected you, the things you appreciate about them, and the things that have hurt you. If your parents are living, consider whether you might want to express anything in the letter directly to them.

This concludes the healing section on the root chakra. The main intention of this chapter is to take a clear, honest look at your download and also to assess your addictions, or unskillful behaviors, and consider ways to be in a more responsible relationship with yourself, beginning with lifestyle patterns. Remember that what you cultivate in the present plants seeds that you will reap in the future. Small things matter and it is never too late to begin again.

Gifts of the Root Chakra

Cultivating a conscious relationship with your root chakra opens you to the following rewards.

Safety and Security

Ease of relationship with your body and confidence that you can respond intelligently and intuitively to its needs is an essential condition for happiness. It creates an interior security based on a good relationship with your organismic self. You need not live in fear of your body and resort to primitive methods of force and control or their corollary, which is collapse. Instead, you can remain open and responsive to your body's needs without resentment or fear.

Unconditional Worthiness

If you were raised in a fear-driven environment, unconditional worthiness may seem like a delusion. After all, you need to earn your keep, right? Love without conditions and care freely given are some of life's finer offerings. Unconditional worthiness is a gift channeled through other human beings and has the power to bestow healing upon those who give it as well as those who receive it. Receiving this as an infant is a right of being. To not receive it is a tragedy that can shape the rest of your life. Taking back this basic right of deserving care without conditions by allowing yourself to take compliments with grace and receive needed support is a hidden gift of healing.

The Right to Receive

Related to the above, worry about being perceived as selfish or greedy can block your ability to ask for and enjoy the gift of satisfying your basic needs. The capacity to enjoy the simple gifts that life has to offer, such as a cup of coffee, a beautiful sunset, or a quality item from a store, is grounded in a trust in life supported by being in good relationship with your body and others. There is a big difference between enjoying beauty and the material aspects of the world and grasping onto them compulsively. Receiving with enjoyment is a way of saying thank you.

Ease with the Material World

The ability to navigate obstacles and transform inconvenience into opportunity is the happy outcome of learning to respect the limits and rules of the material world without being confined and defined by them. This is the gift of making peace with the root chakra, accepting its dominion, and treating it with respect. It is only when the limits and requirements of the material world are accounted for and honored that these limits cease to be experienced as impediments to happiness.

Appreciating and caring for your physical body and the apparently mundane aspects of your life releases trapped energy in the root chakra and allows it to move into the sacral chakra, the domain of energy and feeling. When you embrace your roots and face your life on its own terms, energy formerly trapped in resistance to life and addiction is freed to migrate upward and kindle movement in the sacral chakra. This releases you from a life lived in survival-based consciousness, wherein you are in conflict with the fundamentals of your existence, and brings you into the realm of energy where latent possibility can emerge.

Part II
The Sacral Chakra: Your Power Source

Chapter 7

The Sacral Chakra and Emotional Processing

This chapter is divided into two sections. Section 1 explains the role a person's emotional processing system plays in their mental health and overall experience of life. Section 2 explores how the strength of a person's emotional processing system informs their capacity to endure a change process. Since the concept of emotional processing is unique to this paradigm, section 1 starts with a more thorough explanation of what it is and its centrality in human emotional and physical health. The concept of life energy is also explained, as it is a rather squishy concept to begin with and is also not a part of the Western theoretical lexicon. It is, however, fundamental to Eastern conceptual models and chakra theory, and, I would argue, is central to understanding the human experience.

Following this introduction, Riley, Belle, and Joe will illustrate how Little t interferes with the healthy development of the emotional processing system. Riley's experience demonstrates the perils of a chaotic system, and Belle demonstrates the quieter misery of an overly rigid system. Joe demonstrates the subtle phenomenon of energetic confidence and how this is linked to being able to bring language to feelings, a capacity that is shaped during childhood.

The Sacral Chakra in Focus

Location in the Body: Lower abdomen, sacral plexus

Developmental Challenges: The right to feel your feelings without shame or need for external validation; the ability to maintain internal equilibrium and self-soothe in the face of impingements from the body and the world

Threats to Development: Emotional invalidation; shame as a corrective tool; bullying or injustice without emotional support; lack of emotional expression in the home

Primary Developmental Conflict: Balancing the need for social approval and adherence to social conventions with the ability to self-validate and allow feelings to flow without need for permission

Signs of Underdevelopment: Dependence on validation from others in order to legitimize feelings; emotional numbing; constricted affect; lack of awareness of your own and others' feelings; living in your head

Signs of Overdevelopment: Overexpression of feelings, drama, and hysteria; exaggeration of feeling states; allowing feelings to dictate behavior without regard for the impact on others

Conditioned Beliefs: You must have evidence to prove that your feelings are valid. Others must agree with your feelings. It is weak to cry or express helplessness and hurt. It is shameful to be vulnerable.

Associated Addictions: Manipulation of the energetic system in order to artificially create desired feeling states; use of adrenaline, stimulated by exercise, shopping, sex, and gambling to force high-energy states; use of social media, compulsive exercise, or cleaning to distract from emotional pain

Associated Mental Health Disturbances: Major depression, dysthymia, mood lability, anxiety disorders

Gifts of the Sacral Chakra: Ability to affirm and experience the full spectrum of feelings; confidence that painful feelings will resolve into something new and acceptance that pleasurable feelings must end in order to return; capacity to channel energy in response to the challenges of life

SECTION 1: YOUR EMOTIONAL PROCESSING SYSTEM

The function of your emotional processing system is to circulate life energy. The significance of having a well-toned energetic processing center, and its role in your mental and physical health, cannot be overemphasized. When a person's emotional processing system is working well, the person is able to balance internal awareness with external demands. This means they are able to set boundaries, pause, say no when necessary, and take care of their own needs in lieu of meeting others' expectations. The person is flexible enough to change course when needed but also grounded enough to stay rooted in what feels intuitively right to them. There is a balance between awareness of one's own needs and appreciation of the needs of others.

All the qualities listed above rest on the health of a person's emotional processing system, which is established during childhood. During childhood the child learns how to name and manage impulses and feelings of pleasure and pain. This hardwires an orientation to the body and also to life. Children who learn that their impulses are acceptable and can be managed appropriately will enter the world with an inherent confidence and willingness to engage. Children who learn that their impulses are bad, shameful, and dangerous will not possess this confidence and are more likely to shy away from experience or enter recklessly and reinforce the belief that their impulses are bad. This basic orientation to the self and to life establishes either a willingness to engage with life or a tendency to avoid it. Systems that engage get stronger and more resilient and systems that avoid weaken and deteriorate. This is a really big deal because one of the central functions of a human being is to process life energy, and this depends on the strength of the emotional processing system. Life is inherently challenging for everyone. In order to face these challenges, a person must be able to bear up to the darkness and light circulating on the planet and through their own body. To help you fully appreciate this, we will take some time here to further define the concept of life energy.

Life Energy

Because the concept of life energy, or *prana* in yoga parlance, is considered fluffy at best, I would like to give you a primer on what it refers to. As with many things that are glaringly obvious, we rarely pause to consider the subtle miracle of life that is hidden in plain sight. Like light, life energy moves in rhythmic waves of contraction and expansion. This rhythm of peristalsis occurs in the smallest cells of your body, in your organs, and through your whole physiological system. Peristalsis also occurs in your emotional processing system, which expands and contracts in order to move life experiences and feelings through your mind-body system.

In the same way that an unhealthy physical system cannot expand and contract fully to process food or blood (referring to poor peristalsis in the digestive system or heart), an unhealthy emotional system cannot expand and contract fully to process the energy of darkness and light (which we experience as emotion) inherent to life. In order to be a healthy human being, you must be able to grieve, feel joy, and experience pleasure and frustration without getting stuck in patterns of avoidance or numbing. The tendency to hold onto pleasure and avoid pain is natural to the human condition. You must cultivate an emotional system that is willing to experience it all. When your emotional processing system is not well toned and lacks a healthy rhythm of contraction and expansion, you lack confidence that good things pass and will come again and that pain is not permanent. Consequently, your system will lean toward too much contraction (rigidity) or it will become overly expanded (chaos). You will vacillate between these two states, which creates dysregulation and dysfunction. This is a direct consequence of childhood emotional invalidation, which results in a weak sacral chakra and dysfunction.

Work on your sacral chakra begins with insight into how trauma affected your emotional processing system and increased awareness of your habitual orientation to life. Are you a "no" person? Are you often critical and withholding? Do you hold yourself to high, unattainable standards mandated by an invisible authority? These patterns indicate a system that leans toward too much contraction, which is a rejection of life energy. Not having boundaries or structure, and the inability to set boundaries, is indicative of a system leaning toward too much expansion. Both syndromes reflect the same basic problem: a dysfunctional relationship to life energy. Recognizing your default patterns toward contraction or expansion, as well as defining the internal tone of your sacral chakra, can redirect unhelpful, habitual patterns of energetic management that do not serve you. Riley will demonstrate how too much expansion, coupled with equal and opposite contraction, played out in her life, while Belle will demonstrate the more sedate consequences of too much contraction leading to rigidity.

Chaos or Rigidity: Each Exacts Its Price

Riley had the misfortune of being programmed by an unresponsive, abandoning, and sometimes terrifying environment. Consequently, the emotional tone of her interior space was unpleasant, to say the least, fraught with fear and negativity, and therefore necessitated some form of escape via dissociation from an early age. You already have a good idea of the Big T trauma that Riley endured and the toll it took on her root chakra. What is important to understand about her sacral chakra is that each chakra builds upon the stability of the one that comes before. Channeling prana, which is subtle energy, relies on the firm structure of the body, your root chakra, to support it. You can think of your root chakra as the bowl and your sacral chakra as the water. The health of your root chakra supports you in meeting your material needs and provides you with the routine and consistency required to maintain a healthy life in the physical world. If you are lacking this, as Riley was, you will be unable to develop a strong emotional body that is able to safely process both pleasure and pain. We will first explore the consequences of a chaotic emotional system through Riley and then contrast this with Belle's more rigid system.

Emotional Turbulence

Riley suffered from emotional turbulence. If you've ever been on an airline flight and endured the terrifying jumps and gut-dropping plummets of a plane riding unpredictable air currents, then you have an idea of how Riley felt on a daily basis. Her emotional system lacked continuity and coherence, primarily because she lacked the underlying structure of routine, predictability, and safety provided by a strong root chakra. Hence, she was like a plane with no stabilizing system and at the mercy of her own unrestrained impulses and emotions, not to mention the untoward events of the world and the unpredictable and often cruel actions of other people.

Riley's inability to regulate her emotions was a product of the Little t that was endemic to her childhood. The Little t in the aftermath of Big T is often the most damaging aspect of trauma. It is not so much what happened to the person as it is the denial, collusion, and complicity of others that leads to the disoriented, fraught emotional world of the survivor. They cannot trust their own perception of reality—let alone others around them—to see what is obvious and act accordingly.

When Riley was in her twenties, prior to any therapy, her emotional system was severely impaired. She vacillated between being shut down and contracted, like a tightened fist, and being activated and frantic. Her emotional system consequently vacillated between being overly expanded and overly contracted. This earned her the diagnosis of bipolar II disorder, as will be discussed in the next chapter. The problem underlying her mood swings was that she could not manage impingements from the outside world, nor could she safely channel internal sensations and process pleasure and pain. Her energetic system was like old, frayed electrical wiring in a house. The wires sparked dangerously when too much energy was moving through them, leading to risk of a fire. Riley's system would overheat, causing her to either act out erratically or hit the circuit breaker and shut down. Her shutdowns were usually assisted by a sedating substance of some kind, including food, medications, and alcohol, or sometimes cutting, which has a sedating effect. Another way Riley coped was to discharge energy by acting out. She would have tantrums with lovers or break things in her home. These episodes would eventually lead to the destruction of the relationship and leave her in the wreckage of her torturous feelings of shame and guilt.

During our work together, Riley still struggled to manage her energetic system. She put it like this: "Sometimes I just have to scream. Like the energy inside me is so painful. It's like a pressure in my chest that sometimes feels unbearable." I explained to Riley that everyone has strong feelings at times, but that her overwhelm was caused by the injury to her emotional processing system sustained from her childhood trauma. During her therapy, Riley and I focused on helping her strengthen her emotional processing center. She found that doing self-monitoring, so that she was conscious of when she was likely to be triggered and had a plan for how she would respond, gave her a sense of control over her outbursts. She also discovered that by taking care of her basic needs for nutrition and rest, as well as interspersing breathing and relaxation exercises throughout her day, she had more resources to call upon when she was triggered.

Body Mirrors Mind: The Price of Rigidity

In contrast to Riley, Belle's ability to function on a day-to-day basis was generally good. This indicates that her emotional system was strong enough to respond coherently to demands in the environment and to adhere to the external structures that glue society together, which are root chakra capacities. Due to Little t from childhood, signified by her parents' emphasis on proper behavior at the expense of feelings, Belle's emotional system was externally oriented. This means that she was more responsive to cues and demands from others and the environment than oriented to track her own needs and feelings. This left her out of contact with her internal compass. She lacked a clear language for what she felt and what she needed. Ultimately she lacked an overall understanding of what was in her best interest and what she even had the right to ask for. A concrete example of this was her frequent habit of forcing herself to work or do things either that she didn't want to do or that stretched her capacity in an unhealthy way.

Belle's pattern was to tough it out and get through tasks during the workday, teeth gritted and stomach clenched. She frequently used caffeine and sugar to prop herself up in order to complete tasks that she felt she absolutely had to do. These oral habits became crutches she depended on to support her reflex to comply with external demands and meet rigid, often perfectionistic expectations that she herself imposed. It was the habitual nature of her compulsive doing, supported by her oral habits, that eventually became problematic for her and led to the overwhelmed state that brought her to therapy. In the past she had been able to ignore her feelings of overwhelm and anxiety and had relied on wine and food to bring her down in the evenings. Eventually this pattern of coping broke her down, resulting in the frantic woman who presented herself to me for therapy.

In this paradigm, the body is considered an external manifestation of the emotional/energetic system. Hence, it was not a surprise when Belle shared with me, soon into her treatment, that she suffered from IBS. She was initially embarrassed to bring this up to me, but I assured her that I was used to such topics. I explained the above concept to her, which conceptualizes the physical body as an external manifestation of the invisible energy of the emotional processing system. I knew that she was open to such ideas based on our previous conversations, so I explained to her how the digestive system provides a material replica of the emotional processing system.

"Belle," I elaborated one session, "let me try to make this more explicit for you. Your digestive system is designed to take in, process, assimilate, and then release material meant to nourish the body. This system has organs and mechanisms that filter out toxins and then assimilate the nutrients necessary to nourish and sustain your body. This is analogous to what happens in a healthy emotional system. You take in experiences, assimilate them though your heart and mind, release what is toxic or difficult, and then glean meaning from the experiences in order to strengthen and grow. This is why women so often don't remember the pain of childbirth and do it again and again. The meaning of the experience overrides the memory of the pain. This is also why, especially after a person dies, you remember the brilliance of that person's life and filter out the difficult aspects of their personality, which become mere sidenotes to the legacy they left behind." We further discussed how her rigid way of handling her emotions by blocking them out and powering through her days eventually caused her physical digestive system to tighten and shut down, resulting in an unhealthy gut.

Belle resonated with these ideas and they helped relieve some of the shame she felt about her digestive difficulties. She could see that the lack of vigor in her emotional system mirrored the lack of vigor in her digestive system and that both were related to being out of touch with her basic needs. She saw how this was related to the high standards and rigid structure she imposed upon herself. Seeing this connection motivated her to make the changes in both her daily self-care routines and her eating habits previously discussed. This created a sense of self-efficacy and connection with her own system, something that had been lacking for her since childhood.

Energetic Confidence: Holding Your Own

Joe was on time for his usual afternoon appointment with me. He needed to talk and didn't need any prompting to begin. "Work is difficult right now," he began, sighing heavily, wearied by the travails he seemed to continually face. "I have all these personnel problems. It really gets to me. I wish it didn't, but it bothers me. There is this woman on staff. I just don't trust her and I'm having a hard time turning my mind off about it. I feel like she might be preparing to file a complaint through HR or something and it's the last thing I need." Joe paused. He appeared not to know where to go from there, and I too struggled with how to access his inner world and the heavy energy he carried regardless of the apparent problem triggering his anxiety.

Joe suffered from the whack-a-mole syndrome I'd observed in many clients. You take care of one problem and breathe a short sigh of relief and then the next one pops up. What creates this syndrome is not so much the nature of the actual problems the individual faces but rather the energetic orientation the individual has in relation to problems in general. Does the person approach the issue practically, with a take-charge attitude, or are they victimized and helpless? Is the problem unsolvable and unfair or is it just a pain-in-the-ass aspect of life on the planet that needs to be dealt with? These attitudes are not cognitively based but rather are a manifestation of a person's energetic default setting. The attitude the person takes rests on their energetic capacity and level of confidence in their ability to manage obstacles.

The primary problem Joe suffered from was dysfunction in his sacral chakra stemming from Little t in childhood. Because his need for attention was not met by his parents and his sensitive nature was not recognized by them, which will be elaborated upon later, Joe labored under a sense of continual threat that if he did not perform, he would not be accepted. Hence, threats lay everywhere, if not from an employee then from some other looming issue that his worried mind gravitated toward. The source of his sense of threat lay in his own internal knowledge that he lacked confidence in his capacity to stand up to challenges in the world. This was deeply shameful to him—so shameful, in fact, that it was difficult to admit even to himself. After all, shouldn't he be stronger? Shouldn't he be a man?

Living on the knife-edge of being exposed as a fraud is no way to live. Joe was caught between two internal valences: the longing to be approved of and liked and the need to succeed in the role expected of a confident, influential man. He was attempting to solve this dilemma by relying on external proofs of his success. He often mentioned his salary, the bump in pay he expected the following year, and the promotion he might go for when his boss retired. He still held out hope that if he could just clear the next hurdle, he would feel okay. Sadly, I feared that no external accolade or additional zero in his paycheck would be enough to ease the internal rift. When is a man good enough for himself, and what does that even mean?

The Language of Emotion: Owning and Naming Feelings

Accessing feelings that are as yet unnamed and unacknowledged by you but that circulate in your system is central to cultivating energetic confidence. Joe lacked access to his emotions and did not recognize the shame he labored under. He was able to recognize basic emotions in himself and others and could resonate with others who were going through visible challenges. For example, when he described friends and colleagues who were facing medical issues, I could tell that Joe's empathy was genuine. It seemed he could understand emotions that had a visible cause that led to an understandable reaction. But the subtler emotions, like chronic shame or anxiety without apparent cause, were harder for him to feel or understand. It was as though he could name the primary colors but couldn't create shades or nuance with them, let alone paint an interesting or unique tapestry that was meaningful to him. Joe had an especially hard time admitting anything approaching weakness or inadequacy in himself and he judged it harshly in others. He longed to be understood, yet how could he be if he couldn't even understand himself? This led to him feeling very alone in spite of all the people around him. He remained invisible to himself and others, hidden away in his man suit.

Joe's lack of emotional fluency caused him to bypass the world of emotion and default to his root chakra for reassurance. He used his body and external achievements to stabilize himself and remind himself of his value. This, however, did nothing to ease the internal ache. My work with him was designed to help him give language to what was unnamed inside. This was not easy, because the programing as to which feelings are and are not acceptable goes very deep in all of us. As children we learn from our caregivers' responses to us which behaviors gain praise and positive reward and which ones garner shame and reprimand. The feelings and behaviors that cause offense are exiled and relegated to the hidden reservoir that comprises the unconscious.

In emotionally validating environments the child's behavior may be censured, but the feelings driving it are named and validated by caregivers.

Joe did not receive this gift of attention and empathy from his parents. I was hoping that talking more about childhood would open up the hidden world of buried feelings for Joe. This would entail discussing his childhood and naming the feelings that he had exiled. Joe was open to doing this with a little encouragement on my part.

Bringing the Unconscious to Light: Naming Little t

Joe was a sensitive, shy child. He described himself as being socially awkward at school and indicated that he also had struggled academically in the early grades and didn't believe he was very smart. His father was a brusque "man's man," highly successful in his business, with a loud and authoritative manner. Joe looked up to him but described feeling a little afraid of him, especially as a young boy. "He worked a lot," Joe told me when I asked him to describe their relationship when he was a child. "When he came home, I'm sure he was exhausted, so he didn't interact with me much. I understand now. He had a stressful job and just wanted a few drinks, dinner, and to talk with my mom."

I inquired whether Joe had felt left out, and he seemed a little bewildered as to why he would have felt that way. After all, that was adult time. "Joe," I offered after a brief pause, "this is a really good example of you likely having feelings as a child that you didn't even know you had because you didn't have the capacity or awareness to name them." I further explained how children internalize parental standards and identify with the expectations that are taught to them. "Kids want attention," I explained, "and you really looked up to your father. It must have been painful to not matter that much to him when you were a little boy, or at least to feel like you didn't." Joe took this in and seemed to accept the premise. This was a start, I hoped, to helping him see that feelings don't have to be socially approved in order to be real or valid.

In a later session, I continued on the theme of helping Joe unpack feelings that he'd had in relation to his parents as a child. He was able to access his longing for his father's approval and attention and his shame around his struggles in school. He was also beginning to see the connection between his insecurity at work and his unmet need for attention in childhood. I decided to push the envelope and suggested that he begin journaling to see if he could further explore his current feelings of inadequacy by examining some of his old feelings from childhood. He looked dubious. "Joe," I stated firmly, "I want you to do this because journaling is a potent way to make yourself real to yourself. Do you get what I mean by that? Your child self is real and still lives inside of you today. Those child's feelings aren't right or wrong, appropriate or inappropriate," I continued. "They just are and they are yours. You don't need others to approve or validate them. Instead, you validate them to yourself. This is where real self-empowerment begins and it gives you the ground to stand up to others. You can say to someone, 'Hey, I'm feeling this way and it's bothering me. What are you feeling? How can we work this out?' Do you see how this could help with your communications at work and with your wife?"

One of the great, often overlooked tragedies of emotional invalidation in childhood is a lack of emotional fluency and a lack of contact with one's own interior world. Unnamed feelings reside in the subterranean realm of the sacral chakra and exert a downward pull on the personality. In order for a person to process this energy, it first must be given form through words. Words allow energy to become tangible and communicable, thereby allowing it to be processed, first by yourself and then with others. As you free this energy, you become more real to yourself and others respond to you differently because you are more genuine and alive. This ushers you into community with others and helps alleviate the weight of our ultimate existential aloneness.

SECTION 2: ENERGETIC RESILIENCE AND EMOTIONAL GROWTH

The concept of life energy has little role in current Western theories of the personality and mental health. As much as Freud's theoretical model, which emphasizes the primacy of sexual energy, seems antiquated now, he did ascribe primary importance to the role of energy in the personality. Freudian psychology emphasizes sexual, or libidinal, energy. This emphasis on the sexual aspect of energy has muddied the waters and led us to overlook the importance of how a person relates to their visceral impulses, feelings, and desires.

In this embodied spiritual model, sexual energy is considered to be but one aspect of life energy. A healthy energetic system must be able to process it all, including death, disappointment, terror, hopelessness, and joy. The willingness to bear up to life and all that it brings prefigures a person's capacity to grow. These ideas will be further explored next, starting with the concept of energetic resilience. We will then move on to explore active versus passive styles of energy management, the impasse caused by resistance, and the role of choice and free will in the change process. Belle will illustrate the pleasures of increased energetic capacity, and we will conclude with the necessity to bear with the inevitable feelings of chaos that ensue during any change process.

Energetic Resilience: Processing the Darkness

Life is difficult. There are strong energies circulating on the planet and strong energies circulating through your own mind-body system. You must live with uncertainty and face inevitable losses. Trusting your own capacity to stand up to and process these uncertainties and losses takes enormous faith, resilience, and practice. The practice of moving toward difficulty and discomfort reinforces and expands your capacity to stand up to, and respond effectively to, adversity. This is fostered in your daily life through small gestures of willingness to try new things and refrain from behaviors that you know are self-sabotaging and numbing. These small but consistent gestures of willingness add up and create momentum and increasing confidence. More becomes possible over time.

When your emotional system is weak, due to either trauma or a pattern of avoidance, you become thin-skinned and your emotional resilience deteriorates. This is a terrible problem for individuals who were overly pampered in childhood or felt conditionally accepted by parents and caregivers. Belle, for example, was allergic to any negative feedback due to her conditional feelings of worth, so she did everything in her power to avoid displeasing others. Joe suffered from a similar affliction and had a hard time standing up for and asserting himself in the face of another's disapproval or displeasure. Both had an aversion to potential conflict with others and tried hard to conform as a way to always be in alignment with the standards of others. They each habituated to patterns of compliance based on external standards and consequently lost touch with the needs of their own system and their energetic intelligence.

The lack of energetic confidence and vitality that Joe and Belle suffered from is a pernicious problem in today's society. Because we don't have pranic literacy and so many of us have been trained to sit and take in and regurgitate mind-based data, we have lost touch with our innate organic intelligence. The toll this takes on human beings cannot be overestimated. The damage is not just because energetic depletion is uncomfortable and compromises health, but also because it interferes with the human function as a trauma-processing entity. For many people, purpose is found in using their own suffering to bring light to others. This means that the person must be able to feel, process, and move through difficulty and find a new way to move forward. The ability to bring light to darkness, which means finding meaning in suffering, is one of the greatest accomplishments of a human being. The capacity to bring this light to others, illustrated by Riley, creates a sustaining sense of meaning and gives substance to a person's experience of themselves.

It takes effort to cultivate the energetic resilience necessary to bring meaning to suffering. You must ensure that you are replenishing the inevitable energetic toll exacted by the relentless demands of life. Life exacts a toll on everyone; however, survivors of Big T and Little t have less interior reserves and fewer external supports to call on. Recognition of this energetic depletion is an important step on the healing path. Once you are able to name it and take it seriously, you can begin to cultivate a more respectful and compassionate relationship with your needs, feelings, and frailties. Belle and Riley both demonstrate this possibility. Joe's willingness to do this work was yet to be determined.

Active vs. Passive Forms of Energy Management

When you have been shut down and carry a lot of unprocessed, negative energy, as Joe did, confrontation with this stagnant energy is painful because you have to feel the negativity inside that has no discernible source. In my opinion, avoidance of this energy explains why so many people won't try meditation or do breathwork or journaling. Quieting down and focusing on breathing, or being in silence without distraction, forces a confrontation with the internal energy that is very uncomfortable. Joe's system was so shut down that he had little tolerance for discomfort. After all, he faced enough of it at work, and in his therapy I was now asking him to voluntarily do things that were unfamiliar and uncomfortable. I strongly believed that if he was going to change, he needed to push himself into discomfort zones that would allow him more access to and appreciation of his inner world. He was in therapy, which was a step, but I wasn't sure he was willing to do more.

In order to move and transform energy, you must move it through the body, through relationship with others, and through action in the world. Active forms of energy management galvanize the movement of life energy. This allows you to bring stagnant energy into the light of consciousness by naming it and then communicating it to others. Examples of this are participating in a recovery group where people are sharing experiences, learning a new skill that challenges untapped areas of your experience and potential competence, or participating in yoga classes or personal growth retreats. In some ways it doesn't matter what venue or technique you choose, as it is your willingness to move into the unknown with others that signifies the change.

I suggested to Joe that, in addition to journaling he could join a men's group. I was hoping that this would start a positive energy cycle. It could connect him with other men and normalize some of the feelings he was having a hard time accepting or even naming, and it would bring him out of his own head and expose him to new venues of activity and connection. When you do something new and different, especially when it's out of your comfort zone, you may decide that it's not for you. The experience, however, is still beneficial, because you learn more about what you want and what you don't want and you are forced to face interior blockages, preferences, and fears. Herein lies the power of yoga studios, 12-step groups, and the numerous other venues designed for people to gather, participate in a shared activity, and discuss and reflect on the thoughts and feelings that have surfaced during the experience. Changing beliefs must be based on new experience and born of a visceral knowing that occurs in reparative relationships. Active engagement with others on the world stage is essential to the healing process.

Resistance: Better the Hell You Know

The problem with Joe's passive coping style is that unprocessed energy becomes more toxic over time and avoidance becomes self-reinforcing as diagnoses, medications, and physical problems accumulate. A passive coping style indicates a pattern of self-soothing that bypasses negative energy without naming or acknowledging it. This coping style is often assisted by activities designed to numb, like eating high-carb/sugar foods, drinking alcohol, taking other drugs, or distracting oneself by watching TV or scrolling on the phone. Active behaviors, in contrast, require expressing feelings verbally, through writing or talking about what one is feeling. Activities such as walking or running, doing breathwork, and meditating also allow negative energy to move and be processed. I knew that in order to overcome his resistance, Joe needed to employ more active forms of coping that would force him to face what he was feeling and allow for corrective experiences. Yet we were up against the wall of his known self and the reality that he was entrenched in rigid patterns of self-management through working, drinking, and watching sports. Because he was numbing himself on a daily basis, he was not in touch with his own pain, which fed his resistance.

Joe made a few stabs at cutting down on his drinking during his therapy. My sense was that these were half-hearted and therefore difficult to sustain. Although Joe did not consider himself to be alcoholic or food-addicted, and he certainly didn't meet the standard criteria, his chosen methods of passive soothing distracted him and numbed the unprocessed energy of his pain. His habits stood in the way of him accessing uncomfortable feelings that were rooted in his developmental history. Those feelings were starting to come into consciousness during therapy, but insight, as I have mentioned, is not enough, because it does not move unprocessed energy or allow for a corrective experience. Joe also lacked a sense of meaning, or "what for?," that might entice him to give up his salves. He needed something that captured his imagination and a place to channel the energy that would be freed up if he was no longer passively soothing himself. He did not do the meditation class I suggested because, like the men's group, he felt it was "not for me." He said he was trying to walk more consistently, but I knew that wasn't enough.

Choice Points

I decided to take a risk and confront Joe about my concerns more directly. "Joe," I began, responding to his lack of direction regarding how to manage his depression, "you are at a transitional time in your life where 'who I have been' is shifting to 'who am I becoming.' And that is really, really hard work. It's an identity shift wherein you are forming a new sense of self that is responsive to the fact that you are getting older and your past ways of finding meaning and satisfaction need to shift. This isn't really about you and your parents anymore. I mean, that's a done deal. The more important thing that needs to shift is your identification with the rules and expectations you were programed with as a child." I went on to challenge Joe about his lack of interest in the activities I had suggested to promote connection with others. He looked a little shame-faced and sheepish, so I paused, wondering if I should push further and bring up his drinking.

The burden and responsibility of free will means that every moment provides a potential choice. It is ever so much more comfortable to choose the familiar way. Past ways of self-soothing and feeling good that may have once worked quite well have outworn their utility and yet you just can't let go. Joe's achievement-oriented lifestyle had served him well in many ways. However, similar to any addict chasing the first high, his efforts to recapture the magic of his twenties and thirties when he was career building were not working. It was time to find new avenues of satisfaction and meaning.

The capacity to make new choices involves the sacral chakra because energy must shift out of old, tired patterns and move into new and unfamiliar channels. We all know conceptually that every moment provides a choice point. You can brush your teeth or not. Chances are, if you were raised with the expectation of brushing your teeth daily, you will repeat this pattern. This is how habituation serves us. However, habituation can also be an impediment when we keep doing something that no longer works. We all know that the common definition of insanity is repeating the same thing over and over and expecting a different result. This all too common ailment is not due to a lack of intelligence. It is instead due to an overreliance on the logical mind, which can justify anything, and to stagnation in the sacral chakra, which does not want to experience the discomfort of moving energy and releasing stagnant, unprocessed emotion.

Engaging the capacity to move into unfamiliar territory, even when it is a relatively small thing like reaching out to a friend or not drinking after work, cultivates courage and energetic flexibility. This is because you are daring to open up the energetic space that your familiar routines obscure. This space allows you to get in touch with source energy, which is where creativity and possibility live. Even when it is painful and seemingly unproductive, when you dare to do something new, it galvanizes the change process, wherein one small change leads to another. It also opens up the necessary space to process toxic energy. You feel your fear and discomfort and move toward it rather than away from it, and by so doing you meet the toxicity head-on, feel it, name it, and let it move through you and thereby transform into something new. This is the evolutionary process on a microcosmic scale, the level of the individual. This process gradually increases your strength and opens you to new possibilities.

I did bring up Joe's drinking again in this session, framing it not only as something that was contributing to his chronic insomnia but also as a habit that was likely interfering with his motivation in therapy. Joe took in this information calmly and said he would give it more consideration. "I know I need to cut back," he admitted. "It's just been a really stressful time, so I guess I've been cutting myself more slack."

Energetic Interoception: Cultivating Instinctive Intelligence

Energetic interoception refers to your ability to name and feel into your energetic state and work like an alchemist to move your current energy into a new state of being. By *energetic state*, I am referring to the emotional, sensate experience of your mind and body in the moment. The negative energetic states that are commonly referred to as depression, anxiety, and panic are infinitely more visceral, carnal, and intimate than those words convey. These states involve the body and tap into the depth of who and what you are. When you are experiencing them, they are eternal, which is why they can be so terrifying. Because these energetic states are so overwhelming, yet also so private and difficult to explain, they feel very threatening, and the instinct is to contract against them and try to expunge them. You feel something is very wrong, most likely very wrong with you. Hence, you grab the cigarette or the cookie or start scrolling on the phone. The work of energetic interoception involves pausing, naming the feeling, and moving toward it. You can call a friend, walk around the block, or take a cold shower. These responses require great resolve, because they move away from numbing and instead mark an agreement to accept the condition you find yourself in. This acceptance will allow you to process and eventually release the feeling.

The behavioral responses listed above sound simple, but they must be cultivated and practiced. Especially when your emotional system has habituated to being dictated by external demands, you lose the simple capacity to interpret and investigate messages from your organic, embodied self. You are so accustomed to overriding your body with demands that after a while you don't even know you're doing it. As your digestion weakens and your sleep deteriorates, it dawns on you that something is wrong. This harkens an awakening; however, in order to wake up and hear the call from your body, you must first clear the space currently taken up by addictive, numbing behaviors.

Belle is a good example of the role that energetic interoception can play in the change process. Because she could no longer sustain her driven lifestyle, she was given the opportunity to take a look at that which she had never questioned. Perhaps being "good" according to others' standards, controlling her diet, and forcing herself to go to the gym, well…"I don't know," she mused one day. "I am beginning to realize that something was missing even before the pandemic." Her reflection provided an excellent opening for her to examine her daily routines of control and notice how she continually felt conflict about her emotional and physical desires. She felt a reflexive shame about her needs and desires and a correlative need to control herself better. "I am learning more about what self-care really means," she continued. "Before I thought it meant I *should* meditate and go to yoga, and I always felt bad for not doing that. Now I am recognizing that self-care starts with accepting what I really feel and need." She went on to share examples of being flexible with herself, such as not forcing herself to go to the gym if she was tired and taking more pleasure in foods that she had formerly restricted and then binged on. Even though this change was subtle and not visible to others, it was thrilling for Belle not to feel so conflicted and guilty all the time. She was appalled that in the past she hadn't even realized she'd felt that way.

The Dialectic Between Chaos and Rigidity: How Change Happens

As human beings, we are in a continual dance between the polarities of organization and disorganization. War begets peace. Reorganization follows dissolution. In your own life, you will go through inevitable periods of disorder, and this is good. Too much stability creates death. You may crave stability and order, yet you will likely notice that when you become too staid and routinized, you begin to calcify and contract. When you become too routinized, your energy slows down and your system loses vitality and flexibility. Because life energy moves in waves of contraction and expansion, it must move in order to be in a healthy rhythm. Life, by definition, is always changing, and to defy this principle defies life itself. Unfortunately, when you have endured trauma and when your energetic system is not well honed, you crave stability and safety to a fault. You can easily contract into a rigid state of avoidance and stasis because of your acclimation to comfort and a lack of confidence in your ability to endure feared chaos. Avoidance breeds stagnation, which is not a healthy state and can beget the very chaos it is designed to avoid.

Joe and Belle were raised in milieus where too much rigidity was imposed and their natural instincts were not honored or given room to flourish. This deprived them of the opportunity to develop trust in their inherent instinctive intelligence. They learned to conform to standards of behavior that did not align with their instincts but did garner social approval. They did what all children do and adapted to the expectations of the environment. This required them to adopt an external reference point for behavior to make sure they were measuring up to the rules and expectations of others. This led to them both losing touch with their interior reference point. The invisible cost of this was that neither of them felt safe in their own skin because they had lost relationship with their instinctive self. The rigidity of their systems allowed them to avoid chaos; however, their energy was also being slowly worn down.

For Belle, the proverbial canary in the coal mine did eventually fall off its perch and land belly up on the cage floor. The feared chaos emerged, forcing her to acknowledge her need and reach out for help. Belle's emotional crisis is a good example of how a breakdown can actually harken an opportunity to change and do remedial work on that which never appeared broken in the first place. Joe had not yet reached a breaking point, and this was problematic. The canary in the coal mine was losing its color and gasping for air, and Joe was taking note. However, he could not get past needing logical reasons and fixes for his malaise. He would talk about being genetically loaded for depression and anxiety due to his family history, and this seemed to comfort him. If it's all in the genes, then what can you do? This reasoning served to heighten his resistance to making active changes.

The culturally acceptable alibi that mental health diagnoses can create was edging in on Joe, providing him with socially acceptable ways of quantifying and legitimizing his ingrained patterns of collapse and avoidance. This moves us into the domain of mental health diagnoses, which can provide labels and pseudo explanations for energetic weaknesses in the emotional processing system.

Take-Home Points for the Sacral Chakra

- Life energy moves in waves. So, too, do your emotions.
- In order to deal with life's inevitable challenges, losses, pleasures, and pains, you must cultivate a hearty emotional processing center located in your sacral chakra.
- The ability to name and validate your feelings is vital to a healthy sacral chakra and begins with naming Little t from childhood.
- Emotional invalidation in childhood (Little t) interferes with your ability to name your feelings and impairs your emotional processing center because you are unable to acknowledge and validate your own feelings.
- Damage to the emotional processing system results in a tendency to be overly expanded or overly contracted, leading to chaos or rigidity in your system.
- Chaotic systems create general chaos in a person's life and relationships. Rigid systems lack resilience and connection with a person's organic needs.
- Rigid systems result in a lack of confidence in relation to a person's own body and holding their own with others.
- The change process is difficult because systems, especially poorly functioning ones, resist change.
- Life offers you choice points that you may or may not take advantage of. The rewards of doing something different are an

increased connection with yourself and a heightened intuitive awareness of your own needs and the confidence that you can make room for them.

- A willingness to engage with energy in an active way by agreeing to be uncomfortable is vital to the change process.
- Establishing a connection to the interior self and developing a capacity to listen to the messages coming from within leads to a new relationship with the self that fills the void created by always seeking something from the outside.

Chapter 8

Mental Health Disorders and Sacral Chakra Dysfunction

This chapter collapses addiction into mental health disorders, based on the understanding that habitual, and hence addictive, patterns of energetic management stem from dysfunction in the energetic processing system. Although exercise addiction, work addiction, and sex and gambling addictions are not addressed here, the premise is that these addictive patterns of energy regulation serve to cover over underlying dysfunction in the sacral chakra. These dysfunctions manifest as affective disorders and disorders that involve self-regulation. Though mental health diagnoses can be beneficial because they lead to treatment, traditional treatments are often inadequate if they don't address the underlying energetic impairment.

In the paradigm offered here, emotional dysregulation is attributed to sacral chakra dysfunction arising from early childhood emotional invalidation. The interior deficit created by Little t lies in the inability to identify, name, share, and understand one's vacillating emotional states. This rupture in the self creates a need to bear down on feelings and vet them for normalcy. The individual now experiences a blockage in their ability to communicate their feelings to others and, even more importantly, to communicate them to themselves. If the censure of feelings occurred early and often in the person's life, then the ability to express the full range of feelings will be limited and the reservoir of the unconscious self will accumulate this unexpressed material. The need to keep this negativity suppressed, alongside the ongoing displeasure at its unwelcome appearance in the form of symptoms, foibles, and rumination, creates an interior tension and darkness, which can later express in both physical and mental health problems.

The following sections discuss the mental health disorders associated with sacral chakra dysfunction. Riley leads our discussion with an exploration of ADD/ADHD and bipolar II disorder. Her story shows how root and sacral chakra impairments manifest in these disorders. We then address various forms of depression with Joe as our guide, while Belle helps us navigate the ways anxiety can manifest and take over a person's life. Joe also makes an appearance in the section on anxiety because depression and anxiety often go hand and hand, as you will see. The intent of the discussion of mental health disorders in the context of energetic regulation is aimed to help further demystify diagnoses and underscore the importance of learning to regulate and manage your energetic system.

Attention Deficit Disorder (ADD)/ Attention Deficit Hyperactivity Disorder (ADHD)

These two closely tied disorders can fit in the category of either a root or a sacral chakra dysfunction because they involve problems with organization and self-structure, which are root chakra issues, as well as issues with impulse control, hyperactivity, and attentional inertia, which are energetic/sacral chakra issues. The etiology of the disorders is thought to be biological, and true ADD/ADHD is considered a lifelong problem. The confounding variable with these diagnoses is that often, but not always, environmental circumstances are a strong contributing factor.

Regardless of the biological or environmental etiology of ADD/ADHD, successful treatment of these disorders for children requires significant parental and educational engagement, accompanied by systematic changes in the home and school environments designed to support the new behaviors. Adults who are receiving treatment for ADD or ADHD need behavioral tools to encourage self-structure in their daily lives. Stimulant medications are frequently used with both adults and children. The stimulants have a focusing effect because they stimulate underactive brain areas involved in attention, executive function, and self-regulation.

Riley's condition was likely not true ADD of a biological etiology but rather was an outcome of her traumatizing developmental environment. Due to her environmental circumstances as a child, she suffered from a poorly regulated nervous system that rendered her unable to balance arousal with stability. She also never internalized appropriate structures allowing for daily positive routines of self-care and execution of tasks. This resulted in the problems outlined below.

Regulation of Time and Energy

Time and energy are features of the sacral chakra that rely on a healthy underlying root chakra. Time is not part of the material world, but it is intimately bound up with it. Trains, for example, which are material and functional, would not run in a useful or safe manner if not for time. The ability to harmonize the energetic world of time with the material world of solid things such as trains provides the underpinnings of a functional life. Because Riley never had skills for healthy self-structure modeled for her, she lacked the ability to navigate her time and energy effectively as an adult. This translated in a very concrete way for Riley, who was frequently late and often missed scheduled appointments.

An unidentified component of many mental health disorders has to do with having enough self-structure to allow you to navigate the movement of time and external demands in relation to the capacities of your energetic system. If you struggle with ADD/ADHD, you lack the capacity to self-structure and consequently need external structure and cues in order to self-organize. Without this scaffolding, you tend to be late and disorganized and fail to plan well. Riley, for example, would often "forget" about her taxes or find herself overdrawn at the bank. The height of her dysfunction had occurred before she began seeing me, so these problems had largely resolved when I met her. She had learned to regulate herself through methods of self-structure involving calendars, goal setting, and written reminders. These external cues were essential for her functioning, and she accepted the necessity of tracking herself in an intentional way.

Difficulty with Sustained Attention

As discussed in the previous chapter, Riley lived in her own world as a youth. She was there but not there, a ghost girl, as she later described herself. Due to her chronic dissociation, which was a response to severe trauma, she was unable to focus in her classes at school and was forgetful and highly disorganized in her daily life. When I asked her about her experiences in school, she reported barely remembering anything from her past, including the names of teachers and friends. "I don't know how I graduated," she said ruefully. "I mean, I hate to say it, but I'm sure they just pushed me through."

Sustained attention and learning require that an individual have an underlying sense of overall safety and structure, which are root chakra issues. No one is studying a foreign language, calculus, or biology during a flood or a fire. Riley had basically lived in a fire zone, and her attention was subsumed by the demands of survival and safety. Individuals with the genetically driven form of ADD/ADHD have the same problem for a different reason. These individuals are unable to sustain attention due to lagging development of the frontal lobes of the brain and impairment of the neurotransmitter system. This degrades their ability to drown out competing stimuli, including internal stimuli, such as sensations in the body. The ability to sustain attention allows for learning, exploration, and discovery, which are key to a satisfying life. This makes it incumbent upon individuals with ADD/ADHD, and all parents, to provide the underpinnings of order and structure so that imagination and interest can flow freely.

Difficulty with Task Completion and Goal Setting

For those with ADD/ADHD, problems with sustained attention interfere with task completion and the accomplishment of meaningful goals. "I swear," Riley complained to me one day, "I really intend on doing the daily journaling the way we talked about," she sighed. "Then I get on my email, and YouTube, then someone texts me, and, well, I'm off and running. The dishes aren't done and I haven't cleaned the house in weeks. I feel like I'm losing it!" As I listened to her, I was also thinking about myself and the struggle of living in our modern age, where ADD is stimulated by our electronics. For individuals dealing with ADD/ADHD, attending to details and seeing a project through can feel nearly impossible because their internal focus is constantly competing with external stimuli.

Riley and I addressed this problem by putting her on a social media diet that required "fasts" during the day, where she would turn off her media and attend to her chores and take conscious stock of her goals. This technique is referred to as self-monitoring. It proved helpful in allowing her to get a foothold in her life, wherein media consumption was a treat she allowed herself after she had completed necessary tasks for the day. She reported being successful in her efforts to self-monitor and felt much better as a result of her daily journaling and maintenance of the home. This provides a good example of how ADD/ADHD can wear away an individual's self-esteem and deprive them of the small yet important pleasure of daily task completion.

Poor Impulse Control

A classic symptom of ADHD is the inability to regulate behavior. "Acting out" refers to haphazard behaviors that are done without regard to the consequences of the behavior. In children this behavior can be seen in hitting other children, stealing, fidgeting, disrupting, or talking during quiet time. In adults it is observed in inappropriate social behavior, such as tasteless jokes and reckless sexual behavior, or in private behaviors such as binge eating or drinking and excessive spending.

Riley had suffered greatly from a lack of impulse control throughout her life. As a child it had happened with peers and in relation to her inability to manage difficult feelings, which had led to self-harming behavior and damaging relationships. When the nervous system is unregulated, energies of frustration and restlessness feel overwhelming and need to be externalized through an action. A weak sacral chakra is unable to hold the energy of impulse, allow it to dissipate, and make room for the rational functioning of the brain to intervene with more prosocial, higher-order options. Individuals with ADD/ADHD, including Riley, can benefit from building affect tolerance skills that help them name and channel the uncomfortable, sometimes rogue, energies circulating in the nervous system. These skills will be expanded upon in the section on bipolar II disorder, which we will discuss next.

Attention Deficit Disorder/Attention Deficit Hyperactivity Disorder at a Glance

History: In the early 1900s it became widely recognized in the US that some children required immediate gratification, acted without regard for others, and had difficulty with sustained attention. In 1932 the variables of hyperactivity, impulsivity, and inattention were identified as comprising a distinct condition. It was treated with Benzedrine, a stimulant that had been approved by the FDA as a treatment for symptomatic children. Ritalin was introduced in 1955. At that time the condition was attributed to "minimal brain damage," although those afflicted were generally of average intelligence. In 1968 the DSM-II dubbed the condition "hyperkinetic reaction of childhood." In the 1980s the DSM-III changed the name first to attention deficit disorder and later to attention deficit hyperactivity disorder. In 1994, with the publication of the DSM-IV, three subtypes of the diagnosis were identified: combined, primarily inattentive, and hyperactive. These subtypes were sustained in the current DSM-5.

Etiology: ADHD is thought to arise from genetic factors related to anomalies in brain structure and function; however, there are also strong environmental factors. Children at higher risk include those exposed to lead, premature babies, those who experienced prenatal exposure to drugs and alcohol, or children with epilepsy or who have experienced head injury. There is also consideration that social/emotional factors in the home, such as familial dysfunction and drug addiction, may contribute to the disorder.

Prevalence: There was an increase in prevalence of ADHD from 6.1 percent to 10.2 percent in the twenty-year period from 1997 to 2016.[12] Current estimates for the US are 8.7 percent.[13] Boys are typically diagnosed two to three times more frequently than girls, but this is largely believed to be due to the more disruptive way that ADHD manifests in boys.[14]

Treatment: Cognitive behavioral interventions that teach organizational skills and impulse control are the treatments of choice. Effective treatment with young children requires working with parents to manage environmental factors, including having clear expectations with consistent rewards and consequences. Adults are encouraged to use lists and develop clear expectations of themselves with built-in accountability factors. These interventions can occur with or without medication. Stimulant medication is still the pharmacological treatment of choice. SSRIs are used for concomitant symptoms of depression and anxiety.

Controversies: Controversy about an ADD/ADHD diagnosis surrounds the belief held by some professionals that the conditions are overdiagnosed and many of the symptoms are natural responses of children to the restrictive environment imposed by schools. Professionals and caregivers alike are concerned about the practice of giving stimulant medication to children. Proponents of the diagnosis and aggressive treatment believe that early intervention spares children the consequences of low self-esteem due to underachievement and ostracism by peers and adults.

---

12. Abdelnour, Jansen, and Gold, "ADHD Diagnostic Trends: Increased Recognition or Overdiagnosis?"

13. Bozinovic et al., "U.S. National, Regional, and State-Specific Socioeconomic Factors Correlate with Child and Adolescent ADHD Diagnoses Pre-Covid-19 Pandemic."

14. Hinshaw, "The Role of Gender in ADHD Diagnosis and Treatment."

DSM-5 Diagnostic Criteria: The diagnostic criteria for ADHD are as follows: (A) A persistent pattern of hyperactivity, impulsivity, or inattention that markedly impairs functioning. The child must exhibit at least six symptoms indicating poor attention, including difficulty with concentration, organization, or task follow-through, or six symptoms indicating poor impulse control and hyperactive behavior; (B) Symptoms are present before age twelve; (C) The symptoms occur in at least two distinct environments, e.g., school and home; (D) The symptoms interfere with functioning in these environments; (E) Symptoms are not due to an underlying psychiatric or medical disorder.

Bipolar II Disorder

Bipolar II disorder is characterized by major depressive episodes coupled with agitated depression and hypomanic states. It is distinguished from bipolar I disorder because the individual does not suffer full-blown manic episodes. Hypomania is a milder form of mania and is expressed in less extreme symptoms and behaviors that do not pose as much risk as those seen in manic episodes, which can often include psychotic symptoms. In addition, bipolar I appears to have a strong genetic component and an onset during young adulthood resulting from factors not directly related to early development or sacral chakra impairment. Because it is widely thought to be genetically determined and not necessarily associated with developmental trauma, bipolar I will not be discussed further.

In my experience, bipolar II is a diagnosis often given to individuals who also have symptoms of borderline personality disorder (BPD), since mood lability and erratic behavior are prominent features in both conditions. Riley, for example, had been diagnosed with both disorders and treated with mood stabilizers for many years. By the time I worked with her, she had learned how to manage her mood swings more effectively through self-structure, breathing exercises, and mindfulness, coupled with journaling and support groups. The following bipolar II concepts were useful tools that helped Riley identify and manage her moods on a day-to-day basis.

Emotional Diabetes

Diabetes occurs when blood sugar fluctuates wildly and the body is unable to produce or process insulin, which serves to modulate blood sugar and keep it at a steady level. This provides a useful metaphor by which to understand bipolar II. One day after Riley had ruefully described becoming very agitated at her partner and storming out, I explained this way of looking at her mood swings and agitation: "Riley, maybe this will be a helpful way to look at this problem. You can think about yourself as someone with emotional diabetes. Because of how you were raised, you need extra supports to handle strong emotions, similar to how someone with diabetes needs insulin to modulate highly stimulating, sugary foods. In the same way a diabetic can't modulate sugar, you are unable to modulate emotional discomfort or stimulation. Your system goes wild because your sacral chakra can't hold the energy and process it safely. So, similar to a diabetic who injects insulin, you have to manually inject some reasonable thinking into your response—which means pausing, deep breathing, journaling, and all the other tools we've discussed." Though none of this advice was new to Riley, she was motivated to reinvest in her self-management protocol as a means to protect her relationship from her unmodulated outbursts.

Mood-Driven Behavior

Ideally your moods are like the weather: Some days are cloudy and some are sunny, but your plans remain the same and are not determined by changes in the weather. When you have a mood disorder like bipolar II, moods have too strong of an influence on your behavior and you act on them without thought. You go on an unplanned shopping spree because you feel like it or wake up depressed and call in sick for work. This kind of behavior leaves you feeling out of control in your life and leads to poor self-esteem because you can't trust yourself to do right by your future self. You are also prone to getting caught up in euphoric fantasies that aren't psychotic, as they can be in bipolar I, but are still highly unrealistic. For example, you may purchase things based on a plan that later falls through when your mood changes and the difficulty of sustaining the project becomes clear.

Anger and Agitation

Stressors from other people, traffic, leaf blowers, and difficult bosses and spouses, coupled with everyday inconveniences and the weight of completing the tasks required by daily life, are an ongoing impingement on your nervous system. When you are already not well regulated, your ability to tolerate external impingements is compromised. This leads to feeling overwhelmed and continually under threat from within, due to your own tension and agitation, as well as feeling threat from without, related to the ongoing needs and expectations of others. Mounting internal tension, which you may not even be aware of, coupled with seemingly unrelenting demands from the world, can create an overall sense of desperation that leads to mood swings and acting out. For the emotionally unregulated person, this can result in outbursts of rage and even physically or verbally abusing others. In the aftermath of your unskillful behavior, you likely experience the guilt and low self-esteem that come in its wake. Because your emotional system is already compromised, causing you to be highly reactive as described above, when something actually does go wrong in the environment, such as job loss, rejection, or financial woes, you are vulnerable to being thrown into a more serious depressive state. Major depression will be further explored next with Joe as your guide.

Bipolar II at a Glance

History: Manic-depressive insanity and paranoia was first identified by Emil Kraepelin in 1899. He conceptualized manic-depressive psychosis as a spectrum disorder that is distinct from dementia praecox, or schizophrenia, as it is now referred to. In 1980 the DSM-III replaced the diagnosis with the term *bipolar disorder* to indicate fluctuations between two mood polarities. In

1994 the DSM-IV separated bipolar I from bipolar II in order to account for patients hospitalized for major depression who also experienced elevated moods, which were dubbed hypomanic because they did not reach the severity of a manic episode. This designation holds today in the DSM-5.

Etiology: Bipolar II disorder does have a genetic component and also appears to be triggered by environmental factors, including trauma, stress, sleep problems, and alcohol or substance abuse. It is thought to involve a chemical imbalance and abnormal brain circuitry.

Prevalence: Estimates are that 2.8 percent of the US population experience bipolar disorder in any given year, while 4.4 percent of the population experience some form of bipolar disorder at some time in their lives.[15] Women are more likely to receive a bipolar diagnosis than men, which may not match the actual prevalence.[16]

Treatment: Conventional treatment protocols for bipolar II combine a mood-stabilizing medication, including lithium or lamotrigine, with cognitive behavioral therapy or dialectical behavior therapy, the latter of which is also used to treat borderline personality disorder. Low doses of antipsychotic medications are sometimes added to reduce agitation.

Controversies: There is disagreement about whether hypomania is really a disorder, since it often manifests only in an elevated mood and high-energy states without deleterious consequences. Some experts argue that the diagnosis of bipolar II is fuzzy and often includes patients who have borderline personality disorder. In addition, there is an argument that the agitation and irritation commonly seen in bipolar II patients can also be conceptualized

15. "Bipolar Disorder," National Institute of Mental Health.

16. Dell'Osso et al., "Gender and Sex Issues in Bipolar Disorder."

as an agitated depression, thereby putting the condition in the category of a depressive, rather than bipolar, condition.

DSM-5 Diagnosis: The diagnostic criteria for bipolar II disorder are as follows: (A) Hypomania must be present for at least four days; (B) Three or more of the following symptoms must be present: inflated mood, decreased sleep, pressured speech, racing thoughts, distractibility, increased activity, and engagement in potentially risky or self-destructive behavior; (C) The episode is a distinct change from the person's normal behavior; (D) The behavior is observable to others; (E) The behavior is not enough to warrant hospitalization; (F) The behavior cannot be attributed to a drug. The patient also experiences distinct periods of major depression, which is described next.

Major Depressive Disorder (MDD)

A major depressive episode can create a living hell. The disorder is characterized by circulating thoughts of self-recrimination, feelings of worthlessness and guilt, emotional isolation, and a sense of emptiness and meaninglessness. During an episode, you have no ability to experience pleasure and are drained of energy. In its most severe manifestation, you may literally struggle to take a shower and find any activity requiring attention or alertness, like driving a car, to be painful. Loss of appetite, the inability to sleep or, conversely, the need to sleep all day, and difficulty completing small things like house chores increase the litany of self-castigating thoughts circling like a ticker tape in your head. This can drive you to obsessive thoughts about death, plans for suicide, and even an actual suicide attempt. It is clearly a place no one wants to go to, though in spite of your belief that the condition is permanent, it is not, and it can be treated. This is why intervention and hospitalization, if indicated, are so important.

The following categories explain some of the main features of major depressive disorder (MDD) through the framework of the chakras, with Joe as our guide. Although Joe did not meet the criteria for MDD, he was at risk because he suffered from a general atrophy of his energetic system, which will be discussed next under the category of dysthymia.

Inertia

Depression results from a habituated state of contraction and inertia. When you are in this state, the strength of your emotional system is severely degraded. Your system has habituated to a lack of stimulation, eventually making it difficult for you to tolerate any sort of difficulty or challenge. Though you can still function, it gets harder to do small things. This slow weakening of your energetic system can reach a threshold where it crosses over and you are no longer able to function at all or it becomes extremely difficult. This is the result of a slow and gradual process of deterioration that you may not even notice until you are in a full-blown depressive episode. Conversely, something difficult may happen, like a job loss or breakup, that breaks the proverbial camel's back and throws you into a tailspin.

Self-Castigation

One of the most torturous aspects of major depression is the self-castigation that accompanies the energetic/behavioral inertia. The ongoing mental litany of self-blame and exhortations that come from your own psyche aim to shame you into functioning and insist on tallying all your failings. These exhortations are internalized voices from your early development, or sometimes crystallizations of messages from our consumer culture, regaling you with who and what you should be and everything you are not. At a somewhat deeper and more challenging level, the guilt and self-recrimination may also reflect your unconscious awareness of ways you are not bearing up to your life's work. This is referred to as existential guilt and is perhaps the worst kind of guilt because it reflects a sense of internal failure to discover and embody your purpose. A life of avoidance and comfort seeking can lead to this condition.

Joe suffered from a lot of self-criticism, which he freely acknowledged when I asked him about it. He frequently compared himself negatively to others, whom he deemed more successful than he was. He was also thin-skinned and smarted for days from real or perceived slights. It was because of this tendency to see himself in a negative light and his consequent avoidance of new situations that I worried his low mood could turn into a major depression, wherein he would struggle more with daily functioning than he currently did. Happily, this had not yet occurred, but he was vulnerable to this should anything unexpected occur.

Isolation

In the same way an abusive spouse isolates their partner so that the abuser's behavior can remain unchecked by more reasonable hearts and minds, your depression seeks the same dominion over you. Depression convinces you of your inadequacy, compares you unfavorably to others, and relegates you to the category of loser. It convinces you that you are unworthy of the company of other people, who likely have no use for you anyway. You lose the energy to expose yourself to others' scrutiny due to being worn down by your own self-judgment. You don't even consider disclosing how you are actually doing, which is not well, because of your own shame about it. This withdrawal is dangerous because isolation allows your toxic and dysfunctional thoughts to flourish, unchecked by any alternative voices and perspectives.

Joe was not isolated by any objective criteria. He had a wife and children and he interacted with people at work every day. What concerned me, and why I was glad that he chose to pursue therapy, was that he shared very little of his inner self with others. He had stopped confiding in his wife, he told me, because she seemed to be getting annoyed with his negativity, which left him even more isolated. This was a moment when Joe could reflect that his sense of isolation was not due to a lack of people around him, but rather to an inability to communicate with the people around him. I encouraged him to try opening up more to his wife and share more about what he was learning in therapy, something that he said he was willing to do.

Loss of Pleasure

People suffering from major depressive disorder are unable to experience pleasure in anything, and activities that were once enjoyable are drained of their meaning. This is destabilizing for the individual and fills the person with a sense of deep nostalgia and mourning for the lost self. Joe experienced a sense of flatness and lack of excitement, though he was still able to take some pleasure in sports and had some positive interaction with family, hence he had not fallen into a deep depression. Individuals who have fallen into a major depression experience no pleasure at all and find their days a wasteland of time, wherein they feel trapped and tormented by the weight of moments interminably passing by.

Dysregulation of Sleep and Appetite

The seemingly unremarkable pleasures of a good night's sleep or a good meal are lost when you are suffering from MDD. These small punctuations of pleasure, often coupled with the company of others, are no longer accessible to you. This reinforces feelings of isolation and self-castigation and furthers the negative spiraling of your mind. The ability to experience pleasure in the body and with others is part of the tapestry comprising a life worth living. The inability to do so degrades your quality of life, and it can spiral downward from there. In addition, the cost of dysregulated sleep and appetite is a decline in health and energy. Your own body becomes an enemy when it can't sleep, eat, or otherwise behave, furthering your sense of despair as it also degrades your health. Joe struggled with chronic insomnia and was cycling through medications for this with my agreement that it was important for him to get a handle on his exhaustion. A low dose of an SSRI had provided a calming effect that was proving beneficial.

Hopelessness

When hopelessness arrives on the scene, you become convinced that your despair is permanent and that this will never change. This is a big risk in major depression, because as the depression worsens, reality becomes distorted and you fixate on the idea that there is no outcome other than the ongoing torment you are enduring. Lack of volition and the inability to instigate meaningful change lead to the conviction that the future holds nothing other than a repetition of ongoing pain. This puts you at high risk of suicide and in need of outside intervention.

Major Depressive Disorder (MDD) at a Glance

History: In 1895 major depression was designated by Emil Kraepelin to be part of the manic depressive continuum. In 1917 Freud proposed that depression was a form of melancholy similar to mourning though distinct from it, due to the fact that in depression the ego turns against the self. In the first edition of the DSM in 1952, depression was conceptualized as a reactive neurosis, though it was still included under the primary designation of manic depression. In the 1960s Aaron Beck and Albert Ellis highlighted distorted thoughts and beliefs as being the primary cause of depression. The 1980 edition of the DSM-III identified MDD as its own disorder separate from bipolar conditions, and it currently maintains this status in the DSM-5.

Etiology: The causes of depression are agreed to be multifactorial, including biological, genetic, environmental, and psychosocial factors.

Prevalence: According to the National Institute of Mental Health, 8.3 percent of adults over the age of eighteen suffer from major depression, with women more likely than men, 10.3 percent versus 6.2 percent.[17] Prevalence in youth ages 12–17 is estimated at 20.1 percent.

Treatment: Treatment of depression usually combines psychotherapy with selective serotonin reuptake inhibitor (SSRI) medication. Antipsychotic medications are sometimes added to reduce agitation. Severe depression can be treated with elec-

17. "Major Depression," National Institute of Mental Health.

troshock therapy, which has been modernized and is far safer than it was in the past. Therapy approaches range from depth psychoanalytic treatments focusing on ego conflicts to cognitive behavioral forms focusing on distorted thoughts and behaviors and mindfulness approaches that combine cognitive awareness with self-compassion.

Controversies: Some people believe that depression is overdiagnosed and medicalizes normal reactions to life's fluctuations. Controversy also surrounds the liberal use of SSRI medication, particularly in children and teens. Some argue that the medication is numbing, acts as a Band-Aid, and has been shown to lead to suicidal behavior in teens.[18]

DSM-5 Criteria: For a diagnosis of major depressive disorder, five of the following symptoms must be present for two weeks representing a change from previous functioning and must include the first two: (1) Depressed mood most of the day, nearly every day; (2) Loss of interest in pleasure; (3) Unintended weight loss or gain; (4) Insomnia or hypersomnia; (5) Psychomotor agitation or retardation; (6) Fatigue; (7) Feelings of worthlessness or guilt; (8) Poor concentration or indecisiveness; (9) Suicidal ideation or preoccupation with death.

Dysthymia

In contrast to major depression, dysthymia is diagnosed when you struggle with low-level, chronic dreariness. It's like an endless cloudy day when the sun never breaks through. The dysthymic individual is functional and may not even recognize the depression. It's like living life in a black-and-white movie without a soundtrack and not even realizing it. You don't complain or feel joy, nor do you expect or anticipate much.

18. "Suicidality in Children and Adolescents Being Treated with Antidepressant Medications," U.S. Food & Drug Administration.

Joe fit the diagnostic criteria for dysthymia. He came to therapy of his own volition, so he was aware of his unhappiness. This is because he had felt more buoyancy and hope in the past and therefore knew that something was missing. The following categories highlight aspects of dysthymia that are distinct from major depression.

Emotional Flatline

"Joe," I asked one day, "what do you look forward to? What gives you, I don't know, pleasure? Or if not pleasure, then a sense of, you know, peace or okayness? Similar to those good feelings you have described when you were doing sports and hanging out with your team?" Joe acknowledged not really having much in his life that he looked forward to or enjoyed, other than big games that involved his favorite teams. He also acknowledged not enjoying his last reunion with former teammates or the last family vacation. This was concerning to him, and I shared his concern that his pleasures were becoming more isolated and routinized.

Numbing

When a hand or foot becomes numb after frostbite, you lose feeling in the limb and eventually don't feel any pain. If you are lucky enough to get blood moving back into your limb, you feel pain. In the words of Toni Morrison, from her novel *Beloved*, "Anything dead coming back to life hurts." As it goes with the body, so it goes with the heart and the gut. When your core deadens and is not moving life energy, which involves feeling both mild and intense sensations of pleasure and pain, things slow down, you begin to numb, and your energy becomes heavy. The work of healing is to bring movement and vitality back into the feeling body so that you can begin to feel and move energy again. By moving the stagnant, congealed energy in your sacral chakra, you wake up the feelings that have long lain dormant. This will likely release the feelings of sadness and pain that you have ignored. You will experience increased pain at first, which is a necessary part of the healing process as you address that which you have avoided.

Numbing cuts you off from the vital feedback housed in your emotional body. You lose touch with your instinctive, visceral awareness when you are living in your head and are not connecting with your embodied self and all your fluctuating sensations. Your feeling body ceases to be an instrument for guidance and instead becomes an impediment and something to control and overcome. When you ignore feedback from your embodied self, it stops communicating. Without consistent feedback from your emotions, you begin to live a robotic and mechanical life wherein you function but you don't experience. It's as if you are once removed from your life.

Lack of Meaning

Ultimately, dysthymia is the experience of losing the thread of your own narrative. People can endure almost any torment when they maintain a sense of meaning, which is a guiding "what for?" that informs action and interpretation. Perhaps the best example of this is Viktor Frankl's stark narrative about surviving Auschwitz during World War II, titled *Man's Search for Meaning* (1946). By maintaining his dignity and conducting himself according to his values, Viktor rose above the inhumane conditions of his surroundings and the brutal, demeaning actions of his captors. He noticed that fellow Jews who catered to their captors to gain favor did not fare so well. Even if their bodies survived due to garnering extra nourishment as payment for servitude to their captors, what was most essential within them, their dignity, was destroyed. Losing your unique sense of meaning and integrity kills your soul. When this occurs, you lose your life force and you begin to wither, whether or not you are in a concentration camp. One of the things most concerning about Joe's condition was that his sense of meaning and purpose had diminished. His achievements lay in the past and he exuded a pervasive sense of disappointment about his present life and little direction for the future.

Dysthymia at a Glance

History: Individuals displaying a melancholic temperament have been noted since antiquity, though the term *dysthymia* was not used clinically until 1845. The term was subsumed in the early 1900s under Emil Kraeplin's manic-depressive continuum. In the 1968 version of the DSM-II, persistent depression was classified as a personality disorder. The DSM-III, published in 1980, used the term *dysthymia* to classify low-grade depression lasting more than two years. The DSM-5 has reclassified dysthymia as *persistent depressive disorder (PDD)*, which is based on the idea that it is one of three forms of depression that also include major depression and major depression recurrent.

Etiology: Causes of dysthymia are similar to the current understanding of causes of major depressive disorder (MDD). Predisposing factors include chemical imbalance, environmental stressors, psychological conflicts, and biological/genetic factors.

Prevalence: Estimates are that 2.5 percent of adults suffer from PDD at some point in their lives,[19] with women approximately twice as likely as men to be diagnosed, according to the DSM-5. Estimated prevalence for children is 0.3 percent.[20]

Treatment: Treatment of dysthymia is similar to that of major depression and consists of psychopharmacological intervention, commonly SSRI medications, combined with psychotherapy. Given the chronicity of the problem, long-term therapy is often required. Double depression, which refers to when a person is experiencing an acute major depressive episode on top of dysthymia, also warrants longer-term treatment. Com-

19. "Persistent Depressive Disorder (Dysthymic Disorder),"National Institute of Mental Health.

20. Spoelma et al., "Estimated Prevalence of Depressive Disorders in Children From 2004 to 2019."

mon methods of therapy are cognitive behavioral therapy and insight-oriented psychodynamic therapy.

Controversies: A main area of controversy surrounding persistent depressive disorder is whether it warrants a separate diagnosis or should instead be subsumed under the category of major depression. Proponents of keeping it separate contend that it has a different course than major depression and has its own distinct features. Another area of controversy is whether it is actually an affective disorder or is instead reflective of a larger personality disorder.

DSM-5 Criteria: The diagnostic criteria for persistent depressive disorder (dysthymia) are as follows: (A) Depressed mood most days for at least two years; (B) Two or more of the following symptoms: (1) Appetite dysregulation, (2) Sleep dysregulation, (3) Low energy, (4) Low self-esteem, (5) Indecision and poor concentration, (6) Hopelessness; (C) During the two-year period the person is never without symptoms; (D) Symptoms of MDD may also be present; (E–H) Specific exclusionary criteria, including substance issues or existence of other mental health problems.

Anxiety Disorders

If depression signifies a cataclysmic loss of energy, an electric wire that is flaccid, with no current, then anxiety manifests the opposite problem. Although Belle's system trended toward rigidity, she did not experience the numbness that Joe did but rather felt internally overwhelmed with energy that she could not manage. In this way she resembled Riley and the electric wire that is not insulated and therefore unable to safely channel energy. Belle's rigid system had broken down and was now in a chaotic state. Belle will serve as our initial guide through the various expressions that anxiety disorders can take and Joe will rejoin us along the way. The reason Joe figures in this discussion is because dysregulation of energy can manifest in either depression or anxiety, even if a person largely trends in one direction.

Generalized Anxiety Disorder (GAD)

As you may recall, when Belle started therapy, she was crackling with anxiety and had a wild look in her eyes as she described her heart racing, trouble sleeping, and a pattern of frantic response to relatively innocuous stimuli, like discovering an overdue bill or having trouble with her internet connection. Her energetic system had clearly gone haywire. It was not hard to diagnose her. For billing purposes, I chose the umbrella catch-all diagnosis *generalized anxiety disorder (GAD)*, which is professional speak for "I worry about everything all the time," or my favorite description, "My hair is on fire!"

Generalized anxiety disorder is diagnosed when you can't shut off your thoughts and have lost your capacity to trust in the unfolding rhythm of life. How do you know that the check will clear or that your child's difficulty in math will get better with more tutoring and supervised homework time? When you have GAD, your mind works overtime to keep the plane in the sky. Everything heralds impending doom and you don't trust that, with attention and effort, things often go right and problems resolve as something new is created. The following categories describe common aspects of an individual's experience with GAD.

The Other Shoe

"How are you today?" I began with my standard salutation about six months into my work with Belle.

"I think I'm better," she responded. "I've actually been sleeping better and some of those meditations that you sent over have been surprisingly helpful. I'm still having trouble controlling my worry, though. I mean, realistically, everything is fine. My job is going well and they have accommodated my reduced schedule. The kids are coming along with the online schooling and getting into a routine. But I still find myself worrying about everything. It just feels like the other shoe is going to drop all the time. It's frustrating, really."

Belle and I discussed how her system had gotten so overwhelmed that she had lost the capacity to differentiate between real threats versus tedious things she had to deal with but weren't catastrophic or unsolvable. We discussed her progress using mindfulness tools and how they were helping her to step back from her knee-jerk panic response and approach issues in a more systematic way. In addition, adding rest and self-care to her day was helping her system manage daily impingements with more resilience. This provided her with a sense of empowerment over her body and its responses, something that she didn't have before meeting with me. We agreed that it would take time for her system to fully recalibrate but she was on her way.

If It's Not One Thing, It's Another

This phenomenon is the whack-a-mole syndrome discussed in the previous chapter in reference to Joe. Anyone who has practiced meditation or struggled with anxiety will corroborate the mind's incessant habit of needing some problem to fixate on. This is an artifact of living in our fast-paced, technology-driven world and is also exacerbated by bodies that have lost parasympathetic resilience and minds that are addicted to external stimuli. In addition, seeking out problems is also just the nature of the untrained mind. Your everyday mind is trained to anticipate problems and fix them and your body is wired to keep pace. The need for closure and to feel some degree of competence in resolving issues is natural; however, it is not realistic to feel you are ever home-free. Hence, it is important to cultivate periods of mindful rest and relaxation, which help both the body and the mind recover and then manage the inevitable impingements that occur.

Your Mind vs. Your Body

"Belle," I asked one day in response to her report of having a racing heart and tight chest, apparently for no reason, "have you heard that phrase

'The body does not lie' or are you familiar with the book *The Body Keeps the Score* by Bessel van der Kolk? Your body does actually have a reason for its responses and it's up to you to listen to what it is trying to say. It's like a small child, really. It can't express things in clear language. The feelings are visceral and sensate and have not yet been translated into ideas that can be expressed through language. Your job is to be an interpreter or translator of your body's signals but not in terms of talking your body out of its reactions or shaming it for having 'no reason' for reacting the way it is. It's like when your kids were infants. If one of them was fussy and crying, you didn't interrogate the baby as to why it was crying or tell it that it had no right to since it was fed, bathed, and had a clean diaper. You soothed the baby as best you could, and if one thing didn't work, you tried another."

The metaphor of treating her body like a small child was helpful to Belle. She recognized that her approach to her body was often critical and even fearful. She learned that moving into the feeling and sensations with an inquiring and accepting attitude helped dissipate them. This attitude toward herself was translating into her waking life and she found herself less prone to be self-critical or demand perfection.

Generalized Anxiety Disorder (GAD) at a Glance

History: In the nineteenth century anxiety was clinically referred to as *pantophobia*, meaning fear of everything, as well as *anxiety neurosis*. It was also lumped in as a symptom of *neurasthenia*, a vague term defined as mental exhaustion. These terms were used to refer to individuals exhibiting both worry and panic reactions. In 1980 the DSM-III split the two conditions so that panic disorder and anxiety neurosis, now called generalized anxiety disorder (GAD), were distinguished. The DSM-III-R emphasized the cognitive aspects of GAD, highlighting thought distortions common to the condition.

Etiology: Generalized anxiety disorder is thought to arise from a combination of factors, including genetics, environmental triggers such as trauma or stress, health problems such as thyroid disorders, and substances such as prescribed medications and stimulants like, for example, caffeine.

Prevalence: An estimated 2.7 percent of the US adult population experiences GAD in any given year, with a lifetime occurrence of 5.7 percent.[21] Estimates for children in the US are about 2.2 percent. Females are more likely than males to suffer from GAD.

Treatment: First-line treatment for generalized anxiety disorder is a combination of SSRI medication and cognitive behavioral therapy focusing on correcting thought distortions and creating more adaptive coping responses. Recent treatments have incorporated mindfulness-based practices such as anchoring the body in the present and teaching breathing and relaxation practices.

Controversies: Some argue that the diagnosis of GAD needs to be more clearly delineated from coexisting personality problems and other mental health disorders that may be causative of a person's worry.

DSM-5 Diagnosis: The diagnostic criteria for generalized anxiety disorder are as follows: (A) Excessive anxiety and worry about work, events, or life stressors, such as finances, occurring most days for six months; (B) The individual finds it hard to control the worry; (C) Worry is associated with three of the following: (1) restlessness or being keyed up, (2) fatigue, (3) poor concentration, (4) irritability, (5) muscle tension, (6) sleep disturbance; (D) Impairment in social or occupational functioning; (E–F) Symptoms are not attributed to a physiological cause or explained by existence of another mental health disorder.

21. "Generalized Anxiety Disorder," National Institute of Mental Health.

Panic Disorder: An Energetic Tsunami

Panic disorder is diagnosed when a person experiences random tsunamis of energetic overload that feel life-threatening, creating fears of having a heart attack or dying. After a person experiences a panic attack, avoidance patterns often ensue, leading to an additional diagnosis of *agoraphobia*, referring to a fear of leaving the house or being in unfamiliar places. Panic disorder can occur without agoraphobia when avoidance patterns are not prominent.

Belle's condition did not meet the diagnostic criteria for panic disorder due to the fact that she experienced a constant stream of anxiety and did not experience discrete panic attacks or agoraphobia. Joe, on the other hand, was reaching a breaking point. It is unclear why individuals' systems fall into different expressions of anxiety, though arguably they all stem from the core dysfunction of a breakdown in communication between mind and body and a dysregulation of the energetic system. The more dissociated a person is from their energetic system and the language of feeling, the more likely it is that the pressure of suppressed emotion will erupt and flood the body.

Joe was visibly shaken. "I went to the ER last week," he announced at the beginning of our session.

"My God, Joe," I responded. "What happened? Are you okay?"

"Yeah, yeah, I think I'm okay," he responded relatively calmly. "Everything checked out, thankfully. They told me I had a panic attack, but I don't know what to think. I seriously thought I was having a heart attack. It was, well, I was pretty terrified." He shook his head, reliving the recent experience, still bewildered by what had transpired. He proceeded to describe having a seemingly normal day when it occurred. He was at work and dealing with the ordinary headaches of his job. He had things to do, some fires to put out, but no more than usual. "I noticed that I was feeling a little lightheaded, so I figured I should eat something and I had a protein bar. But then it really hit me. I felt dizzy and couldn't get a deep breath. Then my heart started racing and, well, I started to think that my left arm was feeling funny and, it's hard to explain, it was like this feeling of doom, overwhelming doom. I mean, I seriously thought I might be dying…" He trailed off and sat silently, as did I. The following categories describe common characteristics of a panic attack.

A Breakthrough of Stored Energy

A tsunami occurs when there is an earthquake or volcanic eruption deep in the ocean. There couldn't be a more apt metaphor for a panic attack. Panic attacks occur when the energies of the mind-body system can no longer be contained by the determined drum of your rational mind's dictates. You are overcome by these suppressed energies and the overwhelming recognition of just how little control you actually have in life.

We all swim in an interior ocean of feelings, sensations, and energy. By necessity, 90 percent or more of this is unconscious, and most of what preoccupies the conscious mind are tasks, projects, and agendas revolving around immediate physical and emotional necessities. The rest of the mind-body experience, the waves of restlessness, dis-ease, and interior conflicts, are drowned out by the exigencies of the day, the tasks that need to be done, and the distractions of everyday life. Individuals vary widely with regard to how much contact they have with their unconscious, nonlinear, embodied selves. If you are interested in your dreams and like to reflect on your feelings and the incongruities in your behaviors and thoughts, then you are someone who is in more contact with your subterranean self.

Joe was not wired to be in contact with his unconscious self. His whole way of life had been structured around performance, output, and image. His consciousness was ensconced in what Eckhart Tolle refers to as "the world of form."[22] As midlife closed in on Joe, however, and the inexorable changes that occur with aging were no longer so easy for him to ignore, the pressure of his subterranean fears and his feelings of disorientation began to build. Seeking out therapy, at his wife's suggestion, was an indication that he knew something beyond his conscious understanding was happening inside. Perhaps it was not a coincidence that beginning to plumb these depths caused a panic attack.

---

22. Tolle, *The Power of Now.*

Fear of Emotional Reality

"Joe," I began, interrupting the silence, "I agree with the hospital's determination that you had a panic attack, and—well, this may surprise you—I don't think that is such a bad thing. In fact, I think it may have needed to happen. You haven't been happy for several years and you haven't felt like you have direction or purpose. I think you've been pushing it down, hoping it would go away, and in some ways feeling like a failure or an inadequate person for even having these feelings. I think this experience can be interpreted as a really strong message from your inner self that it's time to listen, to take stock, and to make some changes. You've already started that process by being in therapy. That was a really big step for you. I'd like you to think of the panic attack as a message from your unconscious mind, and together we can get curious about what it is trying to communicate."

Joe was silent for a moment. "I need to take it slow," he finally said, "get my feet under me, I guess."

Panic Disorder at a Glance

History: Panic disorder was thought to be a biologically based disorder until 1980, when it was included in the DSM-III as its own separate diagnosis. Until then it was viewed as being caused by physiological anomalies.

Etiology: Panic disorder is thought to have a genetic basis due to patients often having a family history of psychiatric disorders. The causes are multifactorial and include genetics, life stressors, a history of abuse, and a lack of environmental support.

Prevalence: According to current estimates, 2.7 percent of adults experienced panic disorder in the last year, with a lifetime prevalence of 4.7 percent.[23] Women experience a higher incidence of the disorder than do men. Children under the age of fourteen

23. "Panic Disorder," National Institute of Mental Health.

are unlikely to be diagnosed with panic disorder, while lifetime prevalence in adolescents is estimated at 2.3 percent.[24]

Treatment: Treatment approaches for panic disorder include cognitive behavioral therapy, which identifies distorted thoughts and establishes more functional cognitive behavioral responses. Insight-based therapy helps the client identify childhood programming that may be contributing to the suppressed anxiety. Mindfulness-based techniques help clients learn relaxation and breathing techniques that can mitigate or even interrupt a panic attack.

Controversies: There is little understanding of the biological basis of panic disorder as well as the role of respiratory dysfunction in the disorder.

DSM-5 Diagnosis: The diagnostic criteria for panic disorder are as follows: (A) Recurrent unexpected panic attacks, defined as a sudden surge of extreme discomfort and fear marked by four of the following symptoms: (1) heart palpitations or accelerated heart rate, (2) sweating, (3) trembling or shaking, (4) shortness of breath or feelings of suffocation, (5) choking sensations, (6) chest pain, (7) nausea or stomach pain, (8) dizziness or feeling light-headed, (9) chills or sensations of heat, (10) numbness or tingling, (11) feelings of unreality or detachment from self, (12) fear of loss of control, (13) fear of dying; (B) Following the panic attack, one month of either (1) worry about the possibility of another one occurring and fears of going crazy or losing control, and/or (2) maladaptive behavior changes to avoid having another one occur; (C) Attacks are not due to the effects of substance use or a physiological cause; (D) The attacks cannot be attributed to the presence of another mental health disorder.

24. Merikangas et al., "Lifetime Prevalence of Mental Disorders in US Adolescents: Results from the National Comorbidity Survey Replication—Adolescent Supplement (NCS-A)."

Specific Phobia

Belle's mother suffered from a phobia of spiders, and although this was not a prominent issue in Belle's childhood, she had always known about it and recalled ways the family had accommodated her mother's fear. She recalled her mother seeing a daddy longlegs in the tub before her bath time and calling in her father. "I remember being a little confused that she seemed so panicked about it and that my father acted like it was no big deal. But then I didn't think about it much." We further discussed how her mother's phobia imprinted her with beliefs about the role of men in relation to the fragility of women.

Simple phobia is diagnosed when you have an exaggerated fear of something that is unpleasant to many people but your fear is intense and takes up an inordinate amount of room in your consciousness. Common phobias range from spiders or snakes to vomiting, flying, or driving. The feelings associated with the phobic object or experience are aversion, panic, extreme helplessness, and fear. In the case of phobias around driving or flying, the risk of something bad happening, which many people suppress altogether, is so real that it takes over your entire perception of the event. In severe cases it interferes with your capacity to function. The following categories highlight how a phobia influences your entire orientation to life.

Control

Phobias stem from an insistence on exerting control over life and avoiding discomfort or pain. They stem from suppressed fears around life's uncertainty and the fact that we are all inherently vulnerable.

Lightning Rod Effect

Your phobia serves as a lightning rod to absorb the energy of your repressed fears about the risks of living and the inevitability of dying. The phobia allows you to organize your energy so you can remain somewhat functional as long as you stay in control of this one particular feared thing or experience. While your phobia allows you to organize the fear in your psyche, it creates an internal tension and vigilance due to always having to live in relation to your fear. Your emotional body remains rigid because you are unable to fully face, name, and process your feelings of fear, sadness, and helplessness in the face of the random and at times seemingly cruel events that occur as life unfolds.

Organization of Life Around Fear

If your phobia is not dealt with, it eventually contaminates other areas of your life. Belle realized that her mother had unfortunately become more rigid and avoidant over time. The use of avoidance to cope can become a habit and a tool to deal with other discomforts or fears. Belle shared that sadly her mother no longer drove and did not like to fly, which greatly reduced her access to new experiences and pleasure.

Specific Phobia at a Glance

History: The word *phobia* is derived from the name of the Greek god Phobos, a terrifying warrior whose shield was designed to inspire "morbid fear" in enemies. Hippocrates documented cases of phobias, as did Descartes and Camus. Freud studied phobias and attributed them to psychosexual conflicts. *Simple phobia* was included in the first DSM in 1952 and has been featured in all subsequent editions of the manual, with a terminology change to *specific phobia* in the DSM-IV. Phobias have been divided into five subtypes: (1) blood injury; (2) specific places, e.g., enclosed or open spaces, heights, or bridges; (3) environments, e.g., storms, floods, or fires; (4) animals; and (5) other, such as vomiting or fear of specific foods.

Etiology: The cause of specific phobia has been attributed to learning through association, what is known as *classical conditioning*, wherein a neutral stimulus (that later becomes the phobic object) is paired with a naturally aversive stimulus, such as a shock. It is also attributed to learning through the modeling of adults or through verbal teaching, e.g., lecturing a child on the danger of strangers. There is also the theory that phobias are rooted in ancestral memory surrounding things that in the past were actual mortal threats, like snakes and other animals. Genetic predisposition is also thought to play a role.

Prevalence: Specific phobia is the most common mental health diagnosis. The current prevalence is 9.1 percent, with estimates that up to 12.5 percent of the population will develop the condition in their lifetime.[25] Women are approximately twice as likely as men to develop a phobia.[26] Usual onset is in childhood or adolescence, with lifetime prevalence in the latter at 19.3 percent.[27]

Treatment: The standard treatment for specific phobia is short-term cognitive behavioral therapy, which challenges the distorted belief while also encouraging the client to engage in alternative behaviors that interrupt avoidance patterns. Exposure therapy and systematic desensitization are techniques that involve exposing a client to the feared stimulus at increasing levels of intensity.

Controversies: Controversy exists around the diagnosis of social phobia specifically, with some arguing that the line between shyness and social phobia is too blurry. It has also been argued that the theory that phobias arise from associative learning is overly broad and not applicable to all phobias.

DSM-5 Diagnosis: The diagnostic criteria for specific phobia are as follows: (A) Marked fear or anxiety of a specific object or situation; (B) An immediate fear response is evoked in the individual; (C) The object or situation is avoided or endured with high anxiety; (D) The fear is out of proportion with the actual threat the object poses; (E) The fear lasts six months or longer; (F) The fear

25. "Specific Phobia," National Institute of Mental Health.

26. Kessler et al., "Lifetime Prevalence and Age-of-Onset Distributions of DSM-IV Disorders in the National Comorbidity Survey Replication."

27. Merikangas et al., "Lifetime Prevalence of Mental Disorders in US Adolescents: Results from the National Comorbidity Survey Replication—Adolescent Supplement (NCS-A)."

causes clinical distress; (G) The disturbance is not attributed to another mental health problem.

Note: Agoraphobia, which is not included here, has a separate diagnosis due to the reasoning that it includes fears of several places and situations rather than being more circumscribed.

This concludes the discussion of mental health disorders associated with sacral chakra impairment. Though management of your energetic system does not replace medication and therapy, it does provide a tool for and a way of understanding your dysfunction that is empowering and can lead to a beneficial outcome in both your physical and mental health.

Chapter 9
Emotional Legacies

This chapter further discusses the consequences of emotional invalidation and damage to the sacral chakra. We will continue to explore Belle's history and how the modeling her mother provided about her body laid the groundwork for her having a tightly controlled relationship to her physical and emotional needs. Joe demonstrates how a restrictive emotional environment can dictate what feelings are even accessible to consciousness. Therapy allows clients to bring to light aspects of their early life that they haven't paused to question before, which can allow more freedom in relation to developing the inner self. Clients, however, differ in their capacity to question or develop an interest in the legacy they were bequeathed, as Joe will demonstrate.

The Hand-Me-Down Girdle

Although Belle did not have clear memories of being a toddler or being toilet trained, part of her therapy focused on making educated assumptions about the tone of those experiences by extrapolating from her later memories. In one session she recalled her mother's horrified reaction when she inadvertently discovered Belle exploring her genitals when she was around five years old. Belle was embarrassed to talk about it with me thirty-five years after the incident, the shame of the event having seared into her limbic brain. She reluctantly disclosed the details: Her mother was stern and disapproving when she discovered Belle examining her vagina in front of a mirror in her bedroom. She admonished her firmly and, after having her wash her hands, explained why her behavior was inappropriate. Belle didn't look at her genitals or masturbate after that incident and was self-conscious about her vagina when she later began having sex. She also found fault with her thighs and breasts and was continually trying to reshape herself to be more attractive. Although she knew now that her behavior as a little girl was entirely normal and healthy, the shame of the event still informed her relationship to her desires and hampered her ability to take pleasure in her body.

The stern censure of natural behavior bespeaks the tone of Belle's early environment and set the stage for the tense relationship she had with her body later in life. As a child, Belle likely experienced her mother's disapproval frequently in subtle, everyday ways involving manners, cleanliness, and social propriety. Because of the early messages Belle received, she learned to push down and restrict her natural instincts and needs. This evolved into a subtle oversight of herself so that she molded her behavior, including the thoughts and feelings she allowed herself to have, to fit internalized mandates passed down by her hypercivilized parents.

Gradually, as therapy progressed, Belle shared more stories about the tenor of the home she grew up in. Her parents, it appeared, were very routine, orderly people. The home was immaculately kept and expectations were implicit but firm. "It was all really formal. I mean, to me it was normal, but, you know, 'Don't laugh too loud,' 'Have your napkin in your lap.' I mean, looking back, it felt so serious. It's not like I was afraid of getting in trouble. I just knew not to cross the line." This was a taking-off point to further reinforce just how much her childhood home had created her stern oversight of herself. Belle considered herself to have a low sex drive, struggled with IBS, and had been in conflict with her appetite for the majority of her adult life. Her innate capacity to be in friendly relationship with her body was disrupted when she was a child, as was her belief that others could accept and appreciate her body with all its vagaries. Hence an unconscious relationship of control and management over her body took root in childhood and shaped her behavior, and even her physiology, without her even being aware of it. This highlights the power of unconscious conditioning from childhood and how it shapes a person's experience in ways that are opaque to the conscious mind until a light is shone on it.

Emotional Straightjacket

"Joe," I reflected one day when there was a lull in the laundry list reporting of events that had occurred over the week, "I notice in our sessions that if there is not something immediately pressing to talk about, you seem a bit lost about where to go or what to do with the time."

Joe agreed with my observation and even seemed relieved that I had made his awkwardness, something he strove to hide, speakable between us. "I honestly don't know what to talk about sometimes. I usually have specific things that have gone on during the week that are bothering me, but this week has been pretty smooth. Nothing really stands out."

This lull in the session provided a good moment for me to give Joe some psycho-education around the purpose of therapy being more than just solving manifest problems. I went on to explain how we all have an emotional tone, or internal set point, and that this wiring is laid down in childhood. "That's why I've asked you to talk about your childhood and why it is so important in helping us understand your sadness and loneliness now. I'd like to know more about how you felt as a boy, because I think that child lives inside of you now and is still not getting very much attention, even from yourself," I added.

Joe had been able to gain some access to his loneliness as a child and his desperation to please his father. I could tell, however, that this younger, more vulnerable part of himself was not yet real to himself. He couldn't help joking about the corniness of "inner child work" and seemed all too ready to make excuses for his father's behavior. We were still swimming in relatively superficial waters. Though Joe was developing some insight into himself, he was not yet emotionally moved enough, or desperate enough, to do the work. Though desperation is something that can seem negative, sometimes it is the experience of being at the end of one's rope, hitting bottom so to speak, that gives an individual the needed motivation to do the emotional work required to heal. Joe was still strongly identified with his father and had internalized cultural views of the strong, authoritative male. He still experienced the lonely little boy he was as a weakness in himself rather than an artifact of his parents' inability to nurture him.

The Emotional Legacy of Manhood

"Joe," I inquired one day, "you've described your father as very driven and serious. What do you know about his upbringing?" I was hoping that by exploring his father's early life, Joe could gain some insight into the limitations of his father's hypermasculine, authoritative style.

"My dad?" Joe began. "You know, funny thing is I really don't know much about his childhood. I mean, he had about five brothers and sisters, but I've never met them and he has no contact. I think it was pretty rough though. He doesn't talk about it much. I guess his dad was alcoholic and then he died when my dad was about fifteen and, well, his mom was kind of a mess and my dad had to take over and support the family."

I reinforced how difficult this must have been for his father and how this necessitated his hard-edged, rigorous approach to life and intolerance of emotion. I summed up the session with these words: "Joe, I think it's important to understand that as much as you admire your father—and he does sound like a survivor, and in that way he is an impressive man—he clearly gave better than he got and that affords you the opportunity to go beyond him. My sense is that you have a sensitive nature, but your role modeling was by a very hard-nosed, pretty insensitive man. I think it's time you began to question that and give yourself room to be your own person." Joe nodded reflectively and seemed to be absorbing my message. I hoped seeing his father more objectively could galvanize his energy to change.

Not every client gets better in therapy. The most a therapist sometimes hopes for is that new seeds are scattered that may take root at a later date. Joe was feeling a bit better and appreciated having a place to vent and problem-solve. How much change would actually occur was unclear. The tenacious hold that early conditioning has on the emotional body cannot be underestimated. The legacy that is handed down from the family of origin is ancient and is passed through generations of ancestors wired by danger and exigency. Change comes slowly and with rigorous effort, born of the quiet and sometimes agonizing process of un-doing. Rewiring the beliefs and habits of energetic and emotional self-regulation are hard-won and require looking beneath the surface waters of everyday consciousness.

The invisible legacy of energetic conditioning is very powerful. We carry the histories of our parents in our bones and this legacy suffuses the atmosphere of our internal world. This conditioning goes deep and you never get over it, in the sense of expunging the lived memory of your parents from your mind and body. You can, however, rise above it. The gift of individuation is granting yourself permission to explore a fuller expression of your authentic self.

Chapter 10
Healing Your Sacral Chakra

This chapter provides you with specific tools to develop more energetic strength and resilience. We first discuss tools to help you balance the sympathetic and parasympathetic branches of your nervous system. The importance of finding pleasurable ways to rest and restore is emphasized. Then we move into common energetic patterns and explain how your identity, housed in the solar plexus chakra, gets wrapped around your default patterns of energy management. This energetic pattern creates a false narrative about yourself that you can then become identified with. Untangling your identity from ineffective energy patterns, and learning new tools to intervene with those patterns, is a fundamental component of the growth process. The problem of resistance is addressed as one of the most common and problematic unskillful energy patterns. The chapter concludes with guided journal prompts exploring your energetic legacy.

Balancing Your Nervous System: Toning the Parasympathetic Response

This section gives you tools to help improve conscious awareness of your breath and will help you utilize your breath to enhance parasympathetic response. Keep in mind that bodies habituate to stress, and if you have been under chronic stress for decades, you will need to tend to your inner body on a regular basis with a generous attitude. Subtle changes will be immediate and more noticeable changes will occur over time. You may wish to go back to the section on the autonomic nervous system in chapter 1 ("A. Nervous System Development" on page 35) to refresh your memory of the complementary roles of the sympathetic and parasympathetic branches of your nervous system. Refreshing that information will hopefully invigorate your resolve to defy the compulsion to do more and undermine the validity of the mantra "No pain, no gain" that so many in this culture have internalized.

The gateway to parasympathetic activation is the breath. I know you have heard the advice to "just take a deep breath" dozens, perhaps hundreds, of times. Most people acknowledge that conscious breathwork has an immediate beneficial effect yet still have great difficulty motivating themselves to do it on a regular basis. My guess is that the resistance to breathwork is because the practice does not appear to accomplish anything concrete, it forces you to step away from tasks that feel urgent, and it also asks you to confront your internalized stress and really feel it. This is overwhelming to many individuals not acquainted with the inner landscape of their mind-body and can even be experienced as making things worse. Seemingly, running on adrenaline and doing "just one more thing" feels easier in the moment, even when you are exhausted and flaming out as you do it.

A primary reason that it feels easier to just keep going is that your momentum and accomplishments allow you to maintain an illusion of control. When you enter the realm of the inner body and the sacral chakra, you are no longer in control. Now you are a receiver and an observer and you may be forced to confront dark energies you have been avoiding. Grief, fear, and longing live in the tissue of your body, easily ignored beneath the hubbub of your daily to-do list. Learning to push past your resistance to observing and feeling what's inside will gradually create new pathways in your brain and musculature that will be self-reinforcing as you start to feel better. The body likes being aligned and in a balanced state. The body also likes and responds to attention. Feeling the salutary effects of this will activate your native intelligence and increase genuine empowerment.

The following exercises are simple and do not require large swaths of time to provide benefit. I suggest starting with one or two practices and experimenting with the effects of the different techniques. Some of the practices are stimulating and some are more calming. The more small practices you can weave into your day the better, because this will consistently reset your nervous system and gradually teach you what a regulated body feels like. Note your resistance before you practice and be very conscious of how you feel afterward. Noting the positive effects of the practices will enhance your motivation to keep doing them. I suggest supplementing the written descriptions you find here with YouTube videos and meditation apps that provide guided video and audio demonstrations.

Breathing Exercises

The following exercises are simple yet effective ways to bring consciousness to your breathing patterns, and they also serve to strengthen your respiratory system. They are all worthwhile, but some may be more effective for your system than others. Experiment with them and note their effects.

Three-Part Breath

Lie down on the floor with knees bent. Put your hands on your lower belly and inhale fully through your nose, allowing your lower belly to rise. Exhale completely and push more air out. Take five complete breaths. Raise your hands to each side of your rib cage and repeat. Do the same thing with your hands on your upper chest. End your practice with five complete breaths filling your lower abdomen, your rib cage, and then your chest. Exhale by emptying your chest, rib cage, and lower abdomen. This exercise is helpful because it brings you in direct contact with the anatomy of your breathing and helps you experience how each part participates in breathing. This exercise also strengthens your overall breathing apparatus.

Lengthening the Exhale

You can do this sitting or lying down. Inhale through your nose, exhale normally, and then push out as much air as you can through your nose or mouth. When you think your lungs are empty, push more air out and continue this process by bearing down and expelling even more air. Over time this will increase your lung capacity. Shallow breathing is often caused by not exhaling fully rather than not taking in enough air. This breathing technique is quite effective at activating your parasympathetic nervous system.

Bee Breath

This and the following exercises are usually done sitting in a chair or a cross-legged position on the floor. Bee breath is an excellent technique for regulating your breathing and calming anxiety. It also brings you into your interior body and helps you associate the sound and timbre of your voice with relaxation. Plug your ears with your index fingers. Inhale fully and then hum softly on the exhale. Continue for several minutes.

Box Breathing

This breathing technique trains you to equalize your inhales/exhales to a rhythm of about five breaths in and five breaths out, with a five-second pause after each inhale and exhale. You can easily follow this method on YouTube. There is also a free app called Paced Breathing that allows you to set timed inhales and exhales with timed pauses in between. This technique is a quick and convenient way to intersperse breathwork into your busy day and goes a long way toward retraining your body to breathe correctly.

Alternate Nostril Breathing

Place your right thumb over your right nostril and breathe in through your left nostril for six counts. You may retain the inhale or immediately exhale through your right nostril for six counts after placing your right ring finger over your left nostril and releasing your right thumb. Inhale through the right nostril, then close your right nostril with your right thumb and exhale through your left nostril. Inhale through your left nostril and continue. Experiment with your own timing and rhythm, feeling free to lengthen or shorten counts and intersperse with retention of air. This exercise balances your sympathetic and parasympathetic nervous systems and can provide an immediate sense of calm.

Kapalabhati Breathing

This is a stimulating breath that can be done when you are tired and need to jump-start your energetic system. Alternatively, it can actually be helpful to do when you're anxious because it activates your parasympathetic nervous system after a few rounds. In this exercise you exhale forcefully through your nose by quickly pulling your belly inward and upward, making a light puffing sound through your nose. Continue for thirty to sixty counts at the approximate rate of one breath per second. Focus on your exhales, as your inhale will happen automatically. Take a full inhalation and exhalation after each set, and note the energetic shift this created in your body. Repeat for two or three rounds.

Wim Hof Method

This method is derived from an ancient yogic breath technique called Tummo breathing and has been popularized recently by Wim Hof. It involves deliberate hyperventilation with extended breath holds. It is a more vigorous and activating method that is contraindicated for people with fragile health or pregnancy, but it can be very effective for rebooting the nervous system and balancing sympathetic and parasympathetic response in those healthy enough to practice it. You can easily find guided practices for this method on YouTube.

Restorative Practices

Engage in the following practices with a generous and curious attitude. The techniques are often pleasurable; however, for some individuals they can actually be stressful due to unfamiliarity with silence, as well as getting in touch with the well of unconscious stress that lies beneath the surface of awareness.

Consider yourself a voyager in foreign territory and pay attention to signs of tension unraveling in your system. Signs of parasympathetic activation include watering eyes, gurgling sounds and movement in your digestive system, longer exhales, softening musculature, and tingling in your limbs. Name and enjoy this loosening and remember that every small change makes a difference and opens a new possibility. Naming what is happening in your body by putting words to your experience is an important technique that brings more conscious awareness to sensate experiences, reinforcing their healing effects.

Yoga Nidra

Yoga nidra is a guided full-body meditation that is meant to be done lying down with headphones on and is also offered at some yoga studios. It is rooted in the yogic tradition and encourages you to feel your body from the inside in a bilateral rhythm. It includes intention setting and offers visualizations that tap into unconscious processes. There are many samples easily accessible on YouTube, and you will find recommendations for specific practitioners in the recommended resources section of this book.

Sound Healing

This practice is done in a prone position with eye covers and ideally occurs in a studio led by guides. Resonant sounds are provided by gongs, singing bowls, and rain sticks. The echoing sounds from the singing bowls and gongs have a positive impact on the central nervous system, as does gathering with others in a dim room with guides who offer touch, aromatherapy, and gentle affirmation of the importance of rest coupled with sound. It is an opportunity to stimulate all your senses and attend to facets of experience lost in visual capture.

Aromatherapy

Scent has soothing or stimulating effects on your nervous system. Aromatherapy is not intended to bring you down from a panic attack or lift you out of a depressive state, and you will be discouraged if you use scent with this expectation. What essential oils can do is enhance ambience and augment your intention to free up time and space for your body to unwind. Experiment with different oils to find ones you resonate with. You can purchase a diffuser for your home and use it in combination with calm music and soft lighting to create a soothing environment.

Yin Yoga

This is a quiet form of yoga done on the floor where participants are guided into deep stretches that are held for three to five minutes. This form of yoga is meant to moisten and stimulate tissues, joints, and fascia underlying your musculature and can enhance mobility and relieve stiffness. Classes are offered in many yoga studios and are usually very peaceful and meditative.

Walking in Nature

Both the rhythm of walking and the sights and smells of the natural world calm the nervous system. There is something inherently settling about being in the natural world, because it reminds you of your place in the larger order. You may choose to rest on the ground, a practice called *grounding*, which allows you to absorb the energy of the earth and appreciate the sky and the many different sounds the wind makes as it flows through trees. This combination of movement, smells, and noises emanating from the natural world encourages physical and emotional release.

Vinyasa Yoga

This is a more vigorous form of yoga that contrasts intense, active movements with slower, passive movements and is often done in a heated room. The juxtaposition of consciously stressing your body with consciously relaxing your body increases your awareness of what relaxation feels like. This develops interoception and enhances your ability to identify your stress level in situations outside of yoga. Many forms of yoga use *savasana*, also known as corpse pose, liberally throughout the practice, which further helps you internalize how to downshift your system after activation.

Floating

This practice is done at a facility where you lie in a pod filled with highly concentrated Epsom salt water so that your body is weightless. You stay in the pod for an extended period of time without any outside stimulation. This practice is not recommended for individuals struggling with high anxiety, because being in a dark, enclosed space in silence for an extended period of time can be triggering. If the thought of silence and weightlessness sounds soothing, it is an option that can help you release and let go. It is highly advised that you don't attempt to enhance the effect of this practice with substances such as alcohol, THC, or psychedelics, as this could result in unexpected and even tragic outcomes. You can float for one to two hours in a pod. Floating also helps with muscle and joint pain and reduces inflammation.

Sauna

Excellent for detoxification and also good for the cardiovascular system, saunas can be a healing and restorative practice to add to your routine.

Cold Plunge/Cold Showers

Wim Hof has also popularized the cold plunge and cold shower. Although it does stimulate a sympathetic nervous system response, it also seems to kick in something deeply salutary. It acts as an immediate mood elevator and has several other research-based health benefits, including lowering inflammation and improving sleep and muscle recovery.[28,29] I suggest you follow Wim Hof's instruction and use his free Wim Hof Method app if you wish to try this technique. He will give you guidance, courage, and inspiration. If you like it and are lucky enough to live in a cold place, use your pool or an outdoor tub for the full-body experience. In addition, many larger metropolitan areas have facilities with cold plunges, which offer camaraderie as well as hot tubs and saunas.

Re-Minding Your Energetic System

In response to conditioning and societal pressures, your energetic system habituates into patterns that are stress-based and far removed from the

28. Czarnecki et al., "Combined Cold-Water Immersion and Breathwork May Be Associated with Improved Mental Health and Reduction in the Duration of Upper Respiratory Tract Infection."
29. Esperland et al., "Health Effects of Voluntary Exposure to Cold Water: A Continuing Subject of Debate."

healthy homeostasis and regulation that are native to your biology. Your body has a mind of its own, and *re-minding* is the process of bringing your body back to its inherent organic intelligence. Mind-made creatures that we are, most of us ignore our energetic state and get caught up in the narrative our mind offers for how we are feeling. People easily default to identifying with nonproductive energetic patterns and lose faith in their capacity to rewire their system. "This is just who I am" is the default stance of a self that has identified with a pattern and lost sight of the possibility of change.

Interrupting ineffective patterns of energy management with novel interventions is deeply challenging and requires firm commitment, patience, and persistence. Your energetic patterns are embedded in the hard drive of your psyche, and your identity can easily get wrapped around them. "I'm just lazy" or "I'm depressed" is a reason not to make hard changes but can also become an alibi that functions as an excuse. The key to energetic competence is learning to ignore the story your mind offers for your current state and refraining from your habitual coping patterns. In essence, you learn not to take the pattern so personally. It's not you; it's a habit of coping. You learn that by going inward and meeting yourself where you are, new awareness and new tools become available. This does not necessarily fix the problem, but it does establish a responsive relationship between your mind and body.

Common forms of energetic defaults that get embedded in identity are described next. Read through the following sections and identify which patterns are most relevant for you. Then answer the journal prompts that follow, which are designed to help you develop a plan of intervention.

Resistance

This is a ubiquitous energetic default pattern characterized by turning away from any activity that requires engagement and effort. Resistance is natural and no big deal when you learn to identify it and then move through it without giving it any power: "Oh, you again. Excuse me, I have work to do." However, when you have allowed it to dominate your system for too long and mentally identified with it as being who you are, as in the aforementioned "I'm just lazy" default pattern, you have to work extra hard to disengage from the belief (mind-based) and redirect stagnated energy into action (energy-based). You are moving down from the solar plexus chakra (identity and narrative: "I'm lazy") into the sacral chakra by ignoring the story and instead re-minding your energetic system.

Re-minding gives your sacral chakra primacy over your mind-dominated solar plexus chakra, which, no offense, is stupid when it comes to engaging with life. The process of pushing aside the worried, obsessive, calculating mind and staying in the moment with your body and allowing contraction and expansion (the syntax underlying the language of energy) to invigorate your energetic system is how the magic happens. It can be painful at first, like getting molasses to start moving through a closed system, but once the movement starts, it takes on momentum and creates a shift that allows for more.

Numbing

Numbing is a severe form of energetic shutdown (contraction) that results from chronic and unaddressed resistance. When numbing takes over your system, you are vaguely aware of your lost vitality; however, you are entrenched in habitual patterns of comfort and so shut down that you can go long stretches without even caring. Numbing is a more serious state than resistance because your wish for something different has receded and you don't experience much conflict. It may sound strange, but conflict is actually a positive thing, because it signifies a longing for something better and can activate motivation to change.

The prescription for coping with numbing is similar to the one for resistance. However, you will need to move toward engagement in a more gentle way, as your system is quite shut down. At first you will feel strong resistance to engage in anything different. This actually signifies a step forward, because now you are feeling some conflict, which, as mentioned above, is a good thing. If you have been numbing for a long time, it will likely be painful to engage your feeling body. This is because the narrative of failure and inadequacy, which has been suppressed by the numbing, will come to the surface, forcing you to face negative beliefs about yourself that precipitated the numbing. It is essential to garner outside support, like finding a trusted friend who understands your struggle and arranging a walk or coffee with them. Making a commitment to a friend or therapist to take a shower, journal, or go to the grocery store can galvanize your will to break through your stagnation and mitigate your self-castigation. As you bring life back into your system, you will need to be firm and intentional in your daily practices due to the unfamiliarity you have with the process of engagement. Prepare to meet resistance daily, and garner your courage and resources to stay the course of kindling your life force.

Collapsing

Collapsing is the physical corollary of numbing, and the two usually go hand in hand. Collapsing can be visualized as a caving in on the self, a shutdown of breath and energy movement, and a default into the belief that the present moment is permanent and there is no hope for change beyond what is. This solidification of the present moment and inability to move into it in an engaged way is intimately related to depression and an overall abdication of your responsibility to manage your life energy. This may sound like a harsh indictment, but it is certainly not meant that way. Rather, it points to a deficit at the center of your being, which is a depletion of life energy that has caused a collapse of your sacral and solar plexus chakras. This is fixable but requires tender effort and support. Feeling the pain of your collapsed state moves you into a more active form of grieving. You may feel shame at your weakness, but remember, this weakness is only a result of lack of movement and practice. You can and will get stronger as you process the pain that has burrowed into your core psychic tissue.

Dissociating

Dissociating is a habit of sequestering your emotional/energetic state away from conscious awareness and distracting yourself with mindless activities, fantasies, and preoccupations. Doomscrolling, buying things online, and watching videos on social media are common forms of mild dissociation. Many people are dissociated from their body and don't notice hunger, thirst, stagnation, pain, or stiffness. If this applies to you, it is important for you to structure in planned times to do breathing exercises and movement as a means to cultivate interoception and conscious awareness of your physical state. As is the case with numbing, as you get more aware of your state, you will likely endure strong feelings of shame and fear about your dissociated state and the possible damage this has created in your life. It is important to find ways to keep these thoughts in perspective so they don't create a default into further dissociation and avoidance. I recommend keeping a journal tracking your negative thoughts as well as your progress. Having a therapist or trusted confidant helps keep you on course and reinforces a kinder relationship with yourself.

Manic/Compulsive Behavior

This energetic pattern occurs when you habitually force action in the face of demands from the internal or external world. You run on adrenaline, and though you appear—and may even feel—highly energized, it is not a pleasant state because it is coupled with tension and a significant amount of mind chatter that is reaching toward a future state. You are doing one thing while the next thing on the list is pressurizing your energy. You may accomplish a lot in this state; however, it creates and sustains a disconnect between you and your body wherein you dissociate from the needs of your physical body and push through fatigue, hunger, and discomfort in order to meet your perceived demands of the situation. Manic behavior is frequently accompanied by a backlash, causing you to shut down and become depressed and overly fatigued.

The intervention for this pattern is to wise up and recognize that what goes up must come down. There is a cost to your behavior, and it will serve you well to interrupt your activity and check yourself sooner rather than later. The narrative that often accompanies manic behavior is the false belief that you can keep going this way and accomplish more and more and more. This is not true, and the price you pay when your energy collapses can be severe. It takes discipline and a certain amount of faith to interrupt the hold of this energetic pattern, and the best strategy is to intercept it before it escalates. Structure in breaks throughout your day. Setting your phone alarm for every hour and doing a minute of breathing is an effective tool. The key is to stay in relationship to your physical and energetic body and show deference to your limits.

Forcing

This energetic pattern is related to manic activity; however, it occurs without the manic drive. Instead, you are tight-lipped and exhausted, pushing forward and hating every minute of it, counting down how long you have to go. There is no pleasure in this way of living, yet what choice do you have? The demands upon you are inexorable and you keep going, wedded to the belief that you have no choice. The antidote to this is rest; however, this feels counterintuitive and difficult, particularly because your system has lost its capacity to naturally release into relaxation. Difficulty relaxing results from years of sympathetic overdrive. This leaves your system in a "go" state, meaning your muscles are tense, your breathing is irregular and shallow, and your heart rate is accelerated. As you get older and lose parasympathetic tonality, it becomes more difficult for your system to find balance. It may take a fair amount of effort and patience to learn how to release tension. The self-narrative that gets built into this pattern is an inner belief that you are incapable of relaxing. Developing the skill of relaxation will be a process and a commitment from which you will reap benefits over time.

Hoarding

Hoarding is a pattern of holding onto and clutching rather than enjoying. This may express in holding onto money by saving and feeling guilt over expenses that you can actually afford. It also can express in overeating and not exercising. Fear of scarcity and suspicion of your own capacity to engage in the flow of life, where energy is given and received in a process of self-renewal, underlie this pattern. It expresses as an overall withholding of positive energy with yourself and others. Inside you may hold the belief that you are selfish or incapable of enjoying life.

Journal Reflections

1. Which of the above energetic patterns do you typically engage in? How does it serve you? Include more than one if you identify several.
2. When did this energetic pattern first develop? How did it serve you at the time?
3. Is there some form of trauma associated with this energetic pattern?
4. What beliefs about yourself underlie the pattern?
5. What beliefs about other people's capacity to meet your needs underlie this pattern?
6. How does your style of energy management harm you and interfere with your growth now?
7. What negative beliefs about yourself does this energetic pattern reinforce?
8. What energetic interventions mentioned in the first half of this chapter about cultivating the parasympathetic nervous system do you feel drawn toward and feel a willingness to practice?
9. What is your plan for implementing the practices you have chosen? What supports might help you make a commitment to using them? Are you willing to engage an accountability partner?

Your Energetic Legacy

As you have learned in this chapter, we inherit patterns of nervous system regulation, as well as our implicit relationship with our body and our emotions, from our parents. We also internalize their overall relationship to life energy. The following journal prompts encourage you to look at your parents' relationship to life energy and consider what was modeled to you and how these patterns manifest in your own life.

1. Consider how your parents related to food, money, alcohol, and other drugs. Which of their patterns did you inherit? Have you overcompensated for their issues by being the opposite? Do you judge them for their problems? What are your judgments and how do they loom in your own consciousness with regard to how you judge yourself?
2. Consider how emotions were handled in your family. Specifically consider how anger, grief, joy, and pleasure were expressed. How did these patterns affect you as a child? Which of these patterns did you inherit and how are you different?
3. Note how the people you are drawn to are either similar to or different from your parents with regard to emotional expressiveness and dominant energy patterns. Is this problematic or helpful, or possibly both?
4. How did your family handle setbacks, struggles, and apparent failures? How did this affect your self-esteem, your relationship to life challenges, and your ability to move forward after a setback?
5. How did your parents model sex, sensuality, and pleasure? Was there open affection expressed between your parents? How did they manage their sex lives? What did they overtly and covertly teach you about sex, masturbation, and your body? How does the way this was handled in your family affect you now?
6. How were bathroom habits handled in your family? How were belching, passing gas, and smells in the bathroom managed? Was there humor, intrusiveness, or discretion? Did discretion border on shame? How does this affect you now?

Gifts of the Sacral Chakra

The source of your personal power lies in your ability to channel life energy. When your body is cut off from prana, most concretely illustrated in diminished breath capacity, you are unable to hold and process life energy, rendering you weak and uncomfortable and in search of something outside of yourself to soothe and satiate you. This may be food, praise, money, or even a problem to solve, which at least distracts your consciousness from your inner malaise. Your energetic system can strengthen once you identify its weakness and begin to shift your attention to rehabilitating your relationship to life energy. The salutary effects of your intentionality and the concrete practices you employ have a cumulative effect that builds momentum over time. The gifts of your efforts are as follows.

Self-Validating

The gift of self-validation means you know that what you feel is real to you, no matter what someone else's opinion may be. When energy is lost looking outside yourself for approval, it leads to a leveling down of your own experience so that you're vetting your feelings against a supposed standard of normalcy. Self-validation means you are real to yourself and can bear up energetically to opposition and criticism without collapse.

Self-Regulating

The concept of stress is essentially referring to problems in the regulation of energy. When sympathetic activation has programmed your nervous system, you become habituated to chronic stress and live at the mercy of your tense, uncomfortable body. In addition, you are at the mercy of unpleasant events in the world. This is the epitome of not feeling empowered. You must be able to process both exogenous (coming from the outside) and endogenous (arising from within) impingements without losing your center. This capacity can be honed, rendering you heartier and more capable in the face of the world because you are well situated within yourself.

Self-Soothing

The ability to prioritize your own needs in the face of unrelenting demands from the world is grounding and stabilizing. Examples of healthy self-soothing are rituals of self-care, such as reading, walking, massage, rich fragrances, and special teas. The inability to self-soothe leaves you stranded in a war zone where your very own body can be experienced as a dragon to slay. Difficulty eating, sleeping, and eliminating are all symptoms of the chronic inability to self-soothe and leave an individual truly without a home.

Engagement

One of the greatest measures of health is the ability to show up for life with the willingness to experience stimulation and impingement upon your mind-body system without becoming dysregulated. All life experiences have some degree of tension or discomfort. Living dynamically requires that you walk into new experiences and allow them to have an impact. This is the opposite of living in chronic resistance and entails saying yes to life and surrendering to its course.

Access to the Rainbow

Your ability to fully feel and to process all feelings, from joy to grief to pain, brings vitality to your life. Ordinary moments can be lifted out of the mundane when the ability to pay attention and be fully present is cultivated. When your capacity to feel is downgraded, referred to as numbing, experiences become less vibrant and meaningful and you become less alive. This relegates you to "living in the head" and being at the mercy of your restless mind without the leavening that emotional tones bring to experience. This condition creates a relentless flatness in a life that has been reduced to checking things off a list that only repeats the next day. This condition also leaves you far less able to respond to and deal with the inevitable difficulties, or the possible tragedies, that life will bring your way.

Trust in Flow

Individuals with a healthy sacral chakra have an implicit trust in the flow of feeling states, pleasant and unpleasant alike. They know feelings can be fully felt, processed, and then released. This is how experience shifts from one thing to the next. As anyone who has achieved something of significance will tell you, difficulties and apparent failure often end up revealing new information that later serves a vital role in the eventual achievement. Without the capacity to trust in flow and relinquish control, you bear down upon experience and fall into rigid patterns where outcomes are known and certainty is maintained. The dynamisms and mystery that make life interesting and alive are lost.

In conclusion, the importance of a well-functioning, responsive, and flexible energetic system cannot be overemphasized. It precedes and sets the stage for identity formation, which occurs in solar plexus chakra development. When the energetic, instinctive capacity of your system is damaged due to sacral chakra impairment, the development of your solar plexus chakra is at the mercy of the conditioned mind. The last part of this book will explore solar plexus chakra development and further reinforce how the development of the solar plexus chakra is influenced by the stability and balance of the root and sacral chakras.

Part III
The Solar Plexus Chakra: Stoking the Fire of Your Purpose

Chapter 11

The Solar Plexus Chakra and the Realm of Identity

Developing an individuated self isn't easy. The solar plexus chakra, which is the realm of identity, rides upon the realities of your root chakra and the energetic capacity of your sacral chakra. The realities of your root chakra refer to your cultural heritage, gender, appearance, temperament, and intellectual capacities. These endowments interface more or less effectively with your family of origin's capacity to welcome and nurture you. How you were received by your early caregivers plays a decisive role in the development of your energetic capacity and interior sense of well-being, which are attributes of the sacral chakra. Your mind forms an idea of self that is based on both the material realities of your incarnation (gender identity, ethnicity, physical characteristics such as height) and, more subtly, the energetic messages you internalized (wanted, good, enjoyed, safe—or their opposites).

How the world outside your family of origin responds to you also plays a defining role in establishing your idea of self. If you are well treated, affirmed, and nurtured in your school and community, this downloads a positive feeling of self and positive expectations of others. The converse is, of course, also true. The rich get richer, so those individuals with a hearty genetic endowment and a nurturing family are more likely to be well treated by others and will come to experience themselves in a positive way, engendering more of the same. This provides the building blocks for a positive sense of self. When life gets difficult, as it does for us all, this person will have access to an internal reservoir of positive feelings and experiences, as well as an external network of social support built from past, affirmative relationships. This contributes to a sense of self that is positive, able to take risks, and flexible in the face of life's challenges.

Throughout this text, you have gotten to know three individuals who had less-than-ideal early experiences, with Riley's being the most problematic. Riley is an outlier because she was able to develop a self worth living from the rubble of an all but ruined life. Due to the extremity of her situation, she was faced with a stark life-or-death decision and she chose to live, initiating her entry into a recovery process. Belle and Joe, on the other hand, had the dubious luxury of putting off the hard work of taking responsibility for changing the course of their lives. This is because the roar of pain had not become deafening, and it is easy to default to the status quo when you are not forced to change. Theirs is the more normative experience in middle- to upper-class America and will be the focus of the following discussion.

This chapter explores the hidden difficulties of bearing a functional, outside-in identity that is based primarily on performance and appearance, rather than being founded on intrinsically sourced values that are worth living for. Belle and Joe will be your guides and demonstrate two different expressions of solar plexus chakra insufficiency loosely tied to stereotypical gender roles. Joe exemplifies the need to prove value through performance, while Belle seeks to please through meeting others' needs. This chapter explores the necessity of wresting identity away from the conditioned roles handed down by the family of origin and culture and forging a path that is more self-determined. Joe will further demonstrate how resistance can shut down the growth process, while Belle's story will show how change can happen through a process of disorganization and reorganization over time. The mental health disorders associated with solar plexus chakra rigidity will be discussed with the intent of further underlining the importance of viewing mental health problems beyond a reductionistic chemical model.

The Solar Plexus Chakra in Focus

Location in the Body: Stomach and solar plexus

Developmental Challenges: The right to act on your own values and intentions; the capacity to fail without collapse of self-regard; effort valued over outcome; ability to maintain motivation in the face of an uncertain outcome; willingness to face conflict without aggression; identity not contingent upon performance

Threats to Development: Emphasis on performance and appearance over feelings; modeling of a "might makes right" moral code; overvaluation of what others think

Primary Developmental Conflict: Balancing the need for autonomous, self-directed behavior with the need to adhere to social conventions and maintain relationships

Signs of Overdevelopment: Dependence on performance to prove your value; self-esteem contingent upon being better than others; conditional self-regard; fear of failure impeding the ability to take risks and learn new things

Signs of Underdevelopment: Passivity; following others; inability to make independent decisions; overly wedded to rules; chronic need for direction and validation; avoidance of risk or learning new things due to feared incompetence

Conditioned Beliefs: You must prove your worth through performance. Failure is shameful and must be hidden. Performance must be approved by others in order to be valid.

Associated Addictions: Appearance and performance at all costs; image trumps substance; working, exercise, and shopping are common expressions of this addiction.

Associated Mental Health Disturbances: Obsessive-compulsive disorder (OCD); obsessive-compulsive personality disorder; narcissistic personality disorder, codependency

Gifts of the Third Chakra: Ability to act in the face of the unknown without certainty of outcome; ability to break down and process new information and new experiences and make meaning from this; a self-generated, coherent narrative of how you came to be yourself; strong internal values that guide self-initiated action independent of others' opinions; unconditional self-regard

A Performance-Based Identity

My understanding of Joe's malaise was that it stemmed from a crisis of identity due to the former bulwarks of his identity being gradually shaved away. Being young, handsome, and on a trajectory for success adds a certain juice to daily life and gives you a "what for?" that creates a needed coherence in your life and a sense of self. Not having this, and not having an alternative plan, is disorienting. What else is there? There is plenty else, of course, but these things involve relationships, exploration, curiosity, and a willingness to learn. When an identity has been forged around meeting standards and performing well, qualities of curiosity and a willingness to explore have not been developed. Hence, the person feels rudderless when old ways no longer work and a new way is not apparent.

I knew insight alone would not be enough for Joe to make changes, but I hoped that gaining some understanding of the developmental causes of his rigid identity could reduce shame and motivate change. Since male identity is strongly linked to the relationship with the same-gender parent, I guided Joe toward talking more about his relationship with his father. Joe's father was very successful in business and had a dominant personality. "Yeah," Joe elaborated one day, "he doesn't mess around. You know what he thinks and he doesn't care if he offends someone. He's super bright too. He didn't have anything handed to him and he managed to really make something of himself. The rest of his family, well, they're kind of a waste."

"It sounds like you really look up to your father, Joe," I interjected. "It also sounds like he could be pretty intimidating, like he had high standards and if you didn't make the cut, well, too bad for you. I can imagine that was hard for you as a child." We went on to discuss his academic struggles and his father's lack of interest or involvement in this.

In later sessions we discussed how, when Joe's athletic ability came to his father's attention, his father began to notice him. "That must have meant the world to you, Joe," I said. "I mean, you were nobody and then suddenly he's out there in the yard dribbling balls with you and cheering you on."

"Yeah, it was pretty cool," Joe agreed. "It was great. We got really close after that."

I paused. "Joe, I think that there was also a dark side to this. I mean, think about it. You're nobody and then you're somebody because you're good at something. What do you think that meant to you on a deeper level?"

The session continued by exploring how Joe was always performing because he was highly conscious of what others thought of him and expected from him. Doing it right as measured by an external standard was fundamental to the task. "I think this gets in the way of pleasure and freedom," I suggested, "and a big part of the problem now is that you are looking for something to give you that same feeling of achievement but the goalposts have moved, so to speak. If a lot of how you see yourself is based on living up to expectations outside yourself, it can be hard to know where to go when things aren't so clear."

A performance-based identity is founded on a conditional sense of worth, which is also related to the root chakra. When your self-worth feels conditional, motivation is derived from fear of failure and external performance trumps the internal value the performance has. Joe was highly motivated and richly rewarded with praise and attention during his years of athleticism. His work life, however, had a very different quality.

Once it was clear that he wasn't going to play professional soccer due to the long odds of getting and maintaining a roster spot and the financial volatility of this career choice, Joe set his mind to achieving prowess in a more stable and traditional career path. The problem was that he had no clear sense of what his skills or interests were, so he ended up floundering.

By the time he came to see me, it was clear that he was feeling trapped in a job that paid well and was secure but did little to feed his sense of purpose or stimulate his interest. Joe's success was hollow because it was not undergirded by an internally derived sense of purpose. What he had achieved didn't hold intrinsic value for him; hence there was no values-based, self-generated trajectory of interest or intention to carry him forward. His development had stalled and the fires of his solar plexus chakra were dwindling when he initiated therapy.

Initiative: Acting in the Face of Uncertainty

Joe had always colored inside the lines and had never challenged the norms and expectations that he had grown up with. "Joe," I inquired one day, "have you ever done anything crazy? You know, have you ever rebelled in a way that might get you in trouble or was not in line with the expectations of your family and friends? You mentioned that your sister was pretty rebellious for a while. Didn't she dye her hair pink or something?"

He responded as I guessed he would, denying any tendencies toward challenging or defying the status quo. And therein lay my therapeutic dilemma with Joe: How do you kindle a hunger for something that has never been tasted? Joe had never taken any real risk or challenged the norms he had grown up with because it had simply never occurred to him to do so.

Adolescence is the time when young people in the Western world test limits and challenge the norms and expectations of family and community. Joe had never risked the conditional love he experienced from his parents by defying their expectations. They likely would have still loved him, but he didn't have a felt experience of that. Hence, he was still living in the romance of his parental triangle, wherein he was the golden child who made their sacrifices worthwhile. Due to his allegiance to their wishes and his conformity to their values, he had not been able to define himself as a separate entity with distinct feelings, needs, and intentions. This can only be wrought by daring to go against norms and expectations by risking failure and censure from others. I was concerned that if Joe couldn't consciously acknowledge his reluctance to veer from the path of conventionally accepted norms and forge his own way based on his desires and interests, then he would remain stuck in his current emotional malaise.

A wonderful illustration of the challenge of identity formation is seen in the Native American tradition of the vision quest. This is a tradition in many tribes where a young person is sent into the wilderness for several days and must survive on their own. The challenge is for the young adult to dig deep into the solar plexus chakra, use their own skills and native intelligence to navigate the perils of the terrain, and come out on the other side having proven their ability to face the unknown and cope adequately. Cultures that implement the vision quest may avoid the adolescent rebellion so common in the West because avenues for individuation are built into the culture. Joe had never been challenged in this way, literally or figuratively. He had walked in lockstep with parental and cultural expectations and never dared to venture out on his own and test his particular skills, interests, and level of competence.

The challenge facing Joe in his life now was finding avenues to express himself and forge a sense of meaning for himself. This would mean taking some risks, likely many false starts, and being willing to fail. He had come up short in his life because he was not in touch with his own passions and interests, nor had he developed the self-esteem to know that he could venture into the unknown and survive. This had left him bereft of interests and a sense of integrity, because secretly he knew that he was living an all-too-safe existence. The work that now lay in front of him was to get back onto the world stage with new, self-chosen endeavors that might light the fires of his motivation and initiative. This would require him to step away from the value system he had inherited from his family of origin and begin the process of true individuation, which lies in cultivating and honing one's own values. He would need to try new things, explore options, and risk feeling like a fool or a fish out of water at times. Could therapy kindle a hunger for change sufficient enough for him to endure this discomfort? This was the unfolding question that had yet to be answered.

What You Resist Persists

The best predictor of future behavior is past behavior. This precept applies to the likelihood of a person attempting suicide, maintaining fidelity in a marriage, or going to the gym. Structures tend toward stability and resist change. This also applies to nervous system regulation, character patterns, and ways of perceiving the world. That said, revolutions do occur. People do get into recovery, transform their health, and otherwise rise as a phoenix from the ashes to transform their seemingly ruined lives. This is what makes human existence so exciting, so creative, and so potentially significant. We are evolving beings with conscious awareness of ourselves that allows us to potentiate change, which begs the question: What potentiates an inner revolution and evolution and what begets stagnation?

Joe provides a good example of sedimented resistance. We discussed energetic resistance in the sacral chakra chapters. Solar plexus resistance is perhaps even more challenging because it edges into the structures of character and selfhood. If you've ever heard yourself say, "That's just not me" or "I'm not a joiner," then you are aware of how options can easily get closed off due to your familiar definition of who you are and what's for you. Joe's therapy was asking him to make changes that threatened some of the basic tenets of how he had constructed his sense of self. Being a strong, successful man, or at least approximating this in the image he projected to others, was deeply rooted in Joe's identity. To admit that this project was not working, and questioning the tenets upon which he had built his idea of himself, was deeply threatening. Even making small changes, like joining a men's group or not drinking as much, was something he was averse to doing even if he couldn't exactly explain why.

Who you think you are is deeply rooted in your conditioning, and most of us are superglued to our idea of ourselves. Even if you identify with being a lazy, depressed loser, you are likely reluctant to give up this identity because it is familiar and safe to know the parameters of your world and to think you know where you stand and what is possible. This is based on having a sense of control. To give up control, even in small ways, throws the whole project up in the air. The limitations we put on ourselves, though confining, also provide safety and predictability. For people whose systems are not acclimated to stress and who are not accustomed to questioning the status quo, safety and predictability will win out. Resistance to change will also be strong when you have benefited from your habits in the past. If they provided you with approval, self-esteem, money, or praise, you will be reluctant to question their utility. When your identity is tied to seemingly laudatory ideals such as "I am a hard worker," and when this has won you a lot of social and economic capital, you will resist letting go of this idea of yourself. It's like pulling on a small thread and fearing that this may cause the whole edifice to collapse.

The key to initiating this kind of deep change is to go one step at a time and allow the process to unfold. And it requires facing significant discomfort, as all change does. For Joe, it would require questioning his alcohol use and most likely stopping it. This is because another essential constituent of growth is allowing yourself to be vulnerable to others. You cannot be vulnerable to others when you are not in touch with your own pain. And you can't be in touch with your own pain if you are continually numbing and distracting yourself. This is where resistance to growth, to discomfort, and to the unknown can sabotage the most well-intended person. Joe wanted to feel better; however, he may not have been ready to heal. You cannot heal if you continue patterns of easing symptomatic distress and avoiding your own pain and vulnerability with others.

Codependency: Losing Me in the We

Belle provides an alternative form of solar plexus chakra insufficiency. While Joe excelled and achieved for others, Belle garnered sustenance for her identity through the nurturing roles she performed for others. Both Belle and Joe were highly dependent on validation from external sources because their solar plexus chakras were tethered to validation from the outside. Belle's primary sense of self was attached to her position as a wife and mother and the affirmation she gained from performing these roles well. She sought therapy after becoming depleted by the overwhelming demands these roles exacted upon her and her inability to keep up with them. The fires of her solar plexus chakra, like Joe's, had been dwindling for years. Belle just hadn't noticed until circumstances pushed her to an intolerable edge.

The first step of therapy for Belle was disentangling her sense of value and purpose from her role in her family and the validation she got from performing needed functions. "Belle," I ventured one day, "I am sure that you are familiar with the term codependency."

"Oh yes," she quickly replied with a smile. "I rang the bell, no pun intended, on the assessment I took. You name it, I'm the star overly responsible, caretaking, people-pleasing mistress of the universe," she laughed, almost happily.

"Well, tell me this," I queried further in a serious tone. "We tend to throw these terms around nowadays, like stress, depression, and now codependency, but do we really know what we are talking about? What do you think it means in your life? What does it mean to ring the bell, as you put it?"

After pausing for a few beats, she answered in a more sober tone. "I guess it means being overfocused on what others need or think. Or what you've mentioned before. What did you call it? External locus of control, I think it was? And then compulsively saying yes or forcing myself to do things I don't even want to do."

Belle gradually shifted her focus from the revolving ticker tape of what she had to do for others to instead determining what her own needs were. This is not as easy as it sounds. After all, when you've lived your life from the outside in, according to culturally approved maps for success, reconnecting with the self is a vague proposition at best. Using the language of the chakras, therapy encouraged her to develop an internal frame of reference by dialing down her mind-based priorities and learning to listen to and receive messages from her body. Receiving encouragement to validate and align with what she already knew was very helpful.

"You know, I have known I have been exhausted for years," she shared with me in one session. "I thought it was due to my failing, something I was doing wrong. It's helpful not to have to judge this and instead just respond like you said, like a mother to a child." She paused and then continued. "You know, when I think about it, before therapy I don't think I even considered that I might have needs or feelings that were different from what others expected." We went on to discuss how her sense of self was fused with what others expected and what her functions for them were. There was no room for an independent, private self. "Gosh, I think I've been so busy ringing the Belle and vaulting the bar of acceptability that I was relating to myself as a nonperson. I always blamed my husband for his high expectations, but now I see it was mostly about me and the pressure I put on myself." I affirmed the importance of this insight and her capacity to take responsibility for her role in the tension in their relationship.

The Self as an Organ of Relationship

The role of relationships in identity formation is a complex topic because your sense of self is largely formed through the network of relationships you exist within. You know yourself through relationship. As a child, you learned who you were largely based on how your caregivers, siblings, and peers responded to and interacted with you. The feelings you allow yourself to have now, the words you are able to use now to convey your feelings, and the actions you dare to take and those you suppress are all based on your early conditioning and exist within a framework of relationship. Ideally, there is room for self-expression and freedom within the confines of conforming to social expectations. In less ideal circumstances, and when the environment is emotionally invalidating, the self calcifies around circumscribed rules dictated by imaginary others. This leaves scant room for humor, play, and the messy mistakes and corrections integral to a well-lived life.

A balanced person is able to navigate a variety of relationships and can express different aspects of themselves in different contexts. A balanced person also enjoys a primary relationship with themselves. This can be experienced by a person as having an ongoing dialogue with themselves. There is a private, experiencing self who is in an ongoing relationship with the relational, public self. In a less balanced, more codependent person, the attachments are more circumscribed and rigid and don't allow room for a private self, as Belle revealed when disclosing that she never even considered what she wanted or needed. The ability to self-reference and prioritize how she felt about things complicated her life in that she needed to make choices, disappoint people, and face fears of being selfish, which was a deadly sin according to her childhood programming. As we explored her relationship to her private self, Belle gained further insight into the origin and function of her negative self-talk and obsession with what others thought of her.

"You know what I've realized about the problem I have harassing myself when I'm alone, all the comparisons I make to other people and how I come up short? Well, I've realized it's related to codependency." We went on to discuss how, because her sense of self, and her value, was externalized and beholden to the views of others, she needed to continually check and evaluate herself on the basis of whether she was living up to externalized standards.

"I think because you were never encouraged to inquire into your own feelings and experiences, you became addicted to the opinions of others," I suggested. "You modeled yourself after your mother, which is what children do, and she taught you quite definitively what was expected of you to be a 'good girl.'" The organ of Belle's self-system became constricted because there was so little room to take in, assimilate, and digest (much like a stomach) new information. Instead, her self-system was forced to process that which was mandated. Much like overeating a dense steak that sits in the gut, the expanding and contracting, peristaltic function of her emotional system became congested with undigested material.

As we delved more deeply into Belle's identity formation, we explored how the self forms itself around the expectations and standards of culture. "Another aspect of this," I suggested during one session, "is that when you lack that primary inner reference point, you are more vulnerable to the conditioning of culture, and this is really dangerous. I mean, media, peer groups, and advertising all put enormous pressure on people to attain an ideal that is just not possible, nor is it desirable. Your pattern of self-harassment is just the toxic echo of all those internalized voices in your consciousness."

"What a nightmare!" Belle interjected. "But it is helpful to know where it's coming from. I hope this can give me some more freedom." We then talked about ways she could expand her repertoire of self and open herself to latent potentialities she had previously written off as indulgent or not for her. "You know," she shared shyly, "I've always wondered about belly dancing. I have been looking at classes in the area. I mean, I probably won't be any good, but..."

I interrupted her firmly. "Belle, the worse you are the better. Have at it!"

Self-Reinforcing Paradigms

One of the most challenging aspects of the change process is that when you change one thing, it has a ripple effect that extends to everything else. This can cause a person to feel chaotic and lost, especially when it affects relationships and past ways of doing things. Belle demonstrated this point not long after the session in which the above conversation occurred. She was having a hard day. She was frustrated with her job and hadn't been able to make it to the gym or her yoga class all week. "I know you said I shouldn't focus on my husband, but I'm just feeling worn down and I feel like he is getting in the way of me making the changes I want to make. He wants to get a new car." She sighed. "Honestly, even a year ago I would have thought nothing of it. I probably would have even been excited, but now..." She looked at me helplessly. "He just doesn't get it. I want to live less materialistically and our car is fine. He wants an electric vehicle and we've been arguing a lot about it. He says that I don't understand his passion for cars and he's also using gas prices as a reason."

Belle's husband's frustration and lack of understanding made sense. He had no real idea of the internal changes she was making in regard to how she saw herself and how she wanted to live her life. He was used to things being a certain way and expected that they would continue as they had been. Belle was now faced with a choice. It would be easy for her to capitulate to her husband's wishes and give in to guilt about her desires, which would cause him discomfort and possibly threaten his feelings for her. Or she could stay the course and try to communicate more clearly what she was feeling and the changes she was trying to make. This would challenge her core issue, which was self-validation and the ability to face external displeasure without collapsing. She would have to move into her sacral chakra and find words for her feelings and bring them into the realm of the solar plexus chakra by sharing them with her husband and envisaging a path forward that he could sign on to.

We all structure a sense of self and meaning that proves itself true over time based on the choices we make, which then reinforce and build out our structure of reality. We make a choice to marry a certain person, live in a certain place, adopt a certain lifestyle, and all these choices then feel inevitable and preclude making changes. For example, when you've chosen a house with a certain mortgage, you can't very well just quit your job. "I'm trapped" then becomes a self-fulfilling prophecy. It is not uncommon to hold quite tenaciously to your way of doing and seeing things even when there are manifest signs that the old ways are no longer working. Many of your patterns and choices may have served you very well at one time, but then they outgrow their usefulness and it calls for a change in the system, which feels like it challenges everything you know to be true. It is tempting to go into all-or-nothing thinking and keep doing the same old thing regardless. At an individual level, this can be seen in people exercising after injury, staying in abusive relationships, or continuing deleterious eating and drinking patterns when there is clear evidence of harm. At the macro level, the way our society is dealing with climate change reveals the same denial and stubbornness that many of us know well in our own lives. Even when reality begins to tip the cost-benefit scale, we often cling, deny, compensate, and equivocate.

It is very hard to admit that what worked in the past is no longer sustainable in the present. The cost of change, however, is also very real, as Belle was experiencing. She certainly did not want to risk her marriage, but she also did not want to go back to the status quo. With no clear path to move forward, she faced a crossroads involving confrontations in her marriage, questioning her job, and throwing past priorities into question. Her solar plexus chakra was expanding and churning, as her root chakra also felt threatened and her sacral chakra undulated with waves of hope and fear.

Disorganization and Reorganization

Belle and Joe exemplify people who built a sense of self based on an unquestioned script handed down by their families of origin and society. The viability of their meaning-making became challenged as time and changing circumstances began to render their inner lives either too turbulent or too flat. In short, their emotional bodies, the silent voice of the sacral chakra, was causing a questioning of identity and past meaning-making, which was breaking through the previously unquestioned structure of their solar plexus chakras. Joe was depressed and Belle was anxious. This was very disruptive to them, causing a sense of inner chaos and disorganization that brought them to therapy. Ironically, though neither Joe nor Belle had suffered the dysfunction that Riley had as a child, they were getting a taste of her world in the sense that their prior experience of order and meaning was now in question in ways that neither of them had ever experienced before.

Life will challenge you in ways that are disruptive and disorganizing. This is how conditions on the planet are for everyone. Some people do enjoy more stability than others. Individuals who grow up in the same town they choose to live in as adults, stay married to one person, and enjoy loving relationships with their family of origin are examples of this. But even these individuals will suffer illness, lose loved ones, or perhaps endure a fire or tragedy of some kind. Society also goes through upheavals where a prior sense of order and stability is thrown into question as a new order emerges. The measure of health in a human being and of a society is the ability of the system to manage the assault on the assumed order and shift in ways that accommodate the changes. The more you resist, argue with, and rigidify against the new conditions and challenges, the more you will suffer and the more reality will punish you.

The ability to reorganize and integrate new information and understandings is exemplified by both Belle and Riley. The resistance to change is exemplified by Joe. Questioning how you do you and how you do life pulls a thread that threatens to topple the entire structure. This is deeply threatening to the ego and at times can feel like it threatens the entire order of what is real and true. These moments of chaos are transitory and a sense of meaning and stability will re-cohere over time, with little glimpses of a new self in the process. Your capacity to endure this movement between disorganization and reorganization is prefigured by the strength of your sacral chakra. The peristaltic movement of energy will allow you to endure the chaos and gain gradual confidence in the reciprocal reorganization into a new and better order.

Belle's experience of questioning her marriage and the shared values that she and her husband had constructed their lives around was destabilizing for them both. Making gradual changes, starting with expressing her own needs and feelings more directly, began a process of change within the marriage that was beneficial. She was eventually able to open up to him about her new self-awareness, and this proved beneficial to him as well. In response, he decided to do some therapy for himself, and their marriage soon took on a different rhythm where they were mutually exploring different lifestyle options. This a good example of how apparent chaos can allow growth and new behavior and help establish a new and more balanced order.

The following chapter discusses what happens when peristaltic movement is resisted and a person calcifies into a rigid adherence to an ego-driven need to maintain a sense of stable identity. Mental health disorders of the solar plexus chakra result from this rigidity. The mental health disorders described here exemplify an overreliance on the rational mind and a refusal to acknowledge its limitations. There is a grand hubris at the root of the following impairments because the individual refuses to acknowledge the limitations of the mind and surrender into a more fluid lifestyle based on feeling and experiencing.

Take-Home Points for the Solar Plexus Chakra

- An externally referenced, performance-based identity is rigid and unsustainable if not connected to an internal reference point that holds equal value.
- A performance-based, externally referenced identity is modeled in the family of origin for many people in this culture.
- Shifts in behavior that challenge identity are strongly resisted because they threaten an individual's primary sense of self. This applies to making positive changes if the change threatens the person's way of thinking about or doing things, particularly if the change threatens their relational milieu.
- Codependency reflects an externally based self that is dependent on meeting standards imposed by others. A codependent identity knows itself only through the roles it performs in relation to others.
- Both codependency and a performance-based identity bespeak a lack of connection to and valuing of a person's own internal reference point.
- The self is an organ of relationship and is formed through relationship. In order to be healthy, it must be able to process different experiences and potentialities throughout life. It also must navigate between the internal world of experience and the external world of expectation.
- Paradigms are self-reinforcing and resist change. In order to sustain a change process, proceed slowly and do not resort to all-or-nothing thinking.

Chapter 12

Mental Health Disorders and Solar Plexus Chakra Impairment

A healthy solar plexus chakra sources from internal values fueled by intrinsic motivation and self-esteem, attributes that are not contingent upon acceptance and validation from others. Solar plexus chakra impairments manifest in a personality that either functions through overcontrol and force or, conversely, is overly passive and inert. In both styles, identity is contingent upon approval from others and conformity to the values downloaded by the conditioned mind and mass culture. The more active, forceful personality tries to garner favor through meeting standards of performance dictated by culture and tends toward domination, while the more passive style attaches to a dominant other and goes along with the status quo in order to garner approval. Both styles manifest the same core issue of not having an internally sourced, stable yet flexible identity.

The mental health disorders associated with both styles will be discussed next, starting with the more forceful styles. Each section will begin with a brief explanation of the condition followed by descriptive categories highlighting defining features of the disorder.

Obsessive-Compulsive Disorder (OCD)

A personality shaped around an excessive need for control and certainty can result in obsessive-compulsive disorder (OCD). This disorder reflects an overreliance on the rational mind with the presumption that through the power of the mind one can circumvent chaos and uncertainty. The diagnosis is made when a person has intrusive, obsessive thoughts that lead to the compulsive performance of rituals that interfere with daily functioning. The intent of the rituals is to achieve a craved sense of control and safety; however, this desired state of control is continually thwarted by the never-ending litany of thoughts demanding yet another repetition of the ritual. This creates an internal pressure and exhaustion that wears the person down and further alienates them from their instinctive intelligence. This disorder is distinguished from obsessive-compulsive personality disorder, which will be discussed separately. The following categories describe common characteristics of OCD.

Overreliance on the Logical Mind

Obsessive-compulsive disorder is an infection of fear caused by distrust of anything that cannot be seen, understood, or dictated by the logical mind. This way of living, which relies so heavily on the logical mind, can have the paradoxical effect of making you feel crazy. When you suffer from OCD, you ignore and take for granted the everyday mysteries and miracles that we are all indebted to and instead obsess over the unseen, looming threats that could potentially spell disaster. For example, the fact that the sun rises every day is overlooked, while the unseen germ that may lurk on the counter is fixated on. The overestimation of the logical mind's power to control and account for unseen threats signifies an inability to acknowledge the mystery of life. It also signifies an inability to feel gratitude for the small gifts that are unearned.

Intrusive Thoughts

Over time your mind grows increasingly unruly and you can't stop yourself from ruminating about your obsessive preoccupations. Your worries may increase and you find yourself obsessing over more things. These thoughts rule your mind and you are unable to let them go until you perform the ritual. In this way, your behavior is similar to any addict's behavior, though in your case you are addicted to an illusion of control driven by your mind. Over time you become increasingly controlled by a mind that has lost contact with a meaningful sense of reality.

Ritualistic Behavior

OCD involves rituals that are performed in order to neutralize intrusive thoughts. These rituals may involve handwashing, extreme sanitization, highly controlled dietary or exercise regimens, the need to check and recheck doors and appliances, or cleaning routines that absorb a great deal of time and energy. At first the rituals provide some relief, but later they begin interfering with your life and become burdensome. They defy reason and part of you recognizes their emptiness, so you seek to hide the behavior from others, along with your secret shame about it. You are living a double life, passing for normal as you also experience firsthand the insanity of attempting to use your rational mind to override instinctive intelligence.

Tragedy

The definition of *tragedy* is when the conscious effort to avoid a dreaded outcome actually results in the dreaded outcome occurring. We can indeed be our own worst enemies, bringing about our own demise by trying to avoid that which we dread. This is the tragic outcome of OCD. The obsessive hand-washer, vigilantly trying to avoid germs, creates dry, cracked hands that run the risk of infection, as the rituals also wear down the microbiome due to oversanitization. The overexerciser, obsessed with controlling the flesh in order to keep it strong and vital, wears down the body and creates exhaustion, injury, and inertia, rendering the person more vulnerable to illness and infirmity. In short, overreliance on the mind is a deeply counterproductive way to live because the supposed solution it intends actually brings about the very thing that is dreaded.

Obsessive-Compulsive Disorder (OCD) at a Glance

History: Obsessive-compulsive disorder was recognized as far back as the fourteenth century, when it was referred to as "scrupulosity" and described individuals obsessed with committing sins and then needing to pay penance. In the eighteenth and nineteenth centuries, sufferers were institutionalized and treatments included bloodletting to rebalance the *humors*, which refer to bodily fluids thought to be associated with certain personality traits. This practice faded at the end of the nineteenth century when Freud introduced the idea that psychosexual conflicts underlie the disorder. Psychoanalysis gave way to behavioral therapy as the preferred form of treatment in the 1970s. OCD was not a separate diagnosis in the DSM until its third edition in 1980. Before this, it was included under the larger rubric of anxiety disorders.

Etiology: OCD is thought to be caused by a variety of factors, including genetics, anomalous brain functioning, chemical imbalance, learning, and distorted cognition where mild threats are exaggerated. Psychoanalytic explanations suggesting psychosexual conflicts as causative have long been debunked.

Prevalence: The lifetime prevalence of OCD in the US is estimated at 2.3 percent.[30] More women than men suffer from the disorder. Onset of symptoms is in childhood or adolescence.

Treatment: Exposure treatment with response prevention is the treatment of choice for OCD. This entails exposing a person to the threat at graduated levels in order to prevent the ritualistic behavior. Cognitive interventions are also used to correct the distorted thoughts. SSRIs are often used in conjunction with the above.

Controversies: The main controversy around OCD is whether it should be classified as an anxiety disorder or be separated into its own category, which is how it is currently classified. Also, there is controversy as to whether mild presentations of the dis-

30. "Obsessive-Compulsive Disorder (OCD)," National Institute of Mental Health.

order in childhood warrant intervention or if it's a developmental phase that the child will outgrow.

DSM-5 Diagnosis: The diagnostic criteria for obsessive-compulsive disorder are as follows: Presence of obsessions or compulsions or both. (A) Obsessions are defined as recurrent and persistent thoughts, urges, or images that are intrusive and the person attempts to ignore or repress thoughts; (B) Compulsions are defined as (1) repetitive behaviors the individual feels driven to perform, and (2) the behaviors are completed to reduce anxiety or prevent a dreaded outcome. There is no logical link between the behavior and the prevention of outcome; (C) The behaviors are time-consuming; (D) Symptoms are not related to a substance; (E) Symptoms are not attributable to another mental health disorder.

Obsessive-Compulsive Personality Disorder (OCPD)

On a less acute and more chronic level, and sometimes concomitant with OCD, obsessive-compulsive personality disorder (OCPD) infiltrates the personality and contaminates all aspects of your life with rigidity and control. You maintain a tightly structured lifestyle wherein things are always in order and time is regimented into neat compartments that ensure tasks are completed to your satisfaction. Although you get a dopamine hit when you check something off your list, eventually you notice that the list never gets smaller and the weight of the unchecked tasks is always weighing you down. You may know that you are living a half life, but you are unable to release yourself from the prison of control you have erected around yourself. All work and no play does indeed make Jack a dull boy, with tight-lipped Jane right by his side toiling away. The following categories highlight prominent aspects of OCPD.

Rigidity

Rigidity refers to doing the same things in the same way all the time. Order is indeed good, as is habit and some degree of routine. The body enjoys and responds well to regularity. In OCPD, however, what may have started as order and consistency has become a sedimented pattern that you are unable to deviate from. This may look like sticking to the same daily exercise routine regardless of how you feel, eating the same thing all the time, or a refusal to travel or even go to restaurants. This is stultifying and begins to shut down your energetic system. Your life contracts, and as it does, your reliance on routine becomes ever greater. Emptiness begins gnawing at the edges of your routine.

Indecision

Obsessive-compulsive personality disorder renders you unable to choose something when you need to make a decision. You are so unaccustomed to navigating the world of choice and preference, let alone tolerating uncertainty, that you have no idea what to do when there is no rule to follow. Back and forth, back and forth your mind seesaws. As soon as you list the pros on one side, you remember the cons and you go to the other. You are racked with doubt and insecurity and already besieged with regret about the decision you didn't make. This sabotages the pleasure and curiosity you might feel navigating the kaleidoscope of opportunities around you.

Judgment

OCPD is accompanied by a secret self-congratulatory superiority garnered from the order of your life and the daily labors you endure to maintain this, yet your self-regard is so conditional and precarious that it breeds anxiety due to the incessant need to retain your status as a performer with an orderly house. And perhaps underneath your silent superiority is a whiff of regret or envy as you hear the laughter and glimpse the joy shared by other, freer souls around you. That is the cost of your secret comparisons. They accentuate your separation and ultimately serve only to isolate you further in the orderly kingdom where you reign supreme.

Dysthymia

When you have obsessive-compulsive personality disorder, dysthymia, a disorder of the sacral chakra, eventually sets in as your routinized lifestyle grinds on and the fires of your solar plexus chakra dwindle to nothing. When the solar plexus chakra is dominated by values downloaded from the cultural mind and is based on the need for control and security, contact with instinctual energy is lost, as is connection with others and a larger purpose. This renders action meaningless, because it is oriented toward control as an end in itself. Life becomes a routinized litany of forced labor where you reign as the unhappy commandant.

Obsessive-Compulsive Personality Disorder (OCPD) at a Glance

History: Before the nineteenth century, obsessive-compulsive personality disorder was associated with religious melancholia. It was later included under the umbrella of *neurasthenia*, which is inadequate tone of the nervous system. Freud expanded upon this in 1908, dubbing the condition "anal retentive" character, referring to problems with toilet training leading to an adult personality overfocused on control. OCPD was included in the first edition of the DSM in 1952 under the term *compulsive personality*. In 1968 the DSM-II changed its designation to *anankastic personality* to differentiate it from OCD. In the 1980 edition of the DSM-III, it was included under the umbrella of personality disorders, and the symptoms of restricted emotional range and an inability to designate tasks were added.

Etiology: OCPD is thought to arise from a combination of genetic, psychological, and environmental factors. It has been associated with strict parenting and rigid handling of toilet training.

Prevalence: OCPD is thought to be the most common personality disorder. Lifetime estimates range from 3 to 8 percent, with men more affected than women.[31]

Treatment: Long-term insight-oriented therapy is the treatment of choice for OCPD and other personality disorders. The goal of treatment is to understand the conflicts and fears behind the individual's rigidity and help the person relate more positively to themselves and others. Medication can be used to reduce concomitant anxiety and depression.

Controversies: There is little research on OCPD and hence some confusion around where the line is between OCD and OCPD.

DSM-5 Diagnosis: OCPD is categorized as a cluster C personality disorder, along with avoidant personality disorder and dependent personality disorder. It is defined as an individual who is preoccupied with order, perfectionism, and control at the expense of openness, flexibility, and efficiency. In order to meet the diagnostic criteria for OCPD, the person must exhibit four of the following eight characteristics: (1) A preoccupation with details, rules, lists and order so the point of an activity is lost; (2) Perfectionism interfering with task completion; (3) Devotion to work at the expense of leisure and friendship; (4) Overconscientious, scrupulous, and inflexible about morality, ethics, and values, not accounted for by a religious or political affiliation; (5) Inability to throw things away; (6) Inability to delegate tasks unless performed according to exact specifications; (7) Miserly with money in order to save for a rainy day; (8) Rigid and stubborn refusal to alter one's ways in spite of the cost of the behavior.

31. Rizvi and Torrico, "Obsessive-Compulsive Personality Disorder."

Codependency

Codependency is a solar plexus chakra disorder because it involves identity and values. It is a more passive expression of solar plexus chakra dysfunction than OCD and OCPD, which express in a rigid identification of the self. In contrast, the codependent individual cleaves onto another person in order to maintain coherence. The person exhibits an excessive need for approval and an overidentification with the values and opinions of others that results from not having yet clearly defined their own values and purpose.

Both Belle and Joe were in codependent relationships. Belle relied on her husband to make her feel like a worthy wife and mother and also let him set the tone for their lifestyle. Joe, on the other hand, allowed his wife to fill many of his relational needs and also allowed her to dominate the relationships with their children. The following descriptions highlight ways codependency lurks beneath the surface in apparently well-developed people. Although Belle exemplifies a codependent personality more than Joe does, the fact that he, too, showed some of these tendencies underlines the fact that whether your solar plexus chakra is under- or overdeveloped, the same underlying cause is an insecure, undefined self. The following categories identify key features of codependency.

Lack of Self-Determination

People reside within a kaleidoscope of decisions, large and small, that is always in motion. As discussed previously in the text, small things, like what you are having for dinner or whether you go to a party, are seemingly insignificant. Yet these decisions do add up and bring you to where you are today. What you chose yesterday will influence what you will choose today. Bigger decisions, like where you will live and whether you will have a family, are informed by the smaller decisions, like what you had for dinner and whether you went to the party.

The gift of choice confers with it a burden of responsibility inherent to human beings, particularly in Western culture, due to our lack of extended networks of community with shared values and predetermined roles. This burden of responsibility can be temporarily alleviated when you align with a partner. Now you have someone with whom you can share the gift and the curse of choice. This apparently releases you from the "Should I or shouldn't I?" dilemma that can easily overwhelm and muddle the mind of an undifferentiated individual. The problem is if you too easily give over the steering wheel to another person, you defer your own growth by catering too much to the other person's needs and values. Belle's therapy focused on helping her first identify and then act on her own individual needs. Joe's therapy stalled when he was unable to identify ways he wished to grow and develop as an individual.

Clinging

Clinging is an anxious form of attachment manifested in compulsive reassurance-seeking behaviors, such as checking up on a partner or difficulty tolerating any separation. This form of attachment bespeaks an insecure sense of self and the need to cleave to someone else in order to feel safe and whole. Because you have placed one person at the center of your world, you need to compulsively monitor and control that person in order to ensure that your needed supply of safety and acceptance will not be cut off. It can become a form of hell if the other person, sensing your neediness and overdependence, pulls away. Even if the person does not do this, your sense of confidence is impaired because deep down you know that your freedom and self-expression are thwarted by your dependence on the relationship. This dependence impedes your ability to voice or even name your own feelings, let alone your ability to explore things that might interest you and to forge other relationships outside the domain of your codependent attachments.

Controlling the Other

The need to control a partner is related to clinging, although it is the other side of the same coin. In this case, the power you exert over another person imbues you with a sense of strength and selfhood that belies your own lack of self-empowerment and ability to function independently. This form of codependency is expressed when you are the dominant person in an abusive relationship. You may enjoy distancing yourself from your needy partner or telling them what to do, because it reinforces a sense of control that you lack in your own life. If the other person begins to differentiate from you, it can be destabilizing and send you into a tailspin of heretofore unrecognized insecurity. In this case, the roles are reversed and you begin to act in an insecure, clinging manner as you seek to reinstate the old order upon which your stability relied.

Limiting Activities

Couples in codependent relationships easily default to doing everything together and limiting outside activities and relationships. You may find yourself spending less time with friends or no longer pursuing hobbies and interests you enjoyed before the relationship. Belle reported that this happened when she first started dating her husband and she allowed her friendships to falter and stopped her dance classes due to feeling more comfortable at home with her husband. Joe, too, reported spending all his time with his wife after they started dating, and though he enjoyed the security of their relationship, he often wondered if he was missing out on other things.

Deferring Responsibility

Allowing your partner to do all the cooking, driving, finances, vacation planning, or social planning, though expedient, can become problematic over time. This bespeaks the proverbial plight of the older woman who, bereft of her husband, does not know how to pump gas or manage the household finances. The older man bereft of his wife and without other social connections after she passes is another common example of this problem.

Codependency at a Glance

History: The term *codependency* grew out of the Alcoholics Anonymous movement in the 1970s and was coined to refer to individuals whose primary partner was substance-dependent. The presumption was that alcoholism was an illness and those supporting the alcoholic also had an illness due to their proximity to, and enabling of, the disease. The term has never been used clinically due to the lack of clarity around whether it does constitute a true clinical disorder. The general criteria is that a person is in partnership with a chemically dependent person and has one or more chemically dependent parents. The term also grew to include individuals who consider themselves people pleasers but who are not necessarily related or close to someone with a substance use problem.

Etiology: The disorder is thought to be caused by being raised in a home where one or both parents were chemically dependent. Trauma survivors and those from disenfranchised populations are more likely to exhibit characteristics of codependency.

Prevalence: Due to the fact that codependency is not an official diagnosis, there is no verifiable data on prevalence, though many individuals self-identify as having codependent traits.

Treatment: Individual and group therapy focusing on boundary setting, self-development, and widening social networks is the treatment of choice for codependency. Codependents Anonymous is a community-based resource offering group support, 12-step work, and sponsorship. Al-Anon and Adult Children of Alcoholics are designed for a similar population.

DSM-5 Diagnosis: Although codependency is not a diagnosis in the DSM-5, there is an overlapping diagnosis called *dependent personality disorder (DPD)*. DPD is a cluster C personality disorder and is included with borderline personality disorder and obsessive-compulsive personality disorder. Diagnostic criteria for DPD does not include dependence on an addicted individual. The disorder pertains to those having a pervasive and excessive need to be taken care of, leading to submissive and clinging behavior. To meet the criteria for dependent personality disorder, five characteristics from the following list must be observed in the individual: (1) Difficulty making decisions without an excessive amount of advice and support; (2) Need for others to assume responsibility for most areas of his or her life; (3) Difficulty disagreeing with others due to feared loss of support or approval; (4) Inability to take initiative on things due to lack of confidence; (5) Going to excessive lengths to obtain nurturance from others; (6) Difficulty being alone; (7) The urgent need to find a partner if loss of a partner is experienced; (8) Unrealistic fears of being left alone and unable to care for self.

Narcissistic Personality Disorder (NPD)

Narcissism is the flip side of codependency and exemplifies a forceful approach to coping with inadequate identity formation. Rather than being self-effacing, the narcissistic individual takes the opposite approach by glorifying and aggrandizing their own needs, perspectives, and gifts. The person's entrapment within their own perspective interferes with their capacity to value the functions and expertise of others and appreciate the fact that, by default, everyone's way of seeing and organizing reality is inherently limited. The overvaluation of self leads to a heaviness of being, which is felt by all who know them, although the person remains blind to this due to how hypnotized they are by their own agenda. Unrecognized by the narcissist, their self-coherence relies on an endless supply of affirmation, attention, and rewards garnered from others and the world. This points to the deep irony at the heart of the narcissistic personality: As much as the person overvalues their importance and purports a sense of superiority to others, they are deeply dependent on ongoing reinforcement from outside themselves. For the malignant narcissist, this is expressed through being in conflict with others, because it gives the empty self something to define itself against.

Neither Bell nor Joe was narcissistic. What distinguishes their issues from narcissism is that, although both were deeply identified with their solar plexus chakra and in need of continual external reinforcement, both had permeable chakras in the sense that they were highly influenced by the perceptions, needs, and opinions of others.

The following section highlights key features of narcissism. Some of it is relevant to Joe and anyone else who suffers from entrapment within a performance-based, hierarchically placed self.

Inability to Endure Criticism

When a person suffers from narcissism, they are unable to tolerate any form of criticism. This is due to an overidentification with their public image and a refusal to face limitations in their way of doing or seeing things. Any questioning or pushback from others is felt as an intolerable assault, because the private self and the public identity are superglued together. Because the person lacks perspective on their limitations, any questioning is experienced as an attack on the core self. The person manages their fragile identity by devaluing others and consciously glorifying themselves through an imagined sense of superiority and excessive verbiage demonstrating their superiority.

Never Enough

Though a narcissistic person may appear to be happy and in control and enjoy wielding power over others, the reality of their existence is that it is governed by an ongoing insatiability because they are always in need of more fuel to feed the fires of the solar plexus chakra. On a conscious level, the person may have convinced themselves that they are special and will somehow be able to overcome the limitations and pains experienced by others, but their preoccupation with the next conquest, achievement, and gratification is exhausting and takes a silent toll. Though the person may enjoy apparent victories, the pleasure of adulation is always transient and the need for ongoing supply drives the moment forward, precluding any chance that any real pleasure is experienced.

Emptiness

A narcissist's insatiable need for more is driven by an innate dread of external supply drying up. This external supply comes in the form of praise, deference, attention, and even conflict. The person is constantly trying to avoid facing the emptiness at the edge of their existence, but part of them knows confrontation with this is inevitable. This moment might involve a bad diagnosis, loss of a relationship, or legal/financial trouble. This moment is always lurking around the edges and the person is terrified of it, albeit on an unconscious level. Hence, the driven quality to the narcissistic existence forestalls the inevitable reckoning that they are forever outrunning.

Devaluation of Others

The narcissistic person's sense of self is so fragile that they are unable to appreciate the gifts and capacities of others. When everything is a competition, the self is experienced as a weapon used to wield control over others. Other people are then experienced as threats that need to be vanquished. This reduces other people to objects that can be manipulated or exploited for personal gain.

Lack of Empathy

Due to the fact that others are not real to the narcissist, they are incapable of empathy, which refers to the capacity to put oneself in another person's shoes. The narcissistic individual wards off pain and sees it as a manifestation of weakness. Pain in another person is construed as failure and causes the narcissistic person to distance rather than console.

Malignancy

Malignant narcissists attack others, while more benign narcissists parasitically feed off the adulation and attention they demand from their entourage. A benign expression of narcissism can morph into more malignancy over time if the individual is never checked by circumstance or censure.

This is similar to how cancer works: The disease ravages the healthy tissue. In the case of narcissism, it is the tissue of the heart that gets eaten away by the self-obsession and the need for more. As the disease progresses and more healthy tissue is consumed, the dark malignancy spreads, resulting in more egregious behavior that, if unchecked, is increasingly corrupt.

Narcissistic Personality Disorder (NPD) at a Glance

History: The concept of narcissism dates back to the Greek myth of Narcissus, the son of a river god who possessed exceptional beauty. He spurned the love of others and subsequently fell in love with his own reflection. The theme of overvaluation of the self at the expense of learning to love has since been explored by philosophers and psychologists alike. It was first construed as a sexual perversion by German psychiatrist Paul Nacke in the late nineteenth century. Freud broadened the idea to include developmentally appropriate phases of self-love that later could grow to allow love for others. Theorists from the object relations school of psychology later expanded on Freud's theories to highlight impairment in narcissistic individuals' relational capacities stemming from childhood. Narcissism was not included in the DSM until the third edition in 1980. Symptoms of the disorder have since expanded to include envy and grandiose traits.

Etiology: NPD is thought to be caused by a combination of genetics, culture, and parenting styles. More individualistic cultures appear to have a higher prevalence of narcissistic individuals. Parenting styles that are overly indulgent, permissive, and overprotective are linked to development of the disorder.

Prevalence: When using the DSM-IV criteria, prevalence of NPD is estimated at 0.5 to 1 percent of the population, with men diagnosed more frequently than women.[32]

32. Stinson et al., "Prevalence, Correlates, Disability, and Comorbidity of DSM-IV Narcissistic Personality Disorder: Results from the Wave 2 National Epidemiologic Survey on Alcohol and Related Conditions."

Treatment: NPD is best treated by cognitive psychotherapy aimed to point out and correct thought distortions including self-importance, perfectionism, and lack of empathy. Insight-oriented therapy can help clarify the developmental roots of these patterns and often reveals narcissistic traits in the parents or caregivers. Medication can treat concomitant symptoms of depression and anxiety, which occur when the narcissist's defenses are no longer working. A complicating factor in treating NPD is that the individual often does not believe anything is wrong with them and instead tends to project blame onto others.

Controversies: There is lack of agreement around what differentiates normal from pathological narcissism, how to study and assess the disorder, and the role of self-esteem in the disorder, as well as whether to distinguish grandiose narcissism from vulnerable narcissism. The former subtype is brash and attention-seeking and appears very confident, while the latter is more neurotic and self-focused in a needy way. Both tend to be exploitative.

DSM-5 Diagnosis: To receive a diagnosis of narcissistic personality disorder, a person must exhibit, starting in early adulthood, five of the following nine characteristics: (1) Grandiose sense of self expressed in fantasy or behavior; (2) Fantasies of unlimited success, power, or ideal love; (3) Belief in one's specialness or uniqueness and a wish to associate only with certain others believed to be special; (4) Requires admiration; (5) Sense of entitlement; (6) Interpersonally exploitative; (7) Lack of empathy; (8) Excessive envy; (9) Arrogance and tendency to devalue others.

Mental health disorders of the solar plexus chakra stem from problems with identity and development of a coherent self. These disorders rely on rigid styles of coping centered on maintaining control over uncertainty and an overvaluation of the power of the mind. People with these disorders can appear highly functional, as exemplified by Belle and Joe; however, the person is mired in driven behaviors that limit their capacity to respond intelligently to life's challenges. The apparent functionality of these individuals lies in the fact that functionality is highly valued in the Western culture regardless of the cost. The next chapter explores the legacy of the cultural mind and its ramifications on the human psyche.

Chapter 13
The Legacy of the Conditioned Mind

This short chapter summarizes the perils of being overly conditioned by culture and the ethos of production and consumption that is endemic in our society. The waters we swim in as a society are damaging to the soul, and people can easily lose themselves in a race to survive in a world where might makes right and truth is malleable and then used as a weapon. Many people with a "good enough" childhood, as seen with Joe and Belle, are still not home free when it comes to forging a coherent identity that can stand up to the developmental challenges encountered throughout the life span, particularly in the current cultural milieu. This is because unless strong values and community are granted to a person early in life, the person will be vulnerable to being programmed by a culture that prioritizes production and consumption over individuation. Reliance on an outside-in identity conditioned to meet standards imposed by society leads to a fragile self that lacks grounding. This sets the person up for burnout and breakdown later in life.

Joe and Belle provide examples of individuals who were blessed with an adequate degree of stability in their early years. Due to emotional invalidation during childhood, however, coupled with a mandate to fit predetermined expectations of who they must be to earn legitimacy, they built identities that fit cultural mandates but failed to sustain meaning during midlife. Joe is a poignant example of a well-meaning, driven man who followed all the rules to live a good life and then found himself disoriented and rudderless in midlife. Belle also reflects this dilemma, though the cultural map she followed was more reflective of common feminine stereotypes around fulfilling the role of a pleasing woman. Both characters reflect the perils of living a life that is overly bound to cultural norms and not in dialogue with the native needs of the body and spirit. There is a way back to the organic wisdom of the self; however, it takes work to get there, and the crutches one has relied on to meet internalized dictates from the larger culture must be forsaken.

The cultural map, which identifies the landmarks of marriage, children, career, and home ownership as markers of success, is not intrinsically connected to a web of meaning that includes community and shared values. Without a larger web of connection, an achievement-oriented, consumer-based lifestyle is simply not sustainable for many people. Though it may look pristine from the outside, this lifestyle is a mirage based upon a glorified ideal that is empty at the core. This is why many individuals resort to divorce, addiction, and other seemingly self-destructive behaviors. These are symptoms of a crisis of meaning and a flailing for satisfaction even when it means destroying everything.

The crisis of meaning that Belle and Joe experienced brought them both to therapy and offered each an opportunity to reconceive themselves, reorganize their solar plexus chakras, and redraw their life maps. Riley did this at a younger age, and though she was in far more crisis at the time, she also had less capital invested in apparent success as defined by cultural norms. In this way she had less to lose, though in another way she had far more to lose since her life was literally on the line.

Undergoing a crisis of identity and reconfiguration of self is clearly not an easy process for anyone, as both Belle and Joe illustrate. The default to not doing the work, exemplified by Joe, is by no means wrong. It often results in more suffering, however, as opposed to when someone consciously faces the acute pain of active self-confrontation and reorganization. This work, when endured and sustained, is far and away worth the effort and its benefits extend beyond the individual because it potentiates the same process in others. This can alleviate the burdens of legacy trauma in one's immediate family, including ancestors, and some would even argue that this is true whether they are living or dead.

The next chapter provides guideposts to do the work of identity reorganization. As will be emphasized but bears stating now, this work cannot be done alone. Becoming a self requires a network of relationships through which you come to know and define who you are all over again. This is a rebirthing of sorts. It is exciting and creative work that requires you to feel, express, and engage. Your foundational chakras move synergistically as energy disperses and reorganizes, potentiating life energy throughout your entire system.

Chapter 14

Healing Your Solar Plexus Chakra: Identity Re-Formation

This chapter highlights key aspects of solar plexus chakra development and asks you to reflect on different dimensions of your identity. We will first address the quality of motivation. You will reflect on your history of motivation in relation to academic, athletic, and social challenges. The influence of your sacral chakra on your motivational drive (solar plexus chakra) will be explored and your current motivational struggles will be addressed as phenomena that are both energetic and identity-based. Next you will be asked to tease apart your private and public selves and reflect on your relationship to each aspect of yourself. You are encouraged to cultivate an inner refuge, where you are free from the mandates and standards emanating from both your private and public selves. You will then explore your relationship to your past, present, and future selves. Reflecting on the relationship between these three expressions of yourself, two that exist in your mind and one that is visible, provides a unique lens through which to view your unfolding identity. Finally, the importance of meaning and community are addressed to reinforce the vital role they play in creating a hearty yet flexible identity.

Cultivating Motivation: Stoking Your Fire

The symbol of the solar plexus chakra is fire. Fire is a powerful metaphor for the role of motivation in your life. Fire burns down what is so that something new can arise. The stomach, located in the solar plexus, also functions to burn through foreign material so that it can be broken down and transformed into something new. Identity development is a process of transforming thoughts and goals into actions, and this too takes energy and a certain amount of force. Work on your solar plexus chakra often requires burning down your current sense of self and meaning-making in order to create new ways of seeing and comporting yourself. Learning how to generate and sustain the volitional flow of sustained motivation is a vital aspect of identity re-formation.

This section encourages reflection on your experience of motivation as a child. Reflecting on how tightly fused outcome was to effort, and how this impacted your self-esteem, can help you understand and work with struggles with motivation in the present.

Historical Loading

1. Reflect on what motivated you as a child. Divide your childhood into three age segments, roughly from 5–12, 12–18, and 18–22. Consider what things you were good at, where you put your energy, what motivated you, and what defeated you. Reflect on how your activities impacted your self-esteem.
2. Consider how others around you reacted to your achievements and your failures. What role did this play in your self-esteem and motivation? Note this down for the three designated age periods and reflect on how this affected your motivation and self-esteem when you entered each subsequent developmental stage.
3. Reflect on the positive and negative behavioral patterns you established in relation to academic, athletic, and social challenges. What level of support did you get from family, teachers, and coaches? How did their support, or lack thereof, affect you, and how does it impact you now with regard to your willingness to reach out for help?
4. What was your level of drive or discipline as a young person? What motivated you and what deflated and derailed you?

5. Reflect on areas where you were highly motivated versus areas where your motivation flagged and you shut down. Reflect on why this was the case.

Present Goals

1. Reflect on current goals in your life and your motivation to pursue them. Can you link motivational struggles you are having in the present with your autobiographical experience of success, failure, and achievement?
2. Based on your reflections above, make a plan that will help you move beyond negative narratives you carry about your capacity to achieve desired goals. Consider ways you sabotage your motivation with default patterns of self-soothing and foreclosure.
3. Reflect on whether you are highly motivated in some areas of your life and less so in others. Why do you think this is so? How can you utilize the resources you have in one area to help you break through barriers in the areas where you struggle?
4. If you are highly successful in one area of your life, such as your career, but avoid another, such as the gym, reflect on how fears of being a beginner and looking incompetent might be sabotaging your motivation to try something new.
5. Reflect on when you are most susceptible to getting overwhelmed and resorting to self-sabotaging or avoidance behaviors. How can you position yourself so you are less likely to succumb to the temptation to sabotage your aspirations? For most people, meditating or exercising in the morning, eating well, not overdrinking alcohol or using numbing drugs, and maintaining an ordered environment are effective tools to counteract the downward pull into the status quo. The more energy you've banked in the positive category of behavior, the less likely you will be to tear this down with a negative behavior.

Motivation and Sacral Chakra Energy

The ways you manage your motivational fire are unconsciously linked to your sacral chakra and the ways you manage energy. This again demonstrates how the chakras synergistically influence one another. The following prompts are aimed to help you identify how you mismanage the fire of your motivation based on negative energy you carry from emotional invalidation during childhood.

1. Identify a goal that you have been unsuccessful in reaching. Diet and exercise goals are common ones, as is the wish to meditate consistently, read more, do less media, or expand your social life.
2. What is the negative story or belief you have about yourself that interferes with pursuing and staying with this goal?
3. Locate the feelings associated with your negative story or belief about yourself in your body. See if you can link negative behaviors, particularly related to sabotaging your goals, to ways that you habitually deal with this painful feeling. At what time in your life did you adopt this pattern of self-soothing or avoidance?
4. Consider why each goal you listed in question one is important to you. How can you move through the negative energy that blocks you and create a different story about yourself? Make a conscious plan for how you can work with feelings of futility, self-doubt, and despair by actively doing something different in the present. Consider active coping tools that involve breathwork, meditative practices, or group work that engages you with others.

The Art of Beginning Again

Learning to begin again is fundamental to maintaining motivation. When you have not been faithful to your plan and have let the thread of intentionality slacken, it takes increased motivation and self-power (as opposed to willpower) to interrupt your default pattern of foreclosure and get back on track. Whether you go on vacation, get sick, or get off track for any other of a host of reasons, it takes effort to resume. This is just a natural energetic principle. It's not personal. You haven't been "bad." The following reflections will help you cultivate a plan for intercepting foreclosure.

1. How do you typically respond when you get off track with one of your goals? Does this often precipitate abandonment of the plan?
2. How do you talk to yourself when you've fallen away from your plan? What are the feelings and emotional tone behind the self-talk? Do these have autobiographical links?
3. What supports can you employ that will help cut through your habitual response to "failing"? Do you have people who will support you in beginning again? Ideally these are people who share similar goals and may also be engaged in a change process.

Duality of Self: Your Public Image and Your Private Experience

Do you characteristically glance at yourself when you pass by a mirror or a darkened window? What are you looking for? How identified are you with your external appearance? Do you identify as "pretty," "handsome," or "good-looking"? Or are you plagued by concerns about not being attractive enough? These questions encourage you to reflect on your self-image and how much of it is entwined with your physical appearance and how others see you versus your private experience of self.

At the most basic level, you have a public self and a private self. Your public self is based on your image in the mirror as well as your job, credentials, education, marital status, and hobbies. Essentially, it is your identity resume. In contrast, your private self is an invisible landscape of thoughts, feelings, impulses, sensations, dreams, fantasies, fears, and worries. Your relationship with these two aspects of yourself, and your ease in navigating between them, is a good measurement of how comfortable you are with yourself.

A lack of alignment between the image of self that you seek to present to the world and the hidden self that only you are aware of creates a great deal of tension. Furthermore, to borrow a quip from the 12 Steps, you end up comparing your insides to other people's outsides. This creates an internal sense of deficit that attaches to the empty, wandering mind. This inner deficit encourages rumination dominated by comparison, judgment, and craving. Many people attempt to fix this internal unrest with further efforts to improve the outside. "Maybe if I lost weight, made more money, or stepped up my wardrobe, I would feel better." This preoccupation with the outside image of self interferes with attention to the inside experience of self. In addition, it is not uncommon to be frightened by your insides and go to great lengths to avoid them. Aversion to your insides and over-focus on your outsides is detrimental because you are left scrambling for yet another distraction that usually leaves you more craven than before. It also puts your precious self-image squarely in the hands of others because you have no inner backup, having invested all your energy in cultivating an image of self for others to consume.

The following journal prompts urge you to explore the inevitable tensions between the image you present to others and the inside self existing under your skin. The more familiarity you have with the exigencies of both worlds, and the more facility you have navigating between them, the more comfortable you will be in your own skin and with others.

Your Public vs. Private Self

1. How preoccupied are you with how you appear to others? How much time do you spend cultivating your resume of worthiness? What aspects of yourself are important for you to highlight?
2. When you think about how you appear to others, does it inspire confidence or insecurity? In what situations is the former true? In what situations is the latter true?
3. Describe the image of self that you seek to show others using five words.
4. What aspects of yourself do you attempt to hide?

5. How large is the gulf between the image you seek to present to others and how you feel on the inside?
6. It is important to have trusted others with whom you are more transparent. Name the people you can be more transparent with, as well as what you share with them that you don't share with others.
7. Reflect on how it would feel to be more open with others about the particular struggles you have. Do you have some people in your life with whom you can risk more? What are your fears about this? What are the potential benefits?
8. Reflect on venues that might allow you to experiment with more transparency. Therapy, 12-step groups, churches, yoga teacher training, and support groups are great options.
9. Are there things you hide even from trusted others? Explore your feelings about these things and what makes them so unspeakable. Consider the Al-Anon phrase "You are only as sick as your secrets."
10. What is the image of yourself that you strive to achieve for yourself? If this question does not make sense to you, reflect on how you need to see yourself and what it would mean if that idea of yourself suddenly fell apart. Examples of this are a very health-conscious person who is diagnosed with a serious illness or a rich person suddenly going bankrupt.

Your Disowned Self

1. What aspects of yourself do you feel ashamed of?
2. What is your understanding of how you came to have these unwelcome qualities? Consider your history, traumas you experienced, and legacy trauma.
3. Do you seek to hide these qualities even from yourself? A way to ascertain this is to consider things that you avoid in your life or things that you get defensive about with others.

4. When you are a stranger to yourself, which is what chronic denial creates, you will experience symptoms. Symptoms are how denied qualities manifest themselves. It's how your body keeps the score. Consider both physical and emotional symptoms that you struggle with and what unwelcome truths about yourself they reveal.
5. Common wisdom holds that "the truth will set you free." How could facing these denied aspects of your disowned self be freeing for you?

Cultivating an Inner Refuge

1. Consider the concept of having an inner refuge, meaning a place where you go inside where all is forgiven. If you don't already have this, consider some ways that you might cultivate it.
2. Do you keep a journal? If you do, do you censor yourself based on fears that others may read it? Are you willing to use a journal as a place for free expression without censure?
3. Do you have a spiritual practice or a self-compassion practice? If not, what are your feelings about cultivating this? If you feel it is not for you, reflect on why that is.
4. Are you able to forgive yourself for past mistakes you have made or harms you may have caused? How can you allow more room for your own fallibility?
5. Do you like yourself? Why or why not? Write down five qualities you appreciate about yourself.
6. What does self-care mean to you? How do you practice this?
7. Reflect on what self-love means to you. Unconditional positive self-regard honors your heart and your engagement with life regardless of outcomes. How might you cultivate this?

Living in Time: Present You, Past You, and Future You

Are you familiar with the flip-books that show a stick figure in progressive positions that, when the pages are flipped quickly at a particular angle, depict the figure running? This is your life. You live frame by frame, each frame representing a small, humble action that predetermines your next small, humble action. There are big moments in a lifetime, like weddings, graduations, births, and deaths, but the majority of your life is lived frame by mundane frame.

The process of living frame by frame, and achieving some level of peace in the monotonous unfolding of time, is a primary challenge in life, particularly in our fast-moving technological age. Life can easily devolve into an endless repeating of the past coupled with an urgent rushing toward the future, which just ends up repeating the past. The vitality and uniqueness of the present, which is always pregnant with possibilities, is easily enveloped by the competing energies emanating from both past and present poles, swallowing you in their vortex.

Time and identity are in a synergistic relationship mediated by choice. The past exerts a strong force that compels you to repeat familiar patterns that reinforce sedimented ideas you have about yourself. These sedimented ideas, or self-beliefs, manifest in your familiar patterns of thinking, feeling, and behaving. The future exerts an equally compelling energy, either enticing, with promised end points and future rewards, or looming, with inevitable losses and endings. Particularly in modern times, learning to live in the present is a feat of mental and emotional athleticism requiring great discipline of mind and impulse.

The following section explores how your identity, and your ability to evolve, involves having a conscious, intentional relationship to time and an active relationship with the present. Your past patterns determine a lot but not all of what you do in the present. Taking hold of the present and making choices that lean into a future that you desire requires an ongoing practice of patience and resolve. Because this is invisible work, happening in the private world of your own mind and body, it can seem unremarkable and not worthy of mention. This could not be further from the truth. The following discussion aims to help you cultivate a more engaged and present relationship to your self as it unfolds in time.

The Weight of the Past

The history of delight and tragedy that each of us carries inside exerts a strong pull on the mind and body. This is neither a good nor a bad thing. The richness of childhood and the visual, sensate memories of love shared with others buoy the soul. These experiences exist alongside memories of broken hearts, and sometimes broken bodies, and the imprints of horror and aversion they have left. Both realities live in your mind-body system and exist side by side in the record room of your being.

Your past informs every aspect of who you are, from your daily self-care habits to your ways of interpreting internal and external events and relating to others. When you recognize that certain habits are not serving you and make a decision to change them, you are taking your identity by the lapels and intervening with your own intentionality on behalf of your future self. You are imagining that something different and better is possible for you. This requires engagement in the present.

Potentiality and Possibility in the Present

Every moment provides a choice point that exists in the present, is somewhat but not fully determined by the past, and is moving toward an unknown but also somewhat predictable future. The drama of human life exists in the present, where the choice to act is made. The most likely actions taken are those that repeat the past. These are your habitual behaviors, some that serve you and some that don't. Your present and future are woven from these threads. Drama occurs when you make choices that defy or counter momentum from the past. This is where will, determination, and intention, which are all components of motivation, are necessary. It is through exerting effort in the present without a known outcome that these qualities also develop. The more you do, the more you can do. These qualities of consciousness (determination and intention), and the ability to imagine beyond a known past into an unknown future, move you beyond the biological domain and into the human domain. Through the alchemy of conscious intention exerted in the present, you ride on the faith that you can re-create yourself into something new.

It should be clear from this discussion that identity is fluid, or at least it can be. You might remember from the former discussions of the sacral and solar plexus chakras that there is a dialectic between chaos and rigidity and that creation occurs in the tension between the polarities. When energy is trapped on either side of the polarity, there is either destruction (the chaotic pole) or stagnation (the rigid pole). A rigid self monotonously re-creates the past through repetitive patterns of energy movement in a dreary present heading toward a predictable future. A chaotic self spins and fragments as energy incoherently reorganizes, only to spin and fragment again. Neither polarity is healthy; in fact, both polarities create their own kind of hell. The tension of creation, and the athletic feat of living in the present, requires the ability to exist in the tension of the polarities of past and future, neither rushing toward completion nor collapsing into what has been.

Acting into Your Future Self

Choosing to act contrary to past momentum and a sedimented idea of yourself requires resoluteness of mind and spirit. The paradox of time is that you have the ability to reconstruct your past and future in the present. That is because your past, present, and future move together on a horizontal plane. The present always carries potential and offers the possibility of reconstructing your identity one frame at a time. Hence, when you do something different in the present, your past reconstructs itself as a prelude to the different choice you are now making. This different choice then shifts what is possible in your future.

Consider an example of how this works. You make a choice to go to an Al-Anon group after being encouraged by your therapist on several occasions. You have resisted it before for opaque reasons, but your anguish about your relationship with a family member pushes you to a new edge that moves you to act. In your Al-Anon group you hear things that shift your way of thinking about your situation and you see how your past behavior has contributed to some of the current dysfunction. You then make a phone call to your family member, during which you relate differently to them using new skills you discussed with your sponsor. After the call, you feel differently about your situation and recognize your responsibility for creating something different in the future. Hence, your past, present, and future selves are all subtly transformed due to this seemingly small choice. That choice was put in motion when you first started therapy. You imagined your way into a new potentiality, and as soon as you did so, life spontaneously reorganized.

Journal Prompts

The following reflections are designed to help you cultivate a more intentional relationship with your past, present, and future selves. These prompts presume that you have goals you are working on that move toward a desired future expression of self.

1. Are there things you are doing in your present life that reflect efforts to act your way into a new future? Examples are embarking on a new job or educational endeavor, working out or taking on a health challenge, or cultivating new friendships or a new hobby.
2. In what ways does your past self either reinforce this goal or threaten to sabotage it? Are there beliefs about yourself that this goal bumps up against and seeks to dismantle?
3. What actions can you take in the present to guard against derailment and default into the past narrative? Examples are having an accountability partner, journaling, or getting into therapy.
4. What are your hopes and fears about your endeavors? How can you work affirmatively with your fears? Can you be proud

of yourself for having the courage to aspire to something new regardless of the outcome?

5. Reflect on other times in your life that you took on a new challenge. How did it either reinforce or undermine previously held beliefs you had about yourself? Was this a positive or a negative experience in your life?
6. How do past experiences with taking on new challenges affect your current confidence and willingness to aspire now?
7. What aspects of yourself are you attempting to develop through your endeavor? You might want to be healthier, more well-read, or more confident socially. How does the self you aspire toward challenge previously held beliefs you've had about yourself?

Identity Re-Formation and Meaning-Making

Many people struggle with a sense of being purposeless or lost at some point in their lives. This commonly occurs during transitional periods in life, most notably adolescence to young adulthood and middle adulthood into older age. These transitional periods require flexibility in identity because who you have been must be reorganized into who you are becoming. While it is true that we are always becoming, this fact becomes much more obvious during transitional times when a destination point for the becoming is unclear.

Life transitions, though sometimes deeply challenging, are also fertile periods where active intention can create a new trajectory. When the transition is abrupt, it can be terrifying, particularly when the transitional space between who you have been and who you are now is not undergirded by a network of family support, community, and a stable framework of identity. Examples of catastrophic identity loss are the death of a spouse or child, being fired from a job, losing significant wealth, or receiving a serious health diagnosis. Suddenly a major pillar of what you have structured yourself around is plucked out from your core, roots and all, and you must move forward into unknown territory without a map.

Interestingly, sudden fame can also derail a person, particularly when they are young. Although it looks positive on the outside, all that accompanies fame can be overwhelming and disorienting and lead to a cascade of bad decisions, drug use, and overall recklessness. More gradual shifts in identity occur in the young college student who leaves home and must make new friends as well as decisions about a future career path. Aging is another gradual transition, as you gradually witness changes in your face in the mirror and the capacities of your body also degrade.

The work of conscious identity re-formation can be empowering because you are actively forging a sense of self through conscious decision-making followed by intentional activity. You are no longer passively following the script from your family of origin or cultural mandates. Instead, you are in the driver's seat and making choices based upon values and intentions that feel intrinsically right. Through this process you discover that you are in a dialectical relationship with life. You act, life responds, and you base your next actions on how life reveals itself to you.

The following reflections are offered as guideposts on the journey toward solidifying a new sense of self based on intentional values. This work requires strength in the first two chakras, because you will be pulling energy from these resources as you face the challenges and opportunities that solar plexus chakra work will require. Solar plexus chakra work also galvanizes energy in the upper chakras. The heart chakra opens as you meet others in a more vulnerable way and feel connected. Your intuition also kicks in as you learn to trust what feels right and what calls you, even when it doesn't make logical sense. Intuition can be thought of as a synergy of qualities from the second and sixth chakras, combining the felt energy of the sacral chakra with the visionary capacity of the third eye chakra.

1. Do you have a sense of what your calling is? Is there something that you have been interested in since childhood? Consider the activities that you gravitated toward or took solace in as a child.
2. When do you feel most like yourself? Are there certain environments or activities where you feel more relaxed and capable?

3. If money and the need to support yourself were of no consequence, how would you spend your time?
4. People often feel that their greatest gift comes from their life struggles. Do you have a gift born of particular struggles that you have had?
5. What are you most proud of in your life?
6. What aspects of who you are would you like to enhance and celebrate? How can you do this starting today? This entails leaning into who you already are.
7. Do you indulge in grandiose fantasies of being a great writer, actor, painter, comedian, or anything else? How much time do you spend actually honing your craft? Think of creative ways that you could enhance your skills and that would connect you with others who have similar interests.
8. What are some areas of life that you haven't explored but would like to? Would you like to learn a language but find it intimidating? How about learning to dance? Or cook? There is so much to explore in the world. Consider your areas of interest and what attracts you to them and what gets in the way of further exploration of them. Consider the interior limits you put on yourself. These limits are malleable and can be reshaped over time as you challenge your known self with unknown possibilities. This creates a more mysterious, flexible idea of self that is freer to participate in the mystery.
9. What are the actual obstacles you face in pursuing these goals? Most often, time and money rear their heads and foreclose the opportunity before you've even engaged. What are some ways that you could adjust your goals and interests to make them more accessible right now? Do you need to do more active planning and saving of money? Are there ways you could manage time more effectively so that you could access more space in your life?

Cultivating Purpose and Community

A vital component of identity lies in cultivating the meaning, or the "what for?," linked to pursuing your intentions. When you are cultivating meaning in your life, your endeavors must have some immediate meaning for you and enhance your present life, rather than being aimed purely at a goal far off in the future. Ideally you are pursuing a feeling of engagement and pleasure in the present that also aims toward a future that glimmers with enhanced possibility. Purpose in the present is most often linked to engagement with others. The following questions are designed to help you cultivate a sense of purpose in the present as you aspire toward a desired future.

1. Reflect for a few moments on when you feel at your best and when your day feels like it has been worthwhile. How often does your feeling of something being worthwhile involve other people? If you engage in solitary activities, like writing, music, or gardening, do your endeavors involve a future imagined audience or group of appreciators?
2. How can you enhance your opportunities to connect with other people right now?
3. Do you participate in any organizations or activities that involve helping others? Is there room in your life to volunteer or join a community organization?
4. Are you involved in a church, self-help group, book club, or any other group activity? Are you willing to consider this? If not, why not?

Developing a strong yet flexible identity is rigorous work because there is no set plan for you to follow. As in the vision quest, identity re-formation requires you to rely on your instincts and intuition (sacral chakra) as you source from the security rooted in your physical body (root chakra) and launch into an unknown landscape to test your abilities in the world relative to others. This endeavor requires risk and the ability to endure false starts, failures, setbacks, and times of self-doubt. It also requires an ongoing willingness to be in dialogue with both the external world and your own experience. It is tempting to shut down and foreclose the process, which is why it is vital to build a community of others who will support you when you waver and cheer you on as you persevere. The gifts of the work extend beyond yourself and are listed next.

Gifts of the Solar Plexus Chakra

The following attributes correlate to having a strong yet flexible identity. These attributes allow you to maintain perspective, direction, and resilience in the face of life's inevitable challenges and setbacks. You are able to take life seriously without taking yourself too seriously.

Flexibility of Identity

A rigid solar plexus chakra houses an identity that is contingent on external validation. Although a person who is anorexic or workaholic may seem internally driven, the values they pursue are externally derived and reflect a craven need to prove themselves worthy. This tethering of the solar plexus chakra to the conditioned mind by definition creates an insecure self due to the conditionality of its own existence.

In contrast, a fluid solar plexus chakra shifts between different reflections of itself that can integrate disparate potentialities within the self. The ability to accept contradiction and imperfection lends ease to your personality, which is able to embrace multiple aspects of experience. Hence, you are able to withstand assaults on your identity, such as criticism or rejection, without shattering. This allows you to be resilient in the face of adversity, since your sense of self is larger than situational successes or failures.

Core Values

A healthy solar plexus chakra is formed around values that are larger than your individual needs and preferences. This means that your sense of your own value is informed by a purpose that extends beyond your immediate satisfaction or survival. A good example of this is the contrast between putting in long hours at work because it is demanded by an institution that you care little about or working long hours driven by your belief in the value of the work you are doing. This fortifies you with the gift of intrinsic motivation. Because your action is based on values, it is distinct from forced labor, which is performed either to acquire money and praise or to avoid punishment.

Boundaries

Poor boundaries can express as either habitually saying yes or habitually saying no. Habitually saying yes is evidence of an insecure self that is unable to adequately protect itself because you are overly dependent on external validation in order to feel real to yourself. Habitually saying no is evidence of an insecure self that cannot handle impingement and thus cannot receive and integrate information and stimulation from external sources. Strong and flexible boundaries, which are gifts of a healthy solar plexus chakra, reflect an identity that is strong, feels real to itself, and is not overly dependent on validation from others. This affords you access to your sacral chakra, where you are able to vet options and make decisions about whether something feels right before choosing to act or not. You sometimes say yes and sometimes say no according to what feels right at the time.

Initiative

Initiative is the ability to take action in the face of ambiguity. There is often no clear right or wrong path, which forces you to make decisions and act without any assurance of the "rightness" of your choice. Taking initiative requires that you step away from the fantasy of an all-knowing authority who can show you the way and instead trust your internal compass and your ability to make a decision "right" by virtue of your commitment and ability to see it through. The gift of initiative is not acting because you know it is the right thing to do, but rather is choosing and acting in the face of your own uncertainty. Your ability to do this gives you the gift of integrity and confidence in your ability to make something right over time through consistent, ongoing engagement.

Conclusion

Base Camp at Mount Everest

We have arrived. And your journey is far from over. In fact, now it is time to begin. As I have reinforced many times, the lower chakras must be strong in order to allow safe and productive access to the higher chakras. Energy that is trapped in survival-based, habitual loops cannot move upward and galvanize artistic and spiritual growth. These domains belong to the higher chakras, starting with the heart chakra and moving upward into symbolic expression (housed in the throat chakra), visionary capacity (the third eye chakra), and spiritual union (the crown chakra at the top of the head). Nonetheless, the work on your lower chakras is spiritual work, even if it seems very mundane. Being human is a privileged position, as difficult as life may sometimes seem. If it resonates with you that we are spiritual beings having a human experience, then working on the lower chakras is a gesture toward embracing your uniquely human being and constitutes a deep learning experience that will assist in your spiritual evolution.

I know that for me, life has been very difficult at times. It is also sweet, and this sweetness outweighs the travail, though I sometimes lose sight of this. This book is aimed to help you make the most of your human experience with the promise that by coming into deeper connection with your human endowment and learning to love who and what you are, more will become possible. The "more" that becomes possible will be unique to you, and that is where the mystery lies.

Acknowledgments

I am so grateful to the professional, talented individuals at Llewellyn Publications who helped bring this book to fruition. Thank you to Liz Stewart for seeing the potential in this book and helping me hone the original text. Great thanks to Andrea Neff for her careful and insightful reading of the text and for making the final edits so painless.

I would also like to extend a warm acknowledgment to Jean Grant Sutton, who started me on my yoga journey in 2008 and has provided unflagging support at key junctures in my life. Deep gratitude to Peter for his unflagging emotional support and technical help. And thanks to my dear friend Michelle for her wise counsel and generous interest in this creative endeavor.

Glossary

affect tolerance: Refers to the ability of an individual to handle intense, pleasant or unpleasant feelings without acting in ways that are destructive to self or others.

Alcoholics Anonymous (A.A.): Founded in 1935, this is a grassroots self-help organization that has gained worldwide appeal and serves as a haven for individuals struggling with addiction. It is a leaderless organization based upon spiritual principles encouraging addicts to surrender their will and learn a new way of living. This way of living is outlined in 12 steps that progressively teach how to live in a more authentic way. A.A. encourages sponsorship and participation in group meetings.

Big T: Trauma involving impingement on the body in a physical or sexual violation, or severe neglect and deprivation of physical needs. It can also involve accidents with bodily injury, a serious medical event, or witnessing the severe injury or death of another. Finally, it can apply to individuals in a life-threatening environmental catastrophe or fire. Experiencing racism or systemic prejudice can also create Big T.

chakra theory: Arising from Eastern traditions of yoga and meditation, this theory suggests that there are seven energy centers aligned through the spine that correspond to developmental challenges central to being human. The balance and health of each chakra is thought to influence overall physical, emotional, and spiritual well-being.

chronic stress: A condition where stress is ongoing and the individual feels unable to impact the situation in any meaningful way. Can result in apathy and depression due to a sense of helplessness. Can result in severe psychological, cognitive, and physical symptoms.

codependency: This refers to when an individual is excessively reliant on others for validation and a sense of self. Often expressed by being clingy in relationships and people-pleasing, a term used to describe individuals who have a hard time saying no. These individuals often become involved with controlling or addicted others to ensure they will not be abandoned.

cognitive processing therapy (CPT): This is a form of cognitive behavioral therapy designed specifically for PTSD. It focuses on distorted thoughts associated with a traumatic event and helps clients both reframe these thoughts and respond differently.

depersonalization: A symptom of dissociation, depersonalization occurs when a person feels detached from their own thoughts, feelings, and identity. It can be experienced as observing oneself from outside the body or as a sense of not being in control of one's own actions. It can be a coping reaction to a horrifying event and can also be experienced more chronically.

derealization: Derealization is a symptom of dissociation wherein a person experiences a sense of detachment from their present surroundings and there is a feeling of unreality. This can occur during traumatic events, such as a car accident, and is a way that the psyche protects itself.

dialectical behavior therapy (DBT): This form of therapy was originally developed by Marsha Linehan as a treatment for borderline personality disorder, though it is currently employed for people with bipolar disorders and other personality disorders. It incorporates a focus on self-awareness, self-regulation, distress tolerance, and maximizing relationships. DBT is a skill-based therapy utilizing both group and individual therapy.

diffuse identity: Refers to when a person is unclear about their values, goals, or emotional experience. These people are easily manipulated by others and often feel lost and anxious. They tend to get into controlling relationships and are vulnerable to addiction. Adolescence is the time when identity is beginning to form, and teens from unstable homes are at risk of not forming coherent values or goals.

dissociation: Refers to the disconnection of the psyche from the present moment and one's emotional, mental, sensate experience. It ranges from mild, wherein a person is not attending to conversation or a television show, to severe, wherein a person loses experience of their present identity and later has no memory of an event. Dissociation is often a response to trauma but also can be a coping mechanism that occurs when a person is bored or preoccupied. It can result in poor memory and difficulty retaining information.

emotional invalidation: Refers to the act of denying, minimizing, or contradicting another person's feelings. Often expressed in episodes of humiliation, bullying, gaslighting, or ridiculing. It can also occur in the form of ignoring or colluding with abuse. More subtle forms occur when a child's emotional needs are not noticed by caregivers. It is very destructive to the emotional growth of an individual raised in a home with an emotionally invalidating parent or sibling.

emotional processing system: Refers to the resilience and vitality of the emotional system. It is what allows people to tolerate new experiences, manage discomfort, and experience impingements without overreacting or shutting down. In this paradigm, it signifies a person's relationship to life energy, or prana.

emotional validation: This refers to recognizing and accepting another person's feelings and emotional experience as true for them, whether or not the listener agrees with the reasons for the feelings. Parents who offer this to children also offer coping skills that help the child respond to the feeling in a way that is socially appropriate and enhances self-esteem and relationships.

engulfment: The experience of feeling overwhelmed or smothered by another person's thoughts, needs, or emotions. Often refers to the experience of a child growing up with needy or overbearing caregivers whose own needs eclipsed that of the child's.

etiology: Refers to the source or cause of a disease. Includes determining the biological, environmental, and social factors leading to various conditions.

existential guilt: The intuitive knowledge that you are not living up to your life purpose. Applies to people who have colored within the lines and not faced up to the challenges that life has given them. Leads to a feeling of despair and hopelessness.

externalization: Refers to when a person acts out an uncomfortable feeling by doing something destructive, blaming others, or otherwise creating external chaos to avoid having to deal with the uncomfortable feeling.

eye movement desensitization and reprocessing (EMDR): This form of therapy was developed to help individuals work through trauma. It was developed by Francine Shapiro in the late 1980s and consists of a structured protocol wherein traumatic memories are held in mind, along with associated beliefs about the self. Bilateral stimulation is then applied, which involves either eye movements, auditory stimulation, or holding pads that vibrate. Through several sessions, this method helps clients process memories and shift negative beliefs about the self.

gaslighting: A technique of intimidation wherein a person attempts to make another person doubt their own reality. Often the person doing the gaslighting makes the other person feel guilty, thereby avoiding accountability for their own actions and maintaining power in the relationship.

heart rate variability: Measures the variation in time between heartbeats and is an overall measure of a person's cardiovascular health and stress resilience. Ideally the variation between heartbeats is high, which indicates that the vagal break is able to slow down the heart, which is an overall measure of the tonality of the parasympathetic nervous system.

iatrogenic effects: Refers to situations where the treatment for a condition causes negative side effects that become problematic. It can apply to situations where a healthcare provider asks leading questions that cause suggestible patients to believe they have a condition that they do not have. It can also refer to side effects from medications or treatments that cause new medical problems to arise in the patient.

internal family systems: A form of therapy designed by Richard Schwartz that views the personality as having several sub-personalities that perform different functions. The therapy focuses on identifying self-parts, learning their function, and finding appropriate ways to express these functions that are not in conflict with the good of the full self.

interoception: A sense of the internal state of the body, including hunger and thirst, fatigue, awareness of tension, and temperature of the body. Also applies to awareness of emotional states. Plays a large role in self-regulation. Lack of this capacity can result in poor self-care, dysregulated emotional states, and poor health.

legacy trauma: This refers to trauma passed down from previous generations who experienced war, oppression, or poverty or were the victims of physical or sexual abuse. It also applies to children of racial or ethnic groups who have experienced systemic oppression.

Little t: Trauma involving emotional invalidation, which can include verbal abuse, minimizing feelings, ridicule, gaslighting, and bullying. Colluding with or minimizing abuse is Little t coupled with preexisting Big T. Lack of emotional mirroring also constitutes subtle Little t. Implicit racism or bias is a form of Little t.

logotherapy: Developed by Viktor Frankl after World War II, logotherapy is based on the idea that having a sustained sense of meaning and purpose is fundamental to human life. This form of therapy stems from his experience surviving a Nazi concentration camp.

mirroring: Refers to reflecting another person's feelings, behaviors, or expressions in a way that is validating and enhances the expressing person's sense of being heard and understood.

neurotic: This refers to a personality trait wherein a person feels highly conflicted about their needs or feelings. This is expressed in chronic feelings of anxiety and guilt. This is not a mental health diagnosis but can underlie mood disorders and anxiety disorders. Neurosis is thought to stem from childhood development creating conflict about the appropriateness of one's needs.

parasympathetic nervous system: The "rest, digest, and repair" branch of the nervous system, it functions to balance sympathetic activation and allows the restorative functions of the body to occur. It functions to decrease heart rate, slow respiration, and promote digestion. The parasympathetic nervous system serves a vital function in maintaining homeostasis.

peristalsis: In the body, this refers to the wavelike contractions and expansions that allow for rhythmic movement in the digestive system, heart, and other organs. In this text, it also refers to the ability to feel and process emotion through expansion and contraction, experienced as feeling fully and then releasing. This can help an individual eventually work through painful things and apply meaning to them.

prana: A concept from Eastern traditions, prana is translated as life force energy and refers to the universal energy that is thought to flow through all life forms. Practices such as yoga, breathwork, meditation, and dietary restrictions are thought to enhance prana. A person's capacity to channel prana is considered to be a central aspect of health in Eastern traditions.

proprioception: The capacity to sense the positioning of one's limbs in space and to regulate coordinated movement and balance. Plays a role in walking, running, throwing, and catching a ball and other movements. Generally more emphasized in a child's development than interoception.

psychotic: This is a condition characterized by a severe disconnection from reality, wherein an individual experiences hallucinations and delusions that they believe are true. It warrants medical intervention and medication because these individuals can act in ways that are harmful to themselves and sometimes to others.

root chakra: The first of the seven chakras, the root is located at the base of the spine and is thought to connect us to the earth and our physical being. Emotional issues connected to the root chakra involve safety, security, and belonging. This chakra is symbolized by the color red and the earth element.

root chakra addiction: Application of a substance, including food, alcohol, cigarettes, or other drugs, that has an immediate calming or stimulating impact on the central nervous system. When this is over-relied upon and becomes a primary way of coping, it gets wired into the nervous system and creates problems with physical and emotional health.

sacral chakra: Located below the navel and encompassing the hips and pelvis, this second chakra is connected to the feeling body and represents the right to feel fully and experience both pleasure and pain. The sacral chakra is symbolized by the color orange and the water element.

sacral chakra addiction: Any repetitive behavior done to artificially stimulate or soothe the nervous system. Examples are exercise, using loud music to create adrenaline, working, shopping, and gambling. When over-relied upon to regulate emotions, it creates physical, emotional, and relational problems.

self-efficacy: A belief in one's ability to succeed. High self-efficacy leads to individuals being able to set goals and self-motivate to actualize them. Low self-efficacy leads to avoidance and lower self-esteem. Self-efficacy can be increased by developing attainable goals and employing support and encouragement from others to maintain focus and accountability.

self-monitoring: A technique from cognitive behavioral therapy wherein a person is encouraged to track their behaviors and identify triggers and patterns with the goal of shifting behavior in a positive direction.

solar plexus chakra: This is the third chakra and is located in the solar plexus, just beneath the diaphragm. It is associated with will, intentionality, and motivation, which are key aspects of self-efficacy. The solar plexus chakra is symbolized by the color yellow and the fire element.

stress: Stress can result when the perceived demands of a situation exceed resources. Can manifest in physiological symptoms, such as headaches or acceleration in heart rate and breathing. Also can manifest in psychological symptoms, such as irritability, anger, or depression, as well as cognitive symptoms, such as difficulties with concentration and decreased ability to think logically.

sympathetic nervous system: Part of the autonomic nervous system, it controls the "fight, flight, or freeze" biological mechanism ensuring survival. It increases heart rate and respiration and releases adrenaline. When activated chronically, as is common for individuals in high-stress environments, the sympathetic nervous system can create many problematic physical and emotional symptoms.

vagus nerve: The longest nerve in the body, extending from the brain stem down through the diaphragm to the internal organs. The vagus nerve plays a large role in the parasympathetic nervous system and helps regulate involuntary functions involved in heart rate, blood pressure, and digestion.

Recommended Resources

The following resources are widely available and will hopefully assist your healing process.

Books

The Body Keeps the Score: Brain, Mind, and Body in the Healing of Trauma by Bessel van der Kolk

This book is a must read for anyone interested in the effects of trauma. Dr. van der Kolk goes over several types of trauma, including war, accidents, and childhood abuse, and illustrates with clear data the impact that the trauma has on a person's brain, physiology, and emotional regulation. Many of my clients expressed a sense of validation and comfort from learning that their peculiarities were not due to an inherent defect in them but instead had brain- and body-based causes due to trauma. The book also goes over several alternative treatments, including yoga and EMDR, and illustrates how these are efficacious.

Breath: The New Science of a Lost Art by James Nestor

This highly engaging and readable book is a deep dive into the science of breathing and the importance of proper breathing for overall health. Nestor performs several experiments on himself, at times to his own detriment, in order to provide confirmation of various theories about the role of respiration in health. He also includes several recommendations and suggestions for better breathing.

Eastern Body, Western Mind: Psychology and the Chakra System as a Path to the Self by Anodea Judith

This is a comprehensive text linking chakra theory to Western psychological theories, including those of Sigmund Freud, Carl Jung, and Abraham Maslow. Judith provides rich information about Eastern psychology and Western theories along with case studies to illustrate her ideas. Readers are also given tools to balance all seven main chakras. If you are intrigued by chakra theory and want to do a deep dive, this is a must read.

The Four Agreements: A Practical Guide to Personal Freedom by Don Miguel Ruiz

This short but powerful book is rooted in Toltec wisdom, which is a philosophy and way of life originating from an ancient civilization in Mexico. The agreements are seemingly simple but can have a profound impact when applied to your life. The agreements are grounded in not being a victim, taking responsibility for all your actions, and conducting relationships with intentionality. The power of cultural conditioning is emphasized.

Higher and Friendly Powers: Transforming Addiction and Suffering by Peg O'Connor

This book is a discussion of addiction and spirituality using tenets from both the 12-step philosophy and the work of William James, a famous American philosopher of religion and psychology from the early twentieth century. This is a great book for people who are interested in the role of spirituality in recovery and want to learn about the life and ideas of William James.

How to Do the Work by Dr. Nicole LePera

This book provides an excellent overview of how trauma, including emotional trauma, affects development. Dr. LePera focuses on taking responsibility for your healing through mindfulness, nutrition, and self-understanding. She offers many tools to help the reader understand their patterns and overcome them. She is known as a holistic psychologist with an emphasis on mind-body healing.

In the Realm of the Hungry Ghosts: Close Encounters with Addiction by Gabor Maté

Maté provides a compassionate and scientifically based understanding of the origin of addiction based on his years of practice treating people with severe drug and alcohol addictions. He discusses his own addictive, compulsive behavior and links all addiction to developmental trauma, societal context, and isolation.

Introduction to Internal Family Systems by Richard C. Schwartz, PhD

This book marks a new understanding of dissociative personality disorder, positing that everyone's personality is comprised of parts, or subpersonalities, that serve different purposes. The reader is encouraged to identify their different parts and honor their functions while also nurturing an internal relationship with the parts that are respectful and compassionate.

Man's Search for Meaning by Viktor Frankl

This book chronicles Viktor Frankl's experience surviving a concentration camp during the Holocaust. His harrowing tale is inspirational because he emphasizes the ever-present ability to embrace choice and free will even when everything has been taken. He developed a new form of therapy from his experience, which he dubbed logotherapy, because it emphasizes the importance of cultivating meaning and purpose in one's life.

Inspiration

Wim Hof: This man took the world by storm in 2017, when he introduced to the public a yogic form of breathing called Tummo breathing and also popularized cold exposure. Hof has broken several world records with physical feats that defy credulity. In addition, he has a warm, accessible personality and conveys a genuine wish to be of benefit to others. His breathing technique is widely accessible on YouTube. He has a free app called the Wim Hof Method Breathing & Cold, which can be accessed through his website, www.wimhofmethod.com.

Recommended Meditation

Ho'oponopono Hawaiian Meditation: This is a beautiful meditative prayer that promotes self-forgiveness and gratitude. There are several versions on YouTube that you can easily access. This prayer is useful when you are feeling down on yourself or are struggling with guilt.

Yin Yoga

Sarah Powers: Powers provides online classes and courses on meditation and yin yoga, in addition to several other offerings. Her yin yoga offerings are excellent and can be viewed through her website, www.sarahandtypowers.com, or purchased separately. She incorporates Buddhist principles into her practices and also offers courses on Buddhist thought.

Yoga Nidra

Ally Boothroyd: Boothroyd provides outstanding yoga nidras that address issues from insomnia to health and the chakras. Her recordings have gorgeous sounds, ranging from the rainforest to chimes, gongs, and silence. Boothroyd is prolific and inspired and is a staple in my own self-care regimen. Her videos are easily accessible on her YouTube channel, Ally Boothroyd | Sarovara Yoga.

Jennifer Reis: Also a gifted yoga nidra practitioner, Reis has a free video on her YouTube channel, Jennifer Reis Relaxation, that provides a twenty-minute journey through the chakras, called "Yoga Nidra: Divine Sleep Yoga Nidra–Healing Chakra Chorus."

Bibliography

Abdelnour E., M. O. Jansen, and J. A. Gold. "ADHD Diagnostic Trends: Increased Recognition or Overdiagnosis?" *Missouri Medicine* 119, no. 5 (Sept.–Oct. 2022): 467–73. PMID: 36337990.

Ainsworth, M. S., and J. Bowlby. "An Ethological Approach to Personality Development." *American Psychologist* 46, no. 4 (1991): 333–41.

Amad, Ali, Nicolas Ramoz, Pierre Thomas, Renaud Jardri, and Philip Gorwood. "Genetics of Borderline Personality Disorder: Systematic Review and Proposal of an Integrative Model." *Neuroscience & Biobehavioral Reviews* 40 (March 2014): 6–19. https://doi.org/10.1016/j.neubiorev.2014.01.003.

Bozinovic, K., F. McLamb, K. O'Connell, N. Olander, Z. Feng, S. Haagensen, and G. Bozinovic. "U.S. National, Regional, and State-Specific Socioeconomic Factors Correlate with Child and Adolescent ADHD Diagnoses Pre-Covid-19 Pandemic." *Scientific Reports* 11, 22008 (2021). https://doi.org/10.1038/s41598-021-01233-2.

Carroll, Lewis. *Alice's Adventures in Wonderland*. T. Y. Crowell & Co., 1893.

Czarnecki, Jan, Katarzyna Nowakowska-Domagala, and Lukasz Mokros. "Combined Cold-Water Immersion and Breathwork May Be Associated with Improved Mental Health and Reduction in the Duration of Upper Respiratory Tract Infection: A Case-Control Study." *International Journal of Circumpolar Health* 83, no. 1 (March 2024). https://doi.org/10.1080/22423982.2024.2330741.

Dell'Osso, Bernardo, Laura Cremaschi, Monica Macellaro, and Rita Cafaro. "Gender and Sex Issues in Bipolar Disorder." *Psychiatric Times* 39, no. 6 (June 10, 2022). www.psychiatrictimes.com/view/gender-and-sex-issues-in-bipolar-disorder.

Diagnostic and Statistical Manual of Mental Disorders: DSM-I. American Psychiatric Association, 1952.

Diagnostic and Statistical Manual of Mental Disorders: DSM-II. American Psychiatric Association, 1968.

Diagnostic and Statistical Manual of Mental Disorders: DSM-III. American Psychiatric Association, 1980.

Diagnostic and Statistical Manual of Mental Disorders: DSM-III-R. 3rd ed., rev. American Psychiatric Association, 1987.

Diagnostic and Statistical Manual of Mental Disorders: DSM-IV. American Psychiatric Association, 1994.

Diagnostic and Statistical Manual of Mental Disorders: DSM-5. American Psychiatric Association, 2013.

Dube, S. R., D. Fairweather, W. S. Pearson, V. J. Felitti, R. F. Anda, and J. B. Croft. "Cumulative Childhood Stress and Autoimmune Diseases in Adults." *Psychosomatic Medicine* 71, no. 2 (Feb. 2009): 243–50. DOI: 10.1097/PSY.0b013e3181907888.

Esperland, Didrik, Louis de Weerd, and James B. Mercer. "Health Effects of Voluntary Exposure to Cold Water: A Continuing Subject of Debate." *International Journal of Circumpolar Health* 81, no. 1 (Dec. 2022). doi: 10.1080/22423982.2022.2111789.

Frankl, Viktor E. *Man's Search for Meaning: An Introduction to Logotherapy.* 1946. Reprint, Beacon Press, 1962.

Hinshaw, Stephen P., and Katherine Ellison. *ADHD: What Everyone Needs to Know.* Oxford University Press, 2016.

Jung C. G. *The Spirit in Man, Art, and Literature.* Vol. 15 of *The Collected Works of C. G. Jung.* Edited and translated by Gerhard Adler and R.F.C. Hull. Princeton University Press, 1966.

Kessler, R. C., P. Berglund, O. Demler, R. Jin, K. R. Merikangas, and E. E. Walters. "Lifetime Prevalence and Age-of-Onset Distributions of DSM-IV Disorders in the National Comorbidity Survey Replication." 2005. *Archives of General Psychiatry* 62, no. 6 (June 2005): 593–602. doi: 10.1001/archpsyc.62.6.593.

Lenzenweger M. F., M. C. Lane, A. W. Loranger, and R. C. Kessler. "DSM-IV Personality Disorders in the National Comorbidity Survey Replication." *Biological Psychiatry* 62, no. 6 (Sept. 2007): 553–64. PMID: 17217923.

Linehan, Marsha. *Cognitive-Behavioral Treatment of Borderline Personality Disorder.* Guilford Press, 1993.

Merikangas, K. R., J. P. He, M. Burstein, S. A. Swanson, S. Avenevoli, L. Cui, C. Benjet, K. Georgiades, and J. Swendsen. "Lifetime Prevalence of Mental Disorders in US Adolescents: Results from the National Comorbidity Survey Replication—Adolescent Supplement (NCS-A)." *Journal of the American Academy of Child & Adolescent Psychiatry* 49, no. 10 (Oct. 2010): 980–89. DOI: 10.1016/j.jaac.2010.05.017.

Mitra, Paroma, and Ankit Jain. "Dissociative Identity Disorder." Treasure Island, FL: StatPearls Publishing. Last updated May 16, 2023. https://www.ncbi.nlm.nih.gov/books/NBK568768.

Morrison, Toni. *Beloved.* Vintage Classics, 1987.

National Institute of Mental Health. "Bipolar Disorder." Last reviewed December 2024. https://www.nimh.nih.gov/health/topics/bipolar-disorder.

National Institute of Mental Health. "Generalized Anxiety Disorder." Accessed June 2025. https://www.nimh.nih.gov/health/statistics/generalized-anxiety-disorder.

National Institute of Mental Health. "Major Depression." Last updated July 2023. https://www.nimh.nih.gov/health/statistics/major-depression.

National Institute of Mental Health. "Obsessive-Compulsive Disorder (OCD)." Accessed June 2025. https://www.nimh.nih.gov/health/statistics/obsessive-compulsive-disorder-ocd.

National Institute of Mental Health. "Panic Disorder." Accessed June 2025. https://www.nimh.nih.gov/health/statistics/panic-disorder.

National Institute of Mental Health. "Persistent Depressive Disorder (Dysthymic Disorder)." Accessed June 2025. https://www.nimh.nih.gov/health/statistics/persistent-depressive-disorder-dysthymic-disorder.

National Institute of Mental Health. "Specific Phobia." Accessed June 2025. https://www.nimh.nih.gov/health/statistics/specific-phobia.

PTSD: National Center for PTSD, U.S. Department of Veterans Affairs. "How Common Is PTSD in Adults?" Last updated March 26, 2025. https://www.ptsd.va.gov/understand/common/common_adults.asp.

Rizvi, A., and T. J. Torrico. "Obsessive-Compulsive Personality Disorder." Treasure Island, FL: StatPearls Publishing. Last updated October 28, 2023. https://www.ncbi.nlm.nih.gov/books/NBK597372.

Schreiber, Flora Rheta. *Sybil*. Henry Regnery Co., 1973.

Siegel, Daniel J. *Mindsight: The New Science of Personal Transformation*. Bantam, 2010.

Spoelma, M. J., G. L. Sicouri, D. A. Francis, A. D. Songco, E. K. Daniel, and J. L. Hudson. "Estimated Prevalence of Depressive Disorders in Children From 2004 to 2019: A Systematic Review and Meta-Analysis." *JAMA Pediatrics* 177, no. 10 (Aug. 28, 2023): 1017–27. https://jamanetwork.com/journals/jamapediatrics/fullarticle/2808878.

Stinson, F. S., D. A. Dawson, R. B. Goldstein, S. P. Chou, B. Huang, S. M. Smith, W. J. Ruan, A. J. Pulay, T. D. Saha, R. P. Pickering, and B. F. Grant. "Prevalence, Correlates, Disability, and Comorbidity of DSM-IV Narcissistic Personality Disorder: Results from the Wave 2 National Epidemiologic Survey on Alcohol and Related Conditions." *Journal of Clinical Psychiatry* 69, no. 7 (July 2008): 1033–45, PMID: 18557663.

Tolle, Eckhart. *The Power of Now*. 1997. Reprint, Hodder Paperbacks, 2001.

U.S. Food & Drug Administration. "Suicidality in Children and Adolescents Being Treated with Antidepressant Medications." U.S. Department of Health and Human Services." Content current as of February 5, 2018. https://www.fda.gov/drugs/postmarket-drug-safety-information-patients-and-providers/suicidality-children-and-adolescents-being-treated-antidepressant-medications.

van der Kolk, Bessel A. *The Body Keeps the Score: Brain, Mind, and Body in the Healing of Trauma*. Viking, 2014.

Wallace, David Foster. *Infinite Jest: A Novel*. 1996. Reprint, Abacus, 2016.

Index

E

F

G

H

I

J

K

L

M

N

O

P

R

S

T

V

W

Y

To Write to the Author

If you wish to contact the author or would like more information about this book, please write to the author in care of Llewellyn Worldwide Ltd. and we will forward your request. Both the author and the publisher appreciate hearing from you and learning of your enjoyment of this book and how it has helped you. Llewellyn Worldwide Ltd. cannot guarantee that every letter written to the author can be answered, but all will be forwarded. Please write to:

Melissa Grabau, PhD
℅ Llewellyn Worldwide
2143 Wooddale Drive
Woodbury, MN 55125-2989

Please enclose a self-addressed stamped envelope for reply, or $1.00 to cover costs. If outside the U.S.A., enclose an international postal reply coupon.

Many of Llewellyn's authors have websites with additional information and resources. For more information, please visit our website at http://www.llewellyn.com.